AF352410

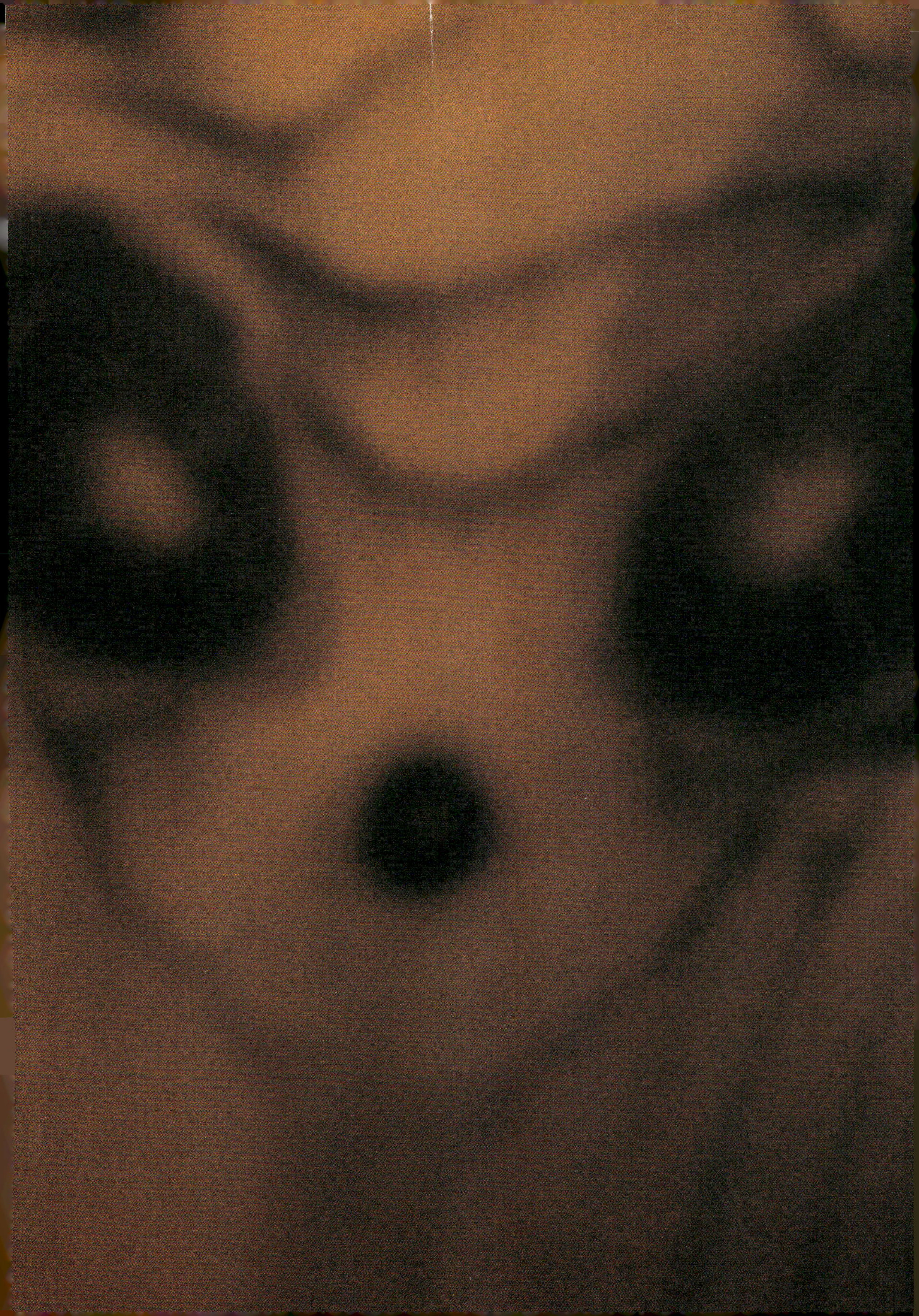

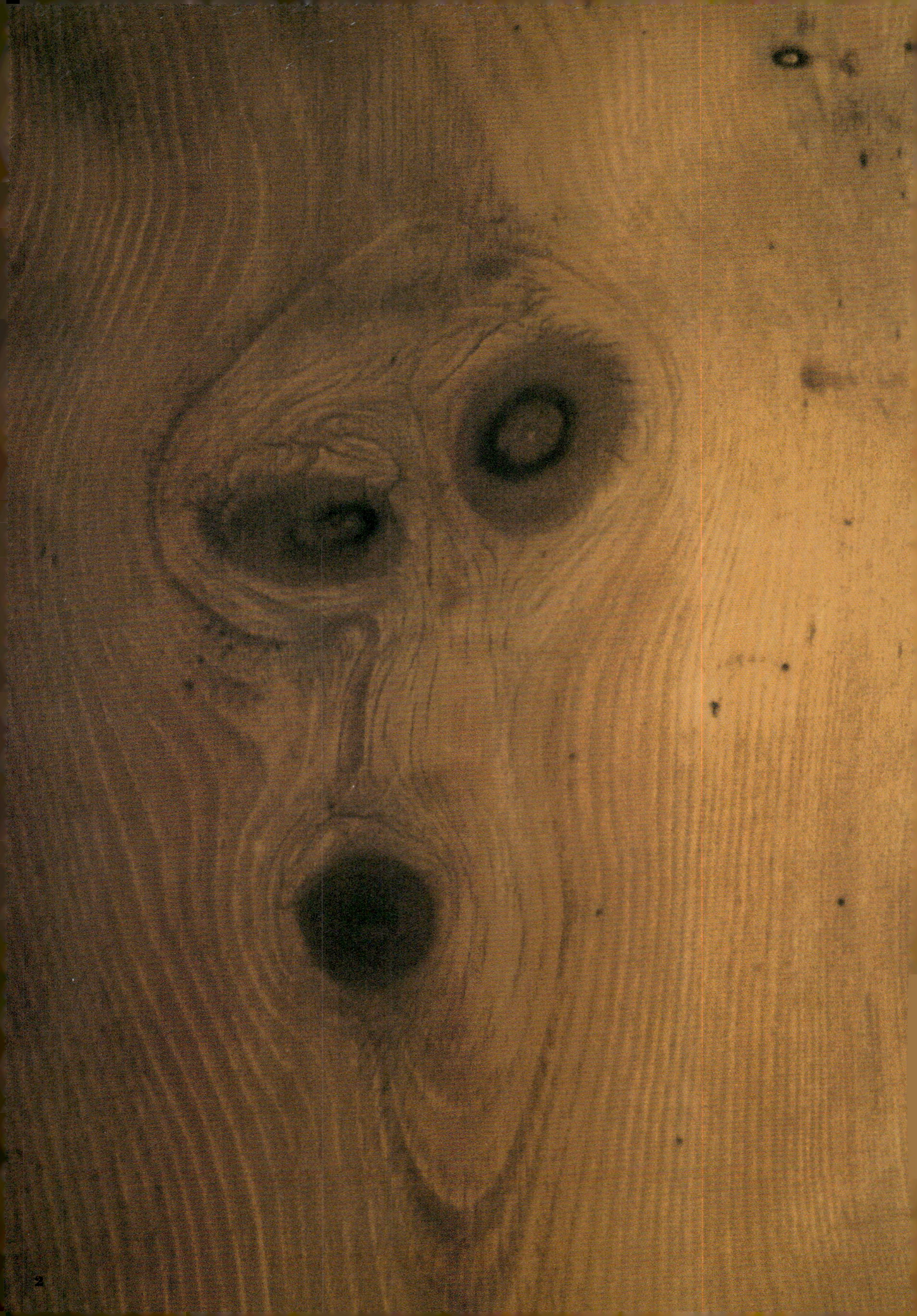

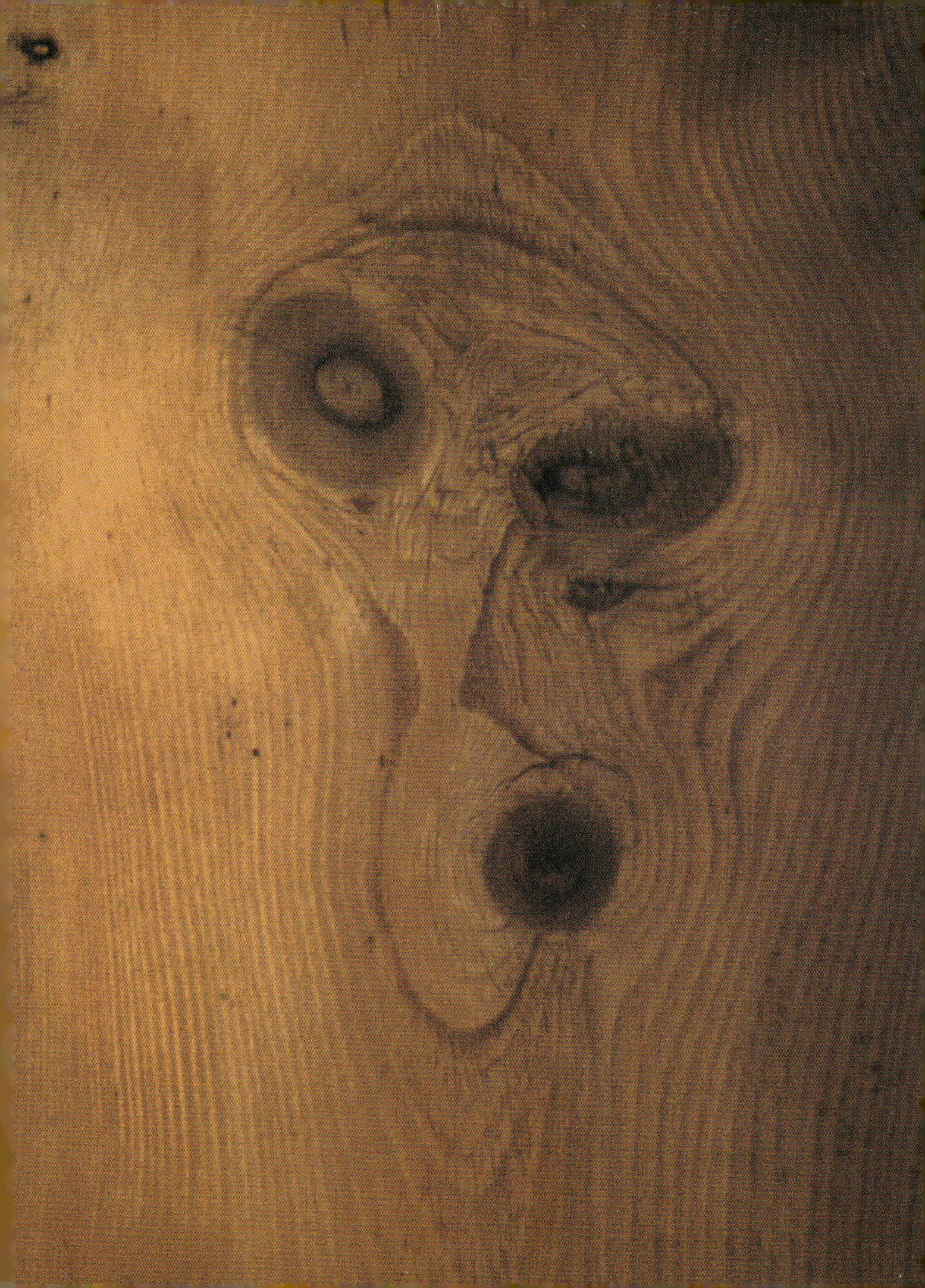

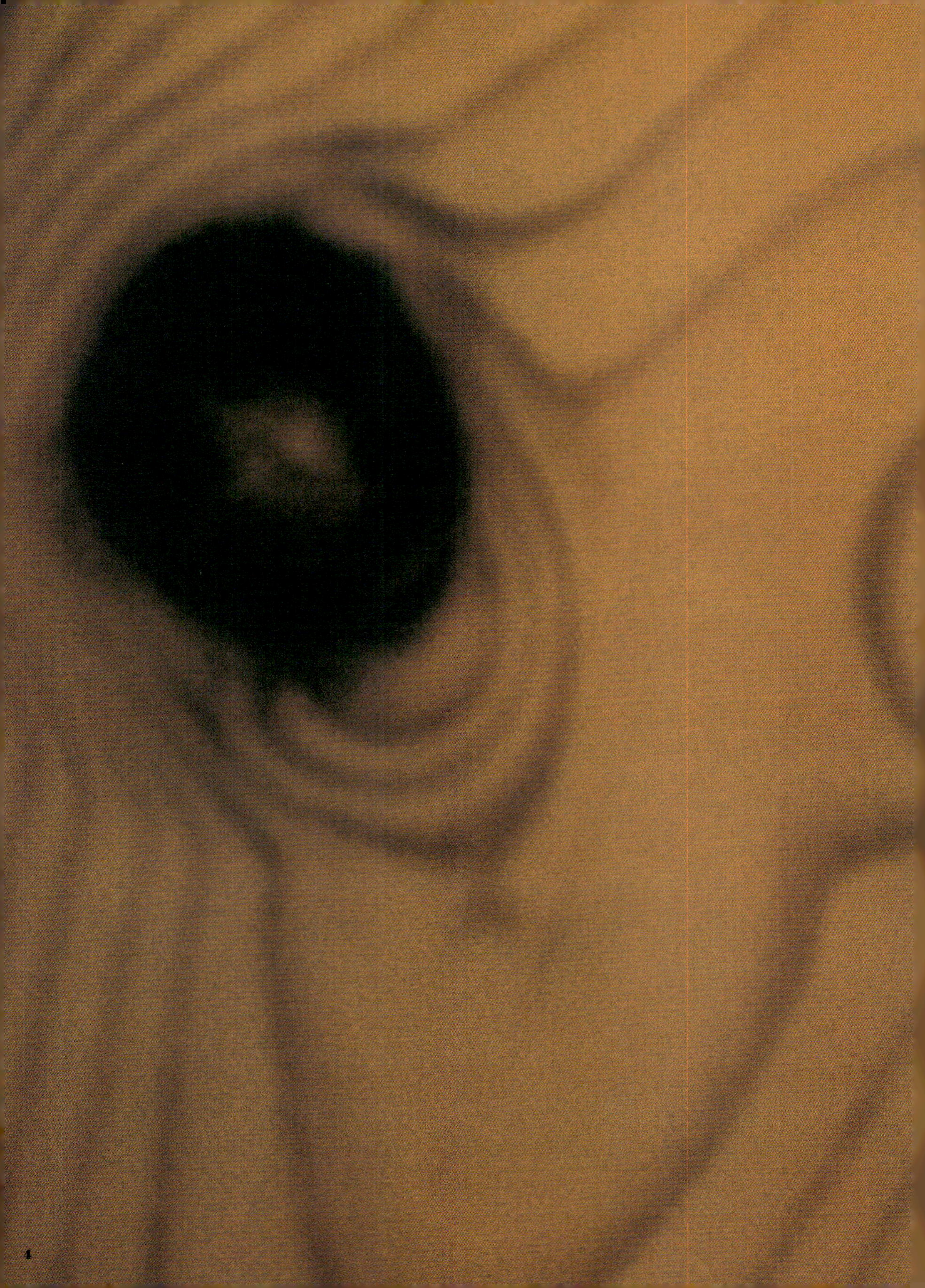

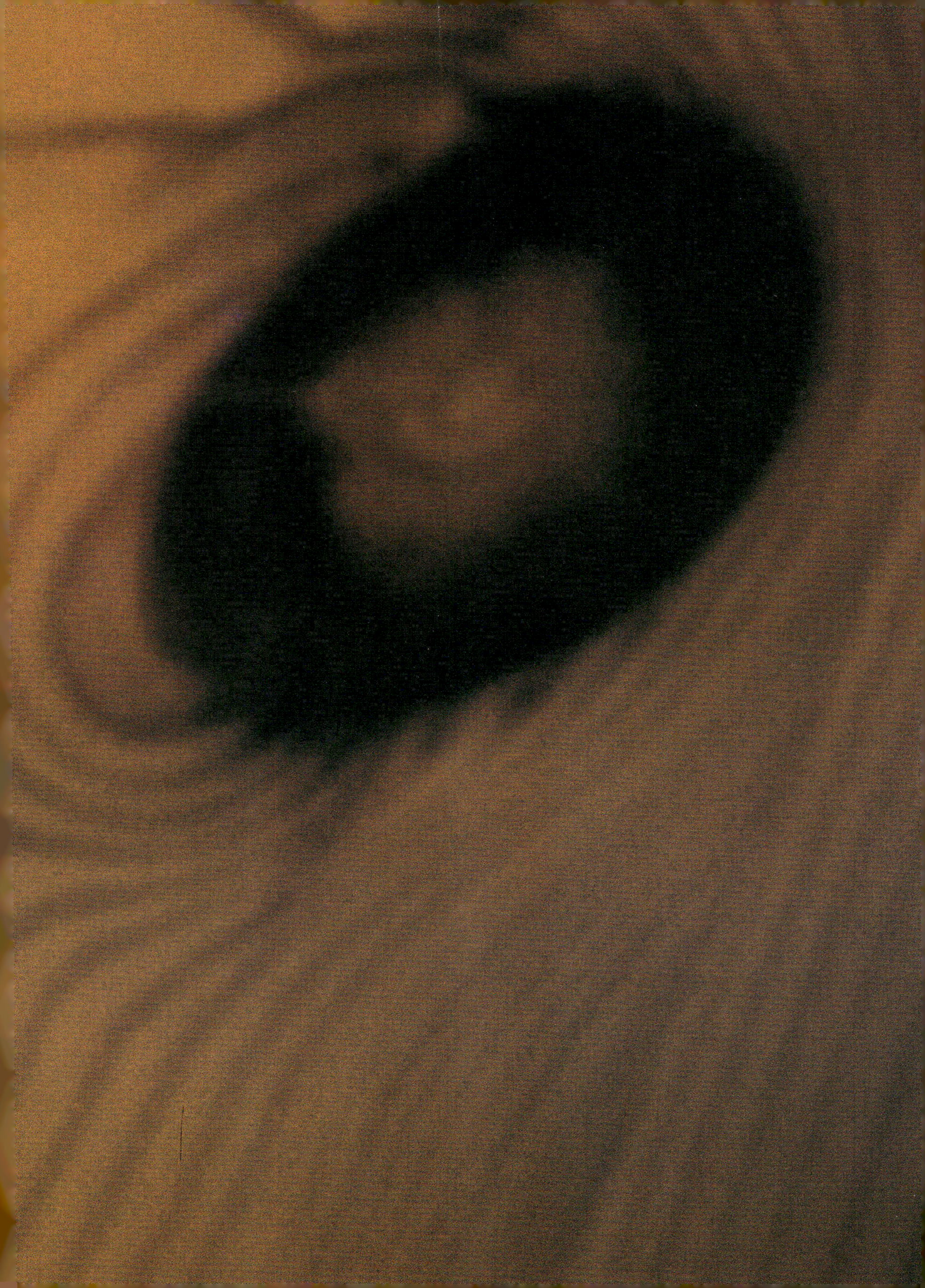

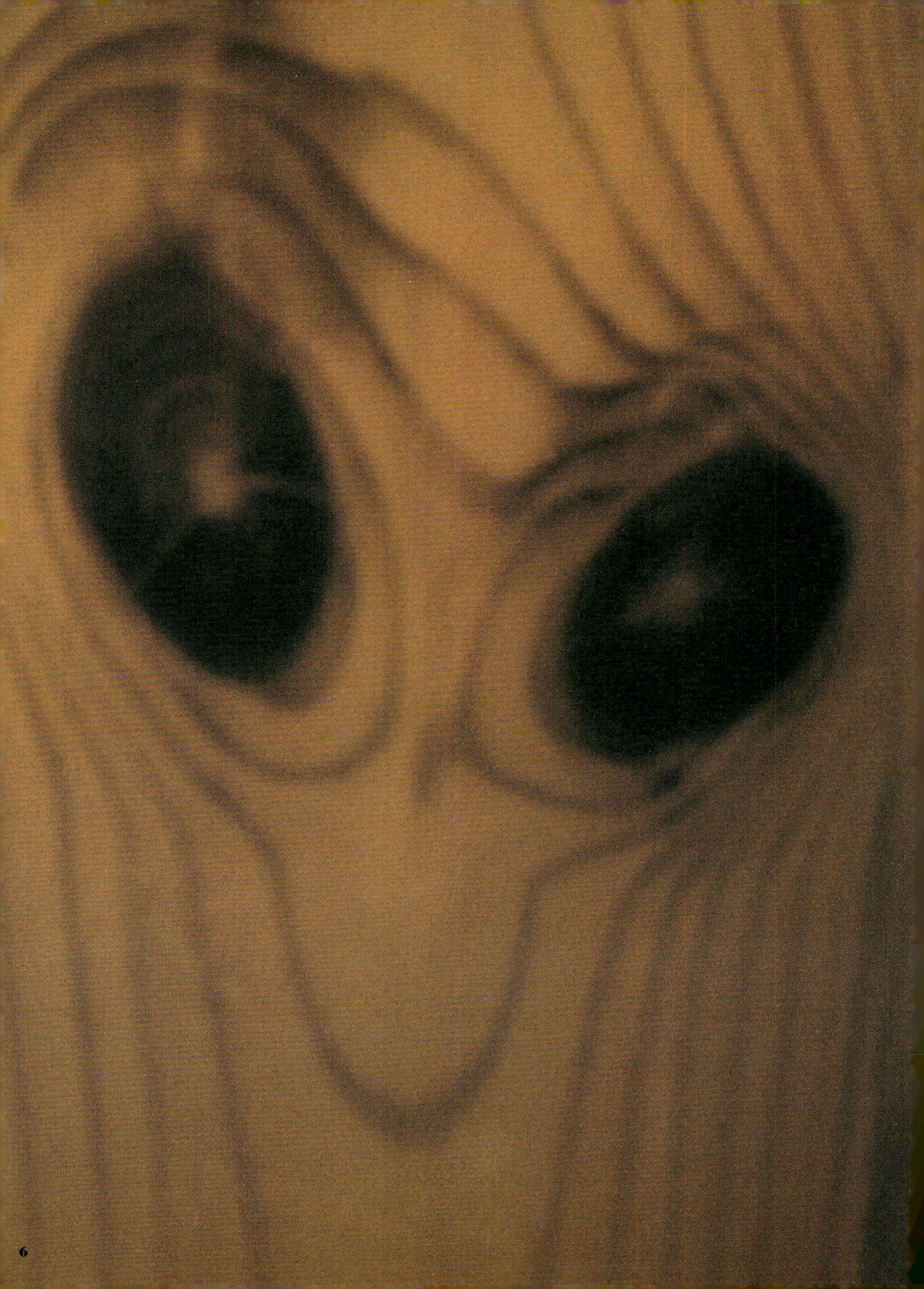

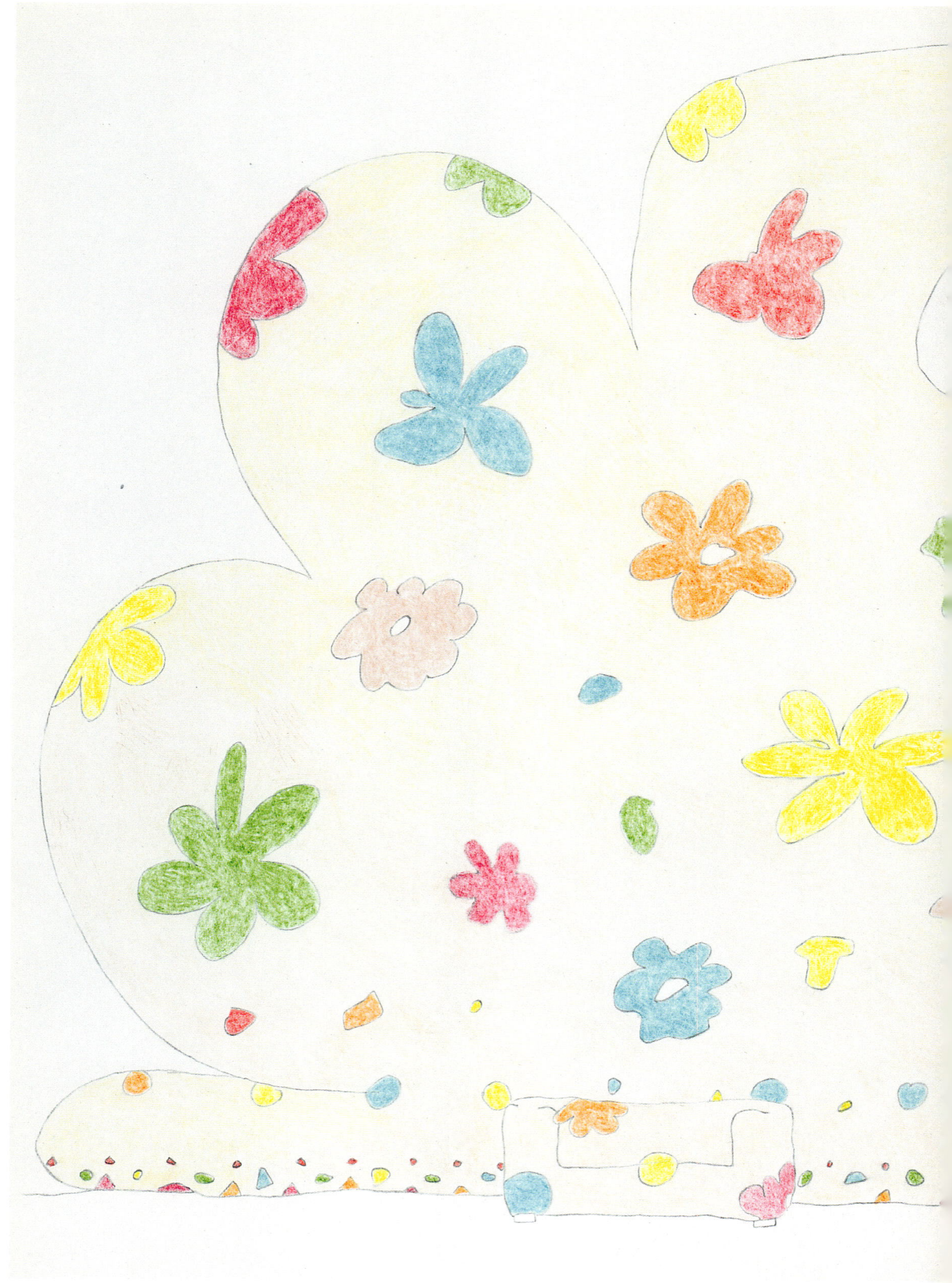

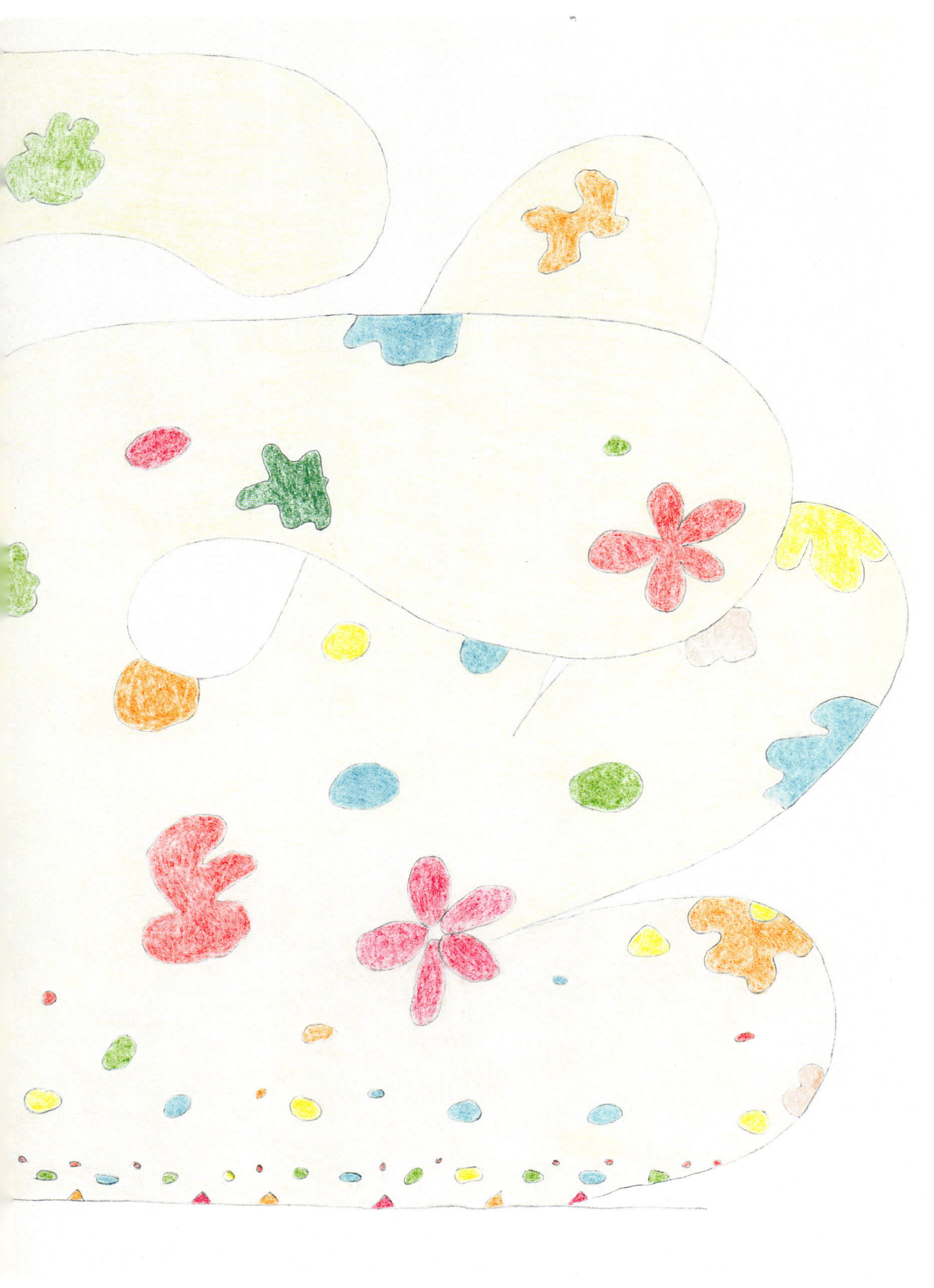

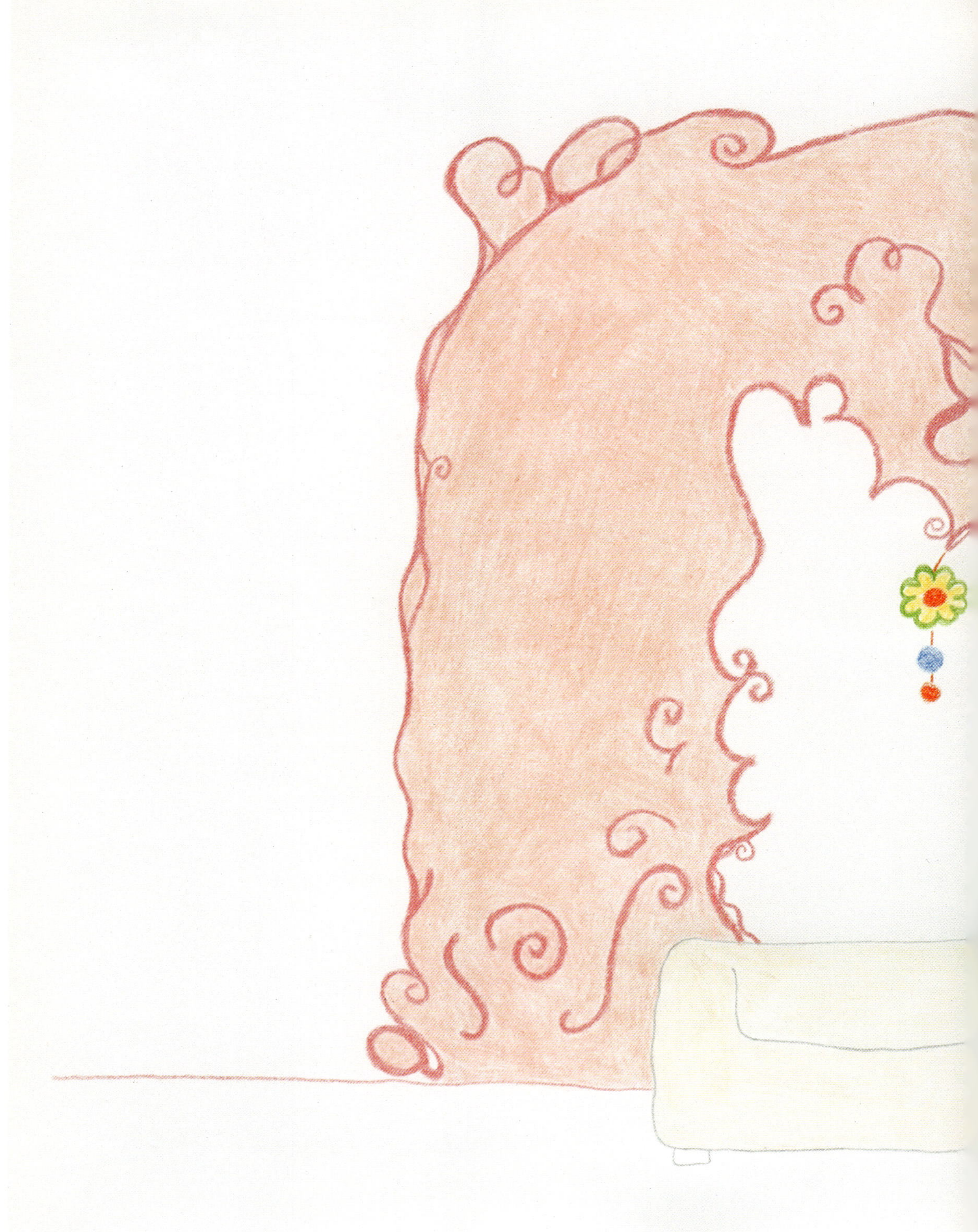

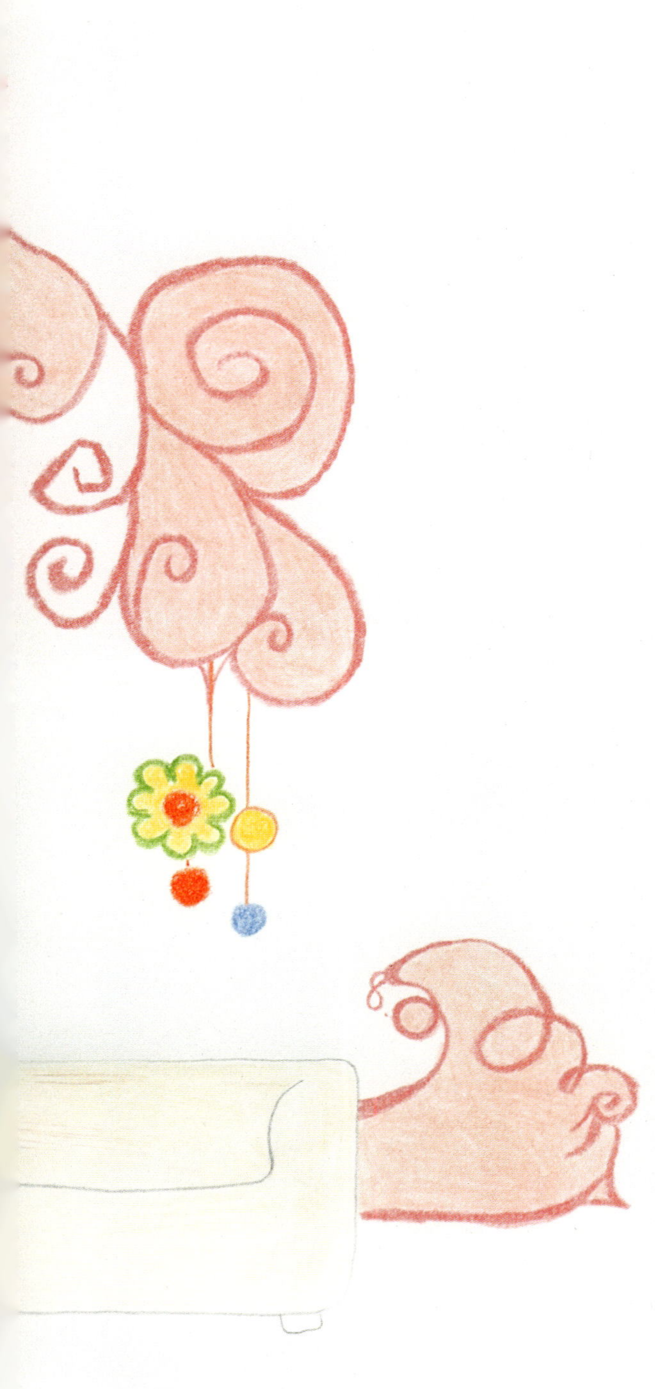

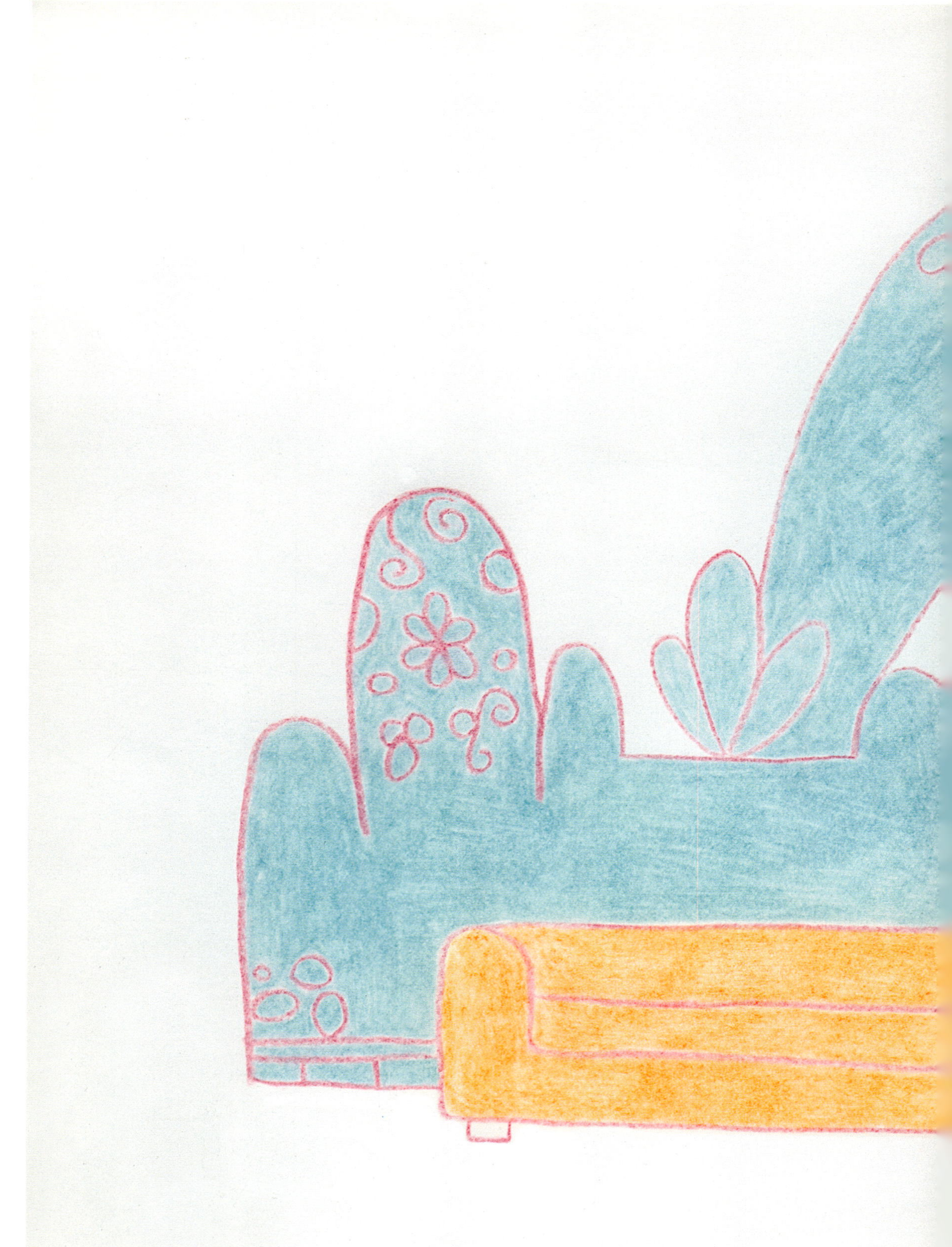

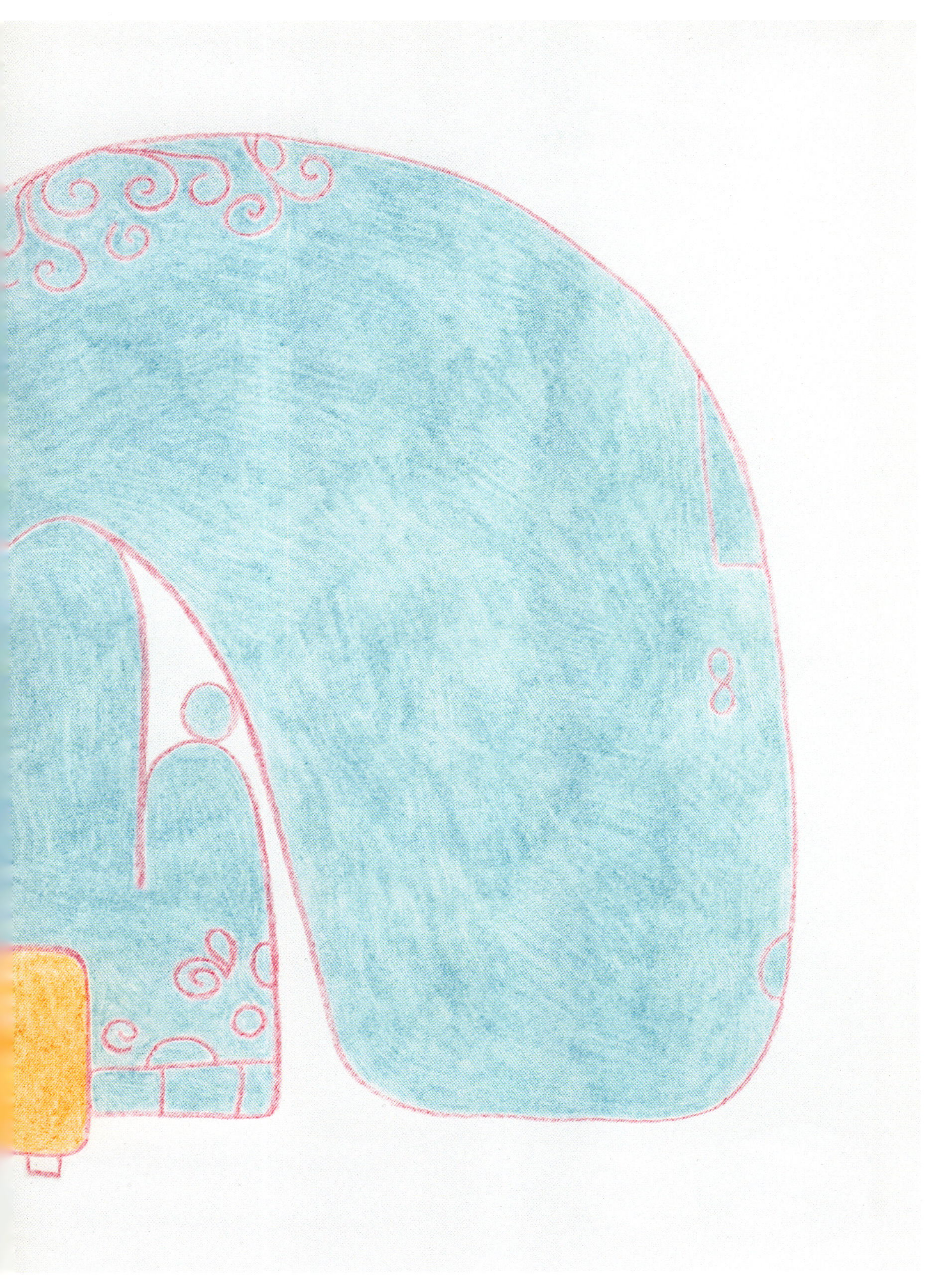

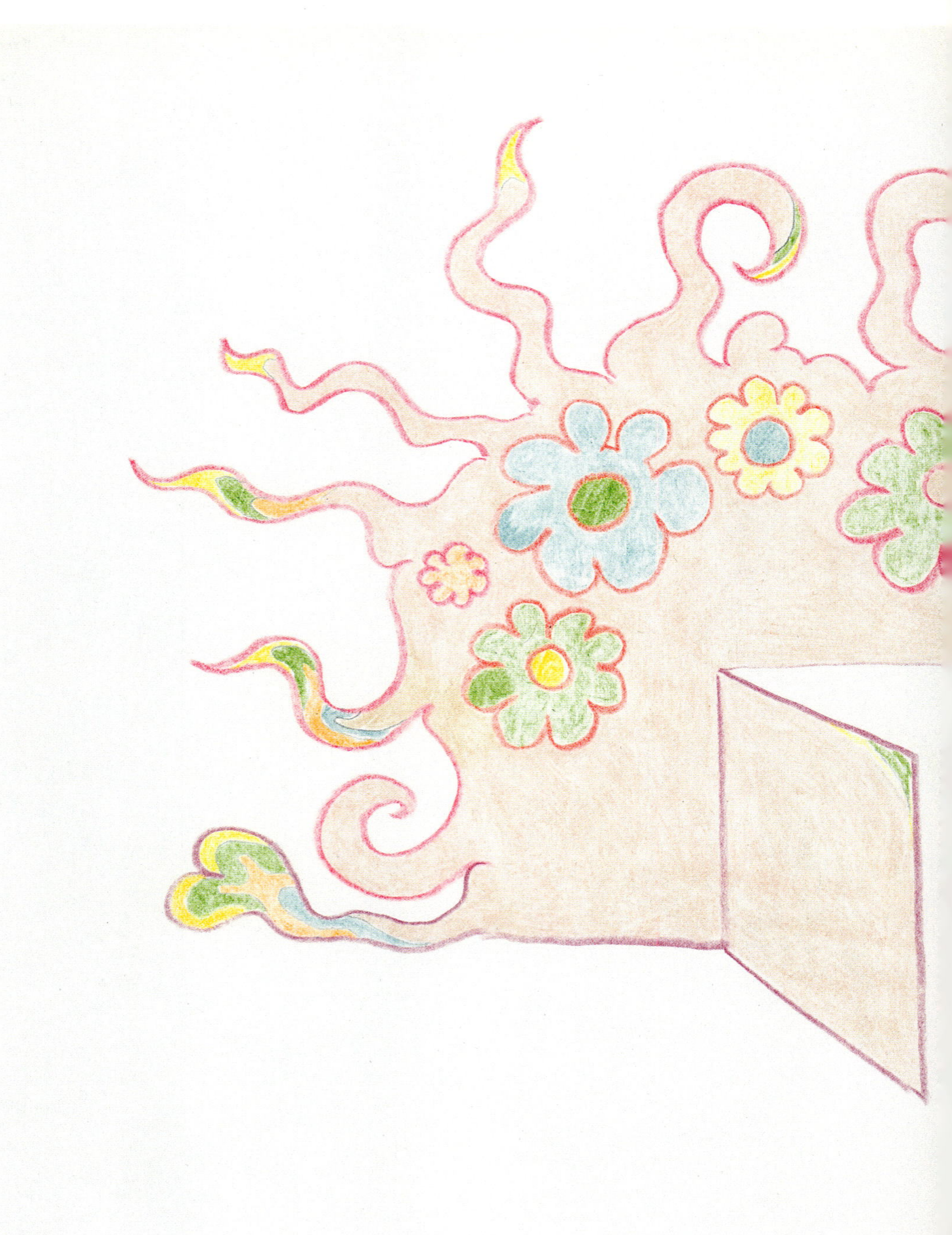

wallpainting + doors

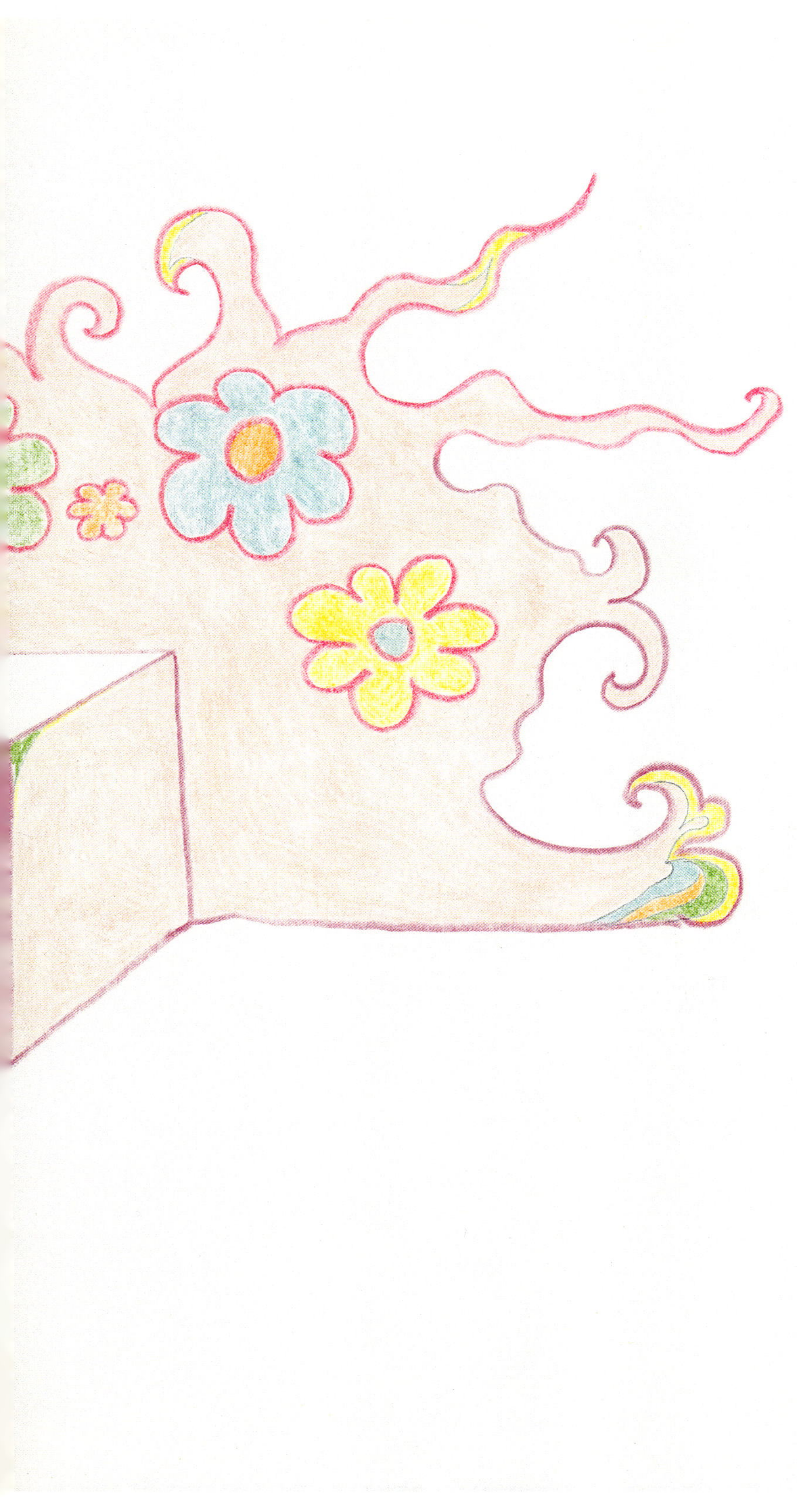

MOST NEEDED

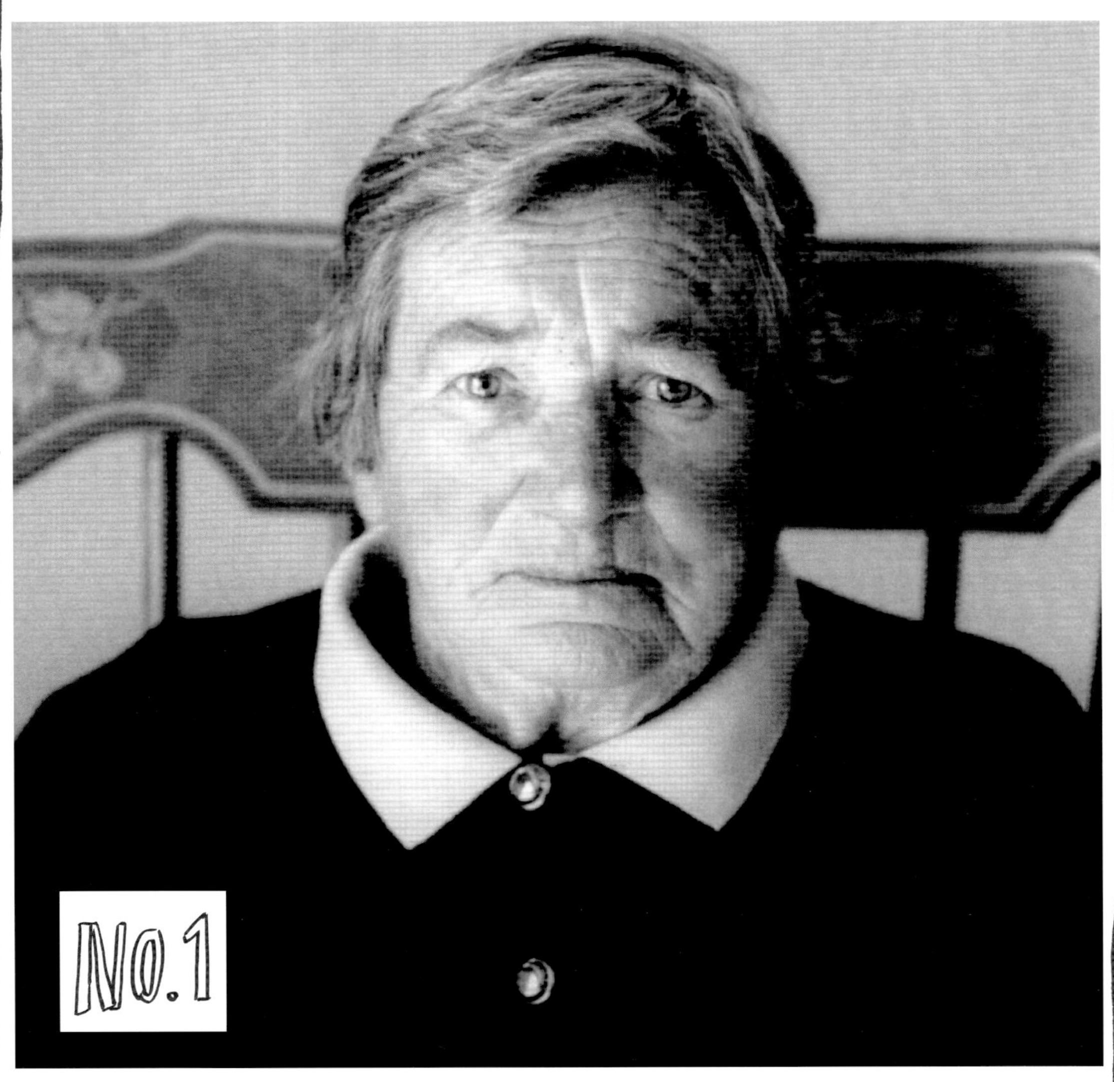

BEAUTY

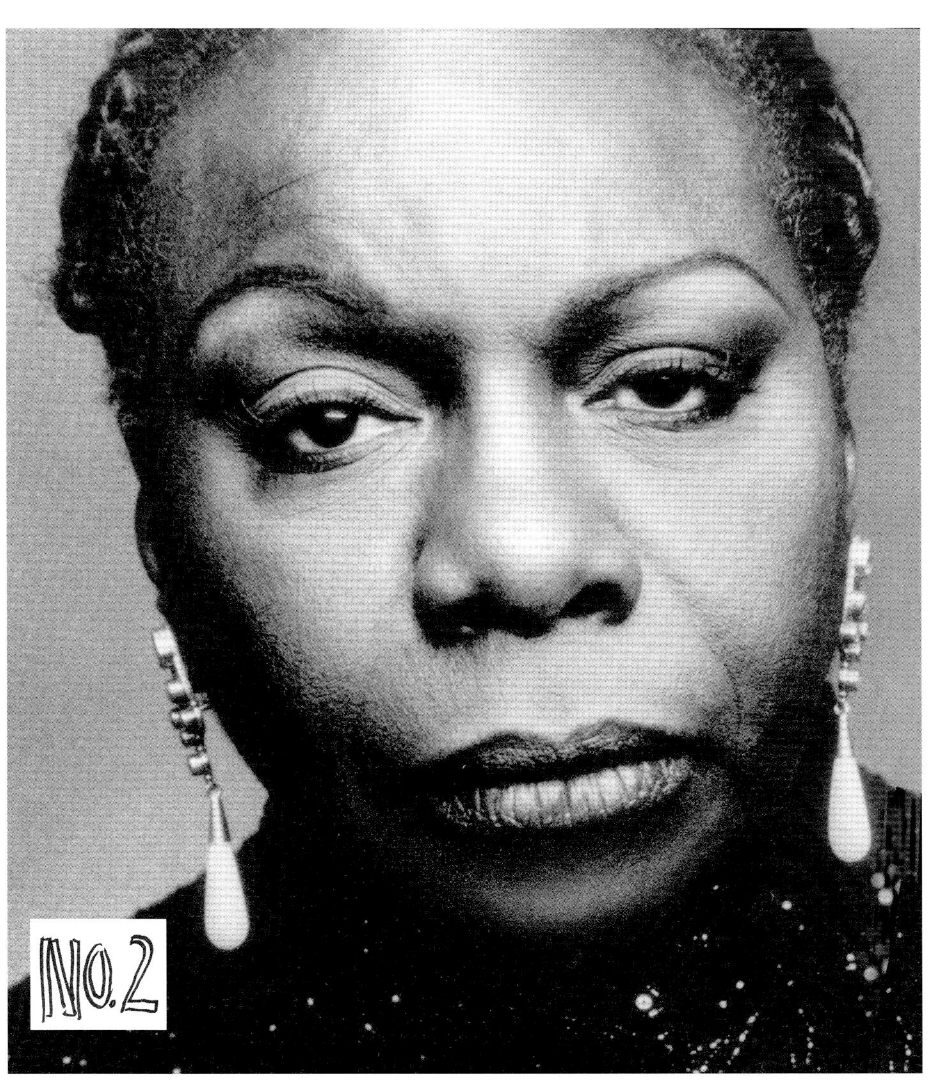

MOST NEEDED
No.2
BEAUTY

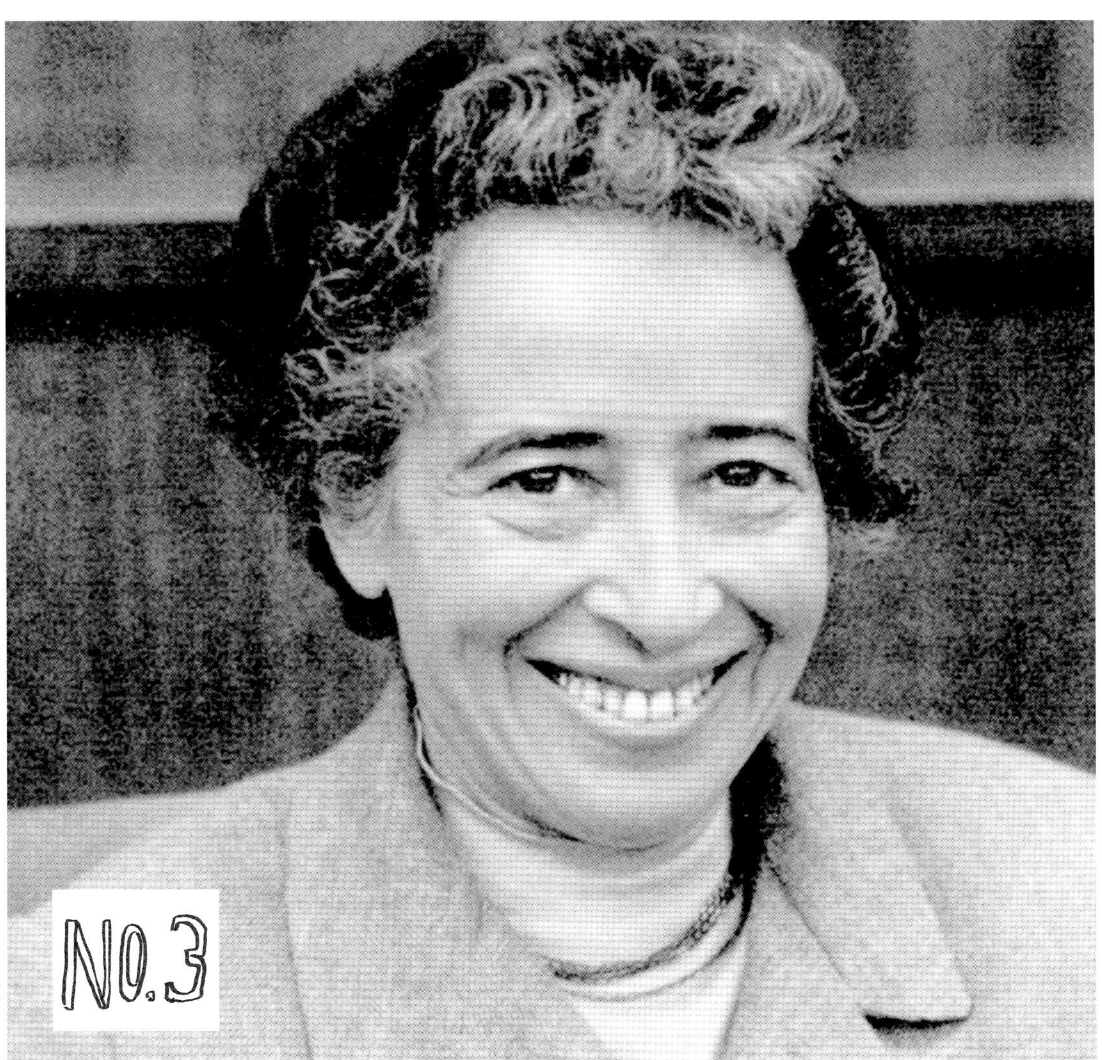
MOST NEEDED
No.3
BEAUTY

MOST NEEDED

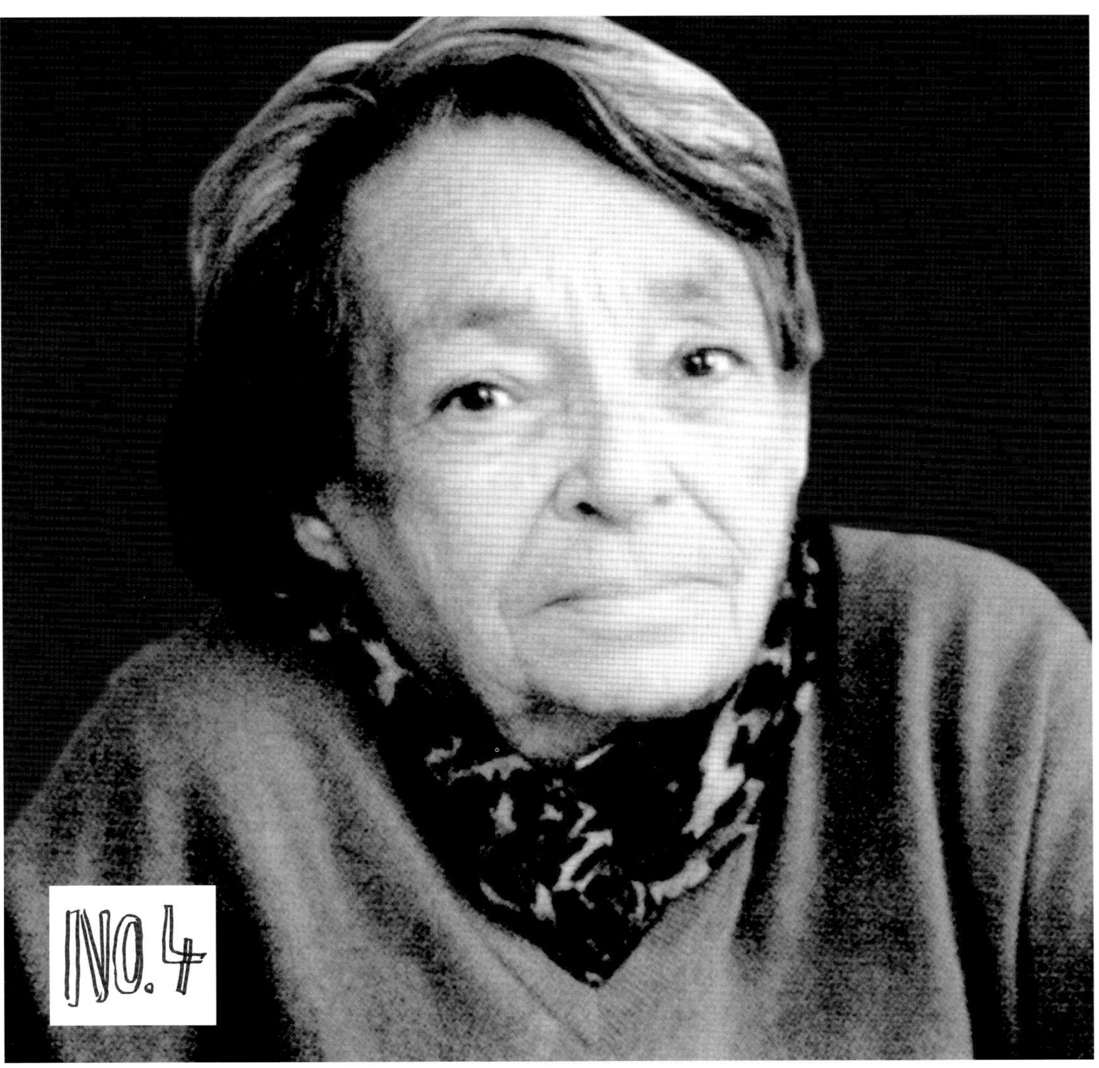

BEAUTY

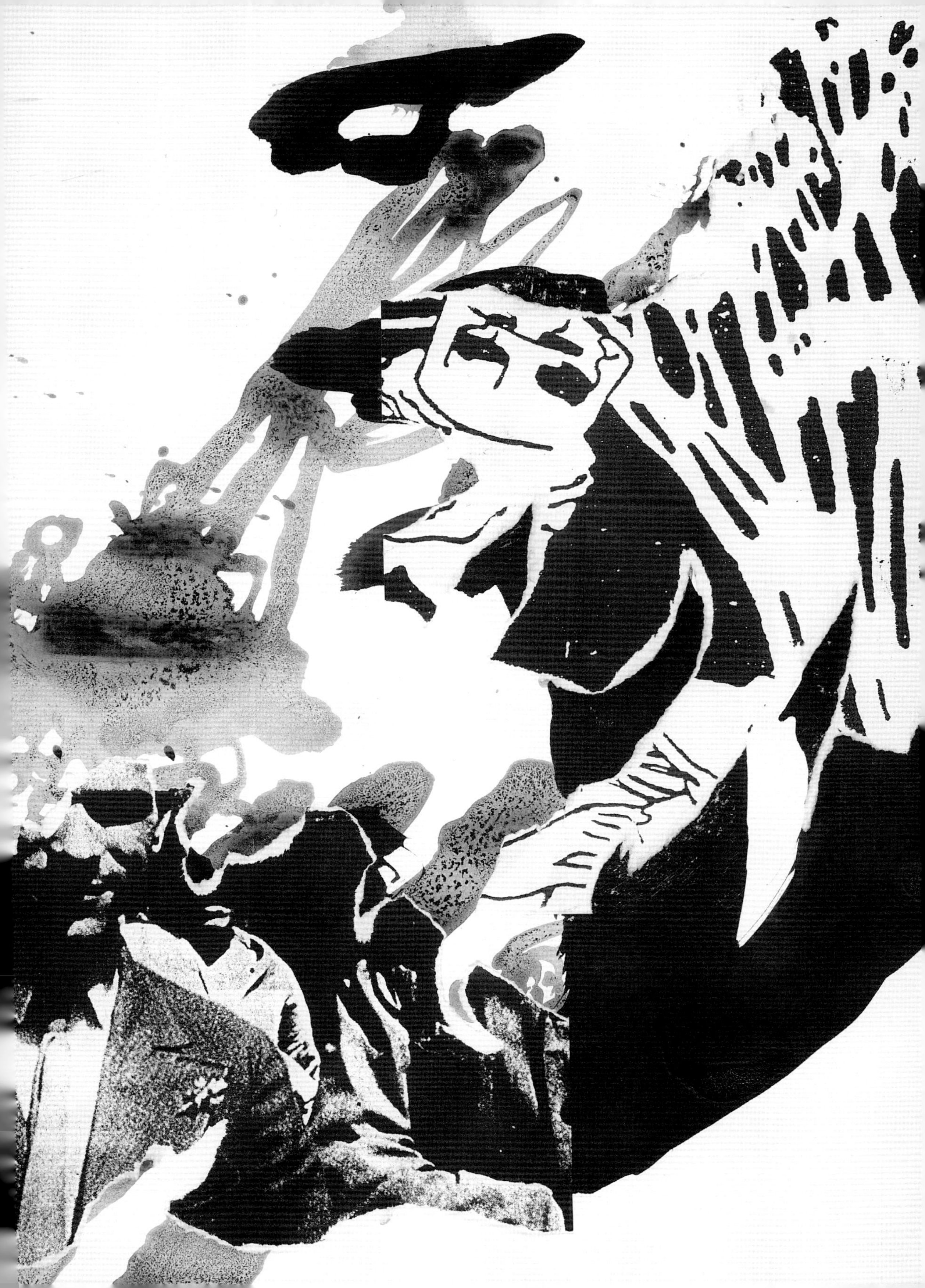

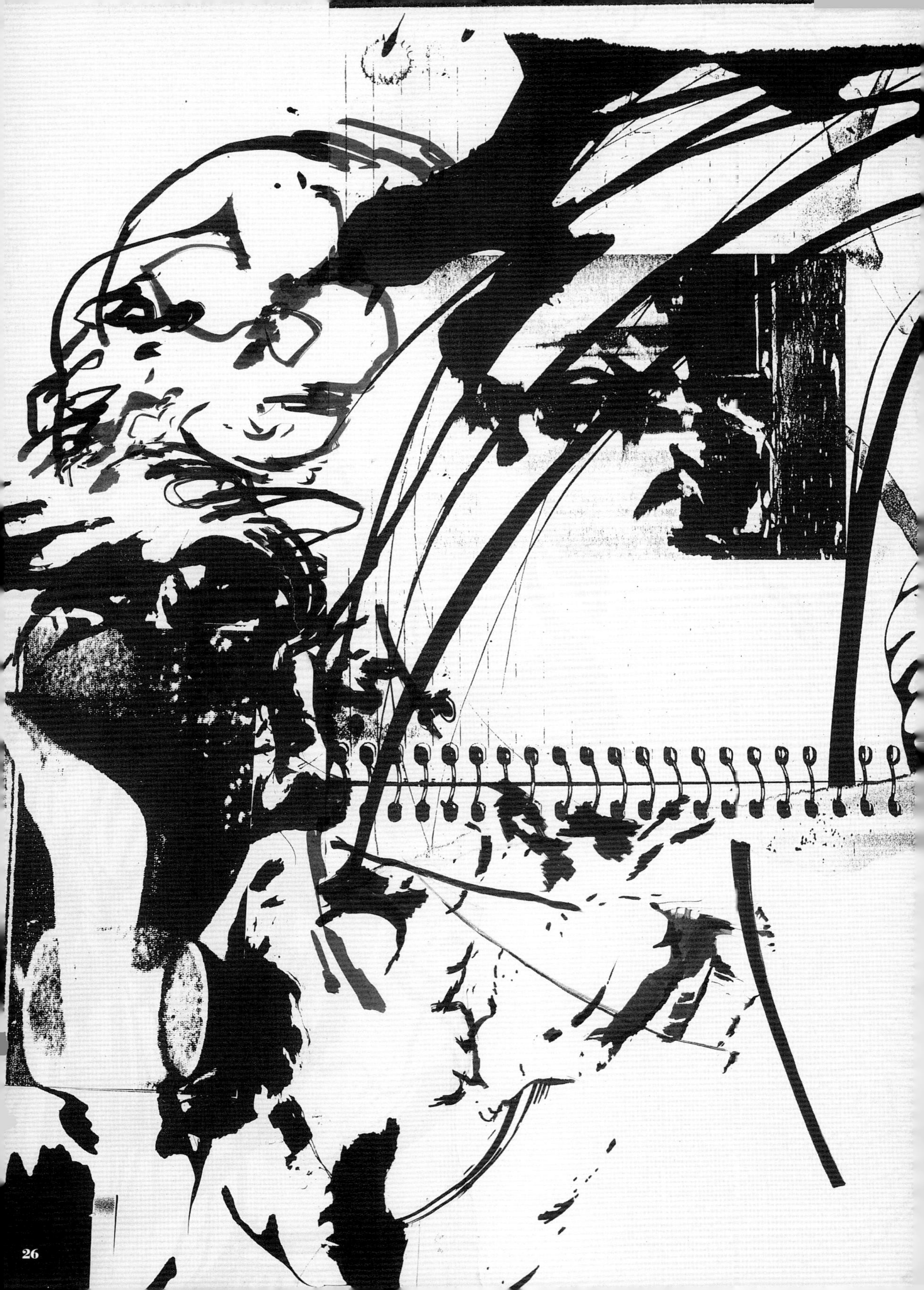

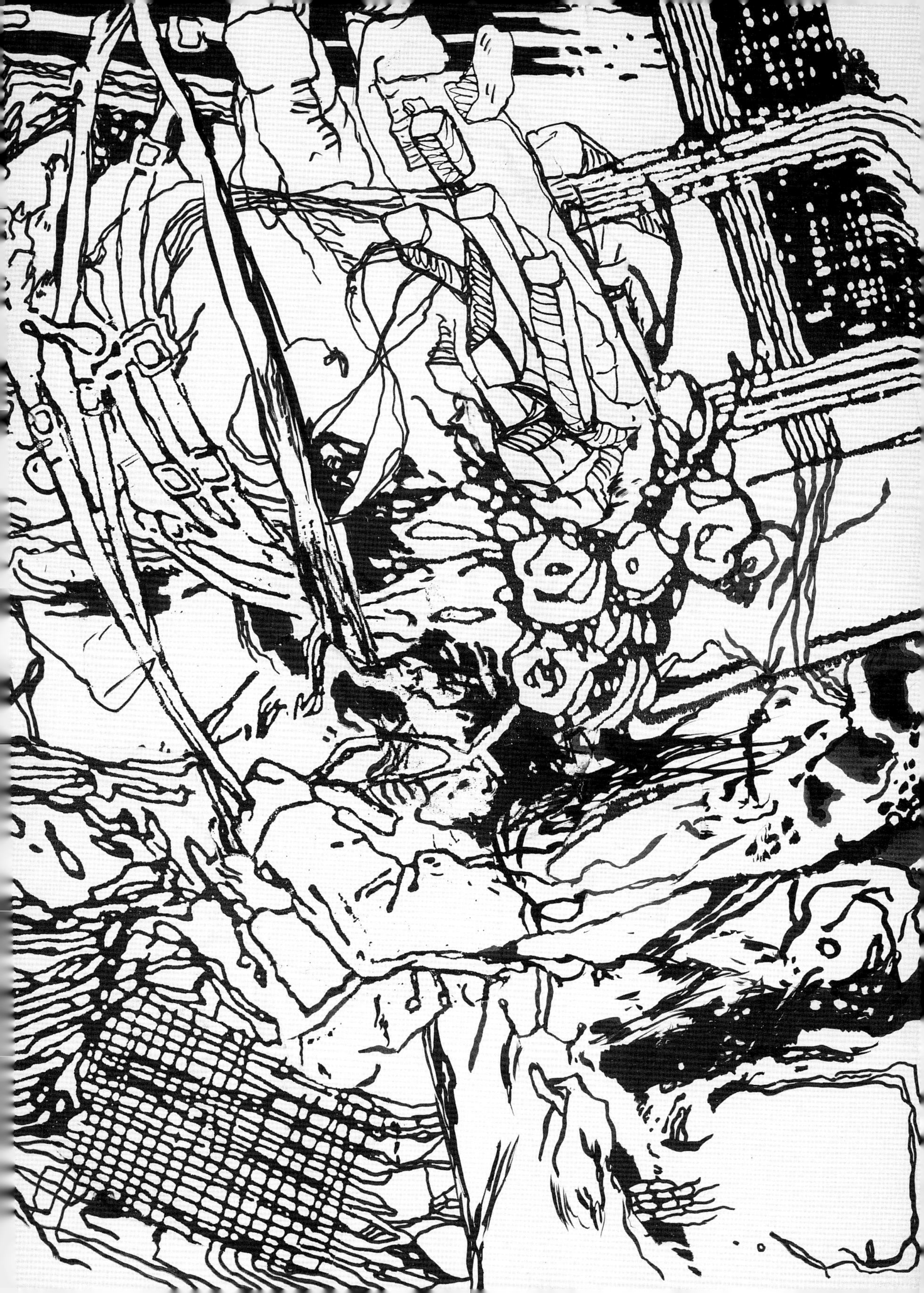

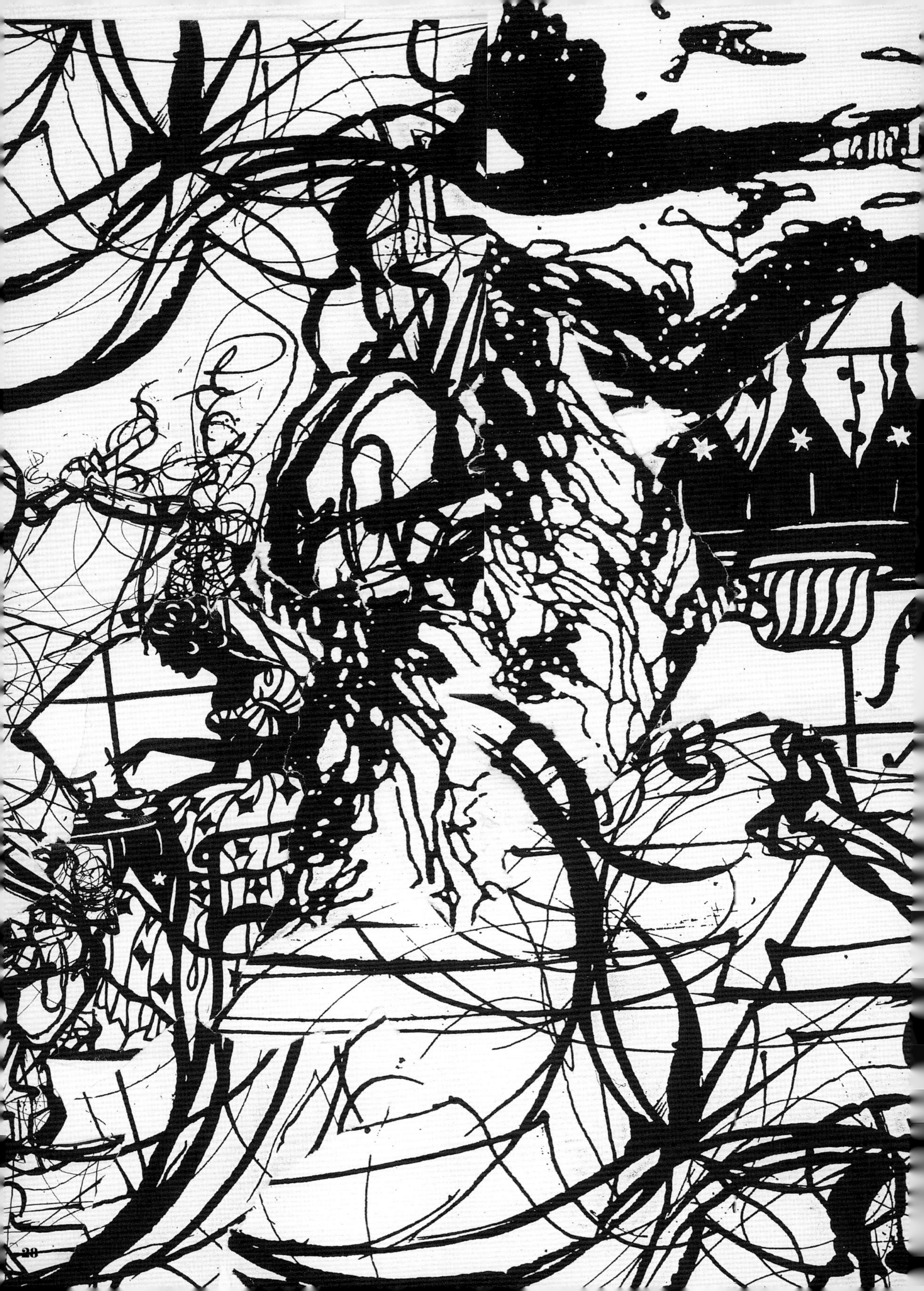

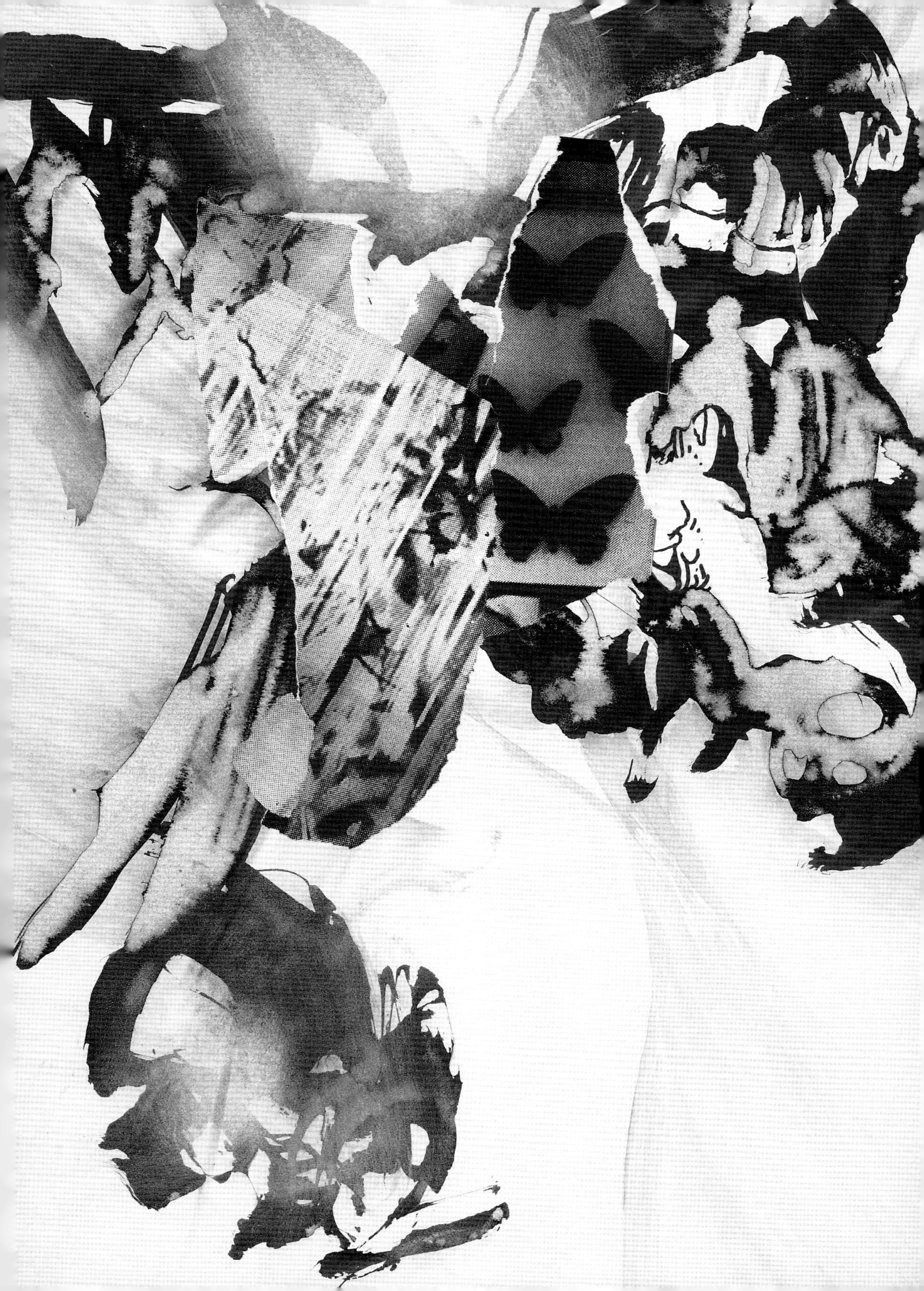

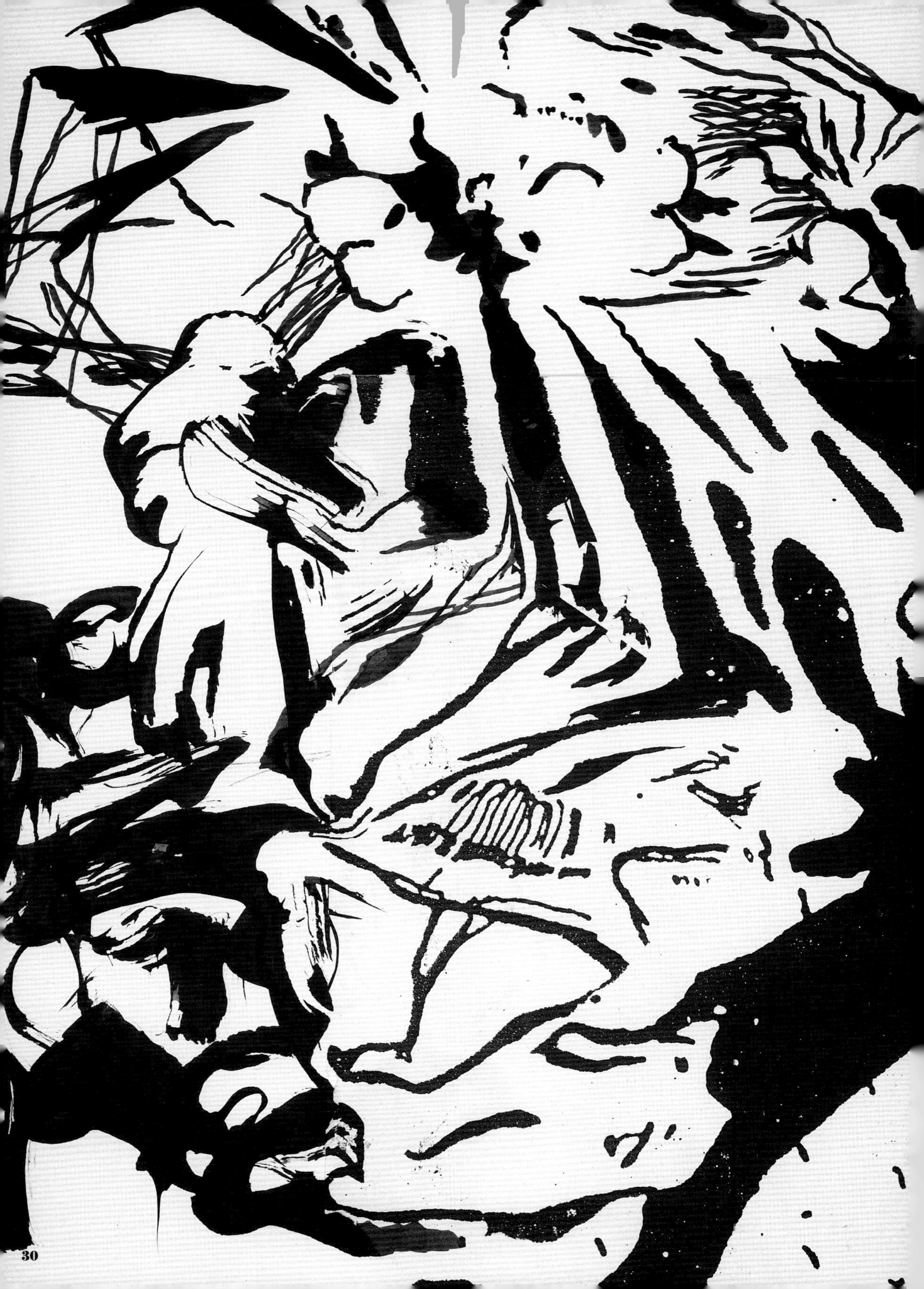

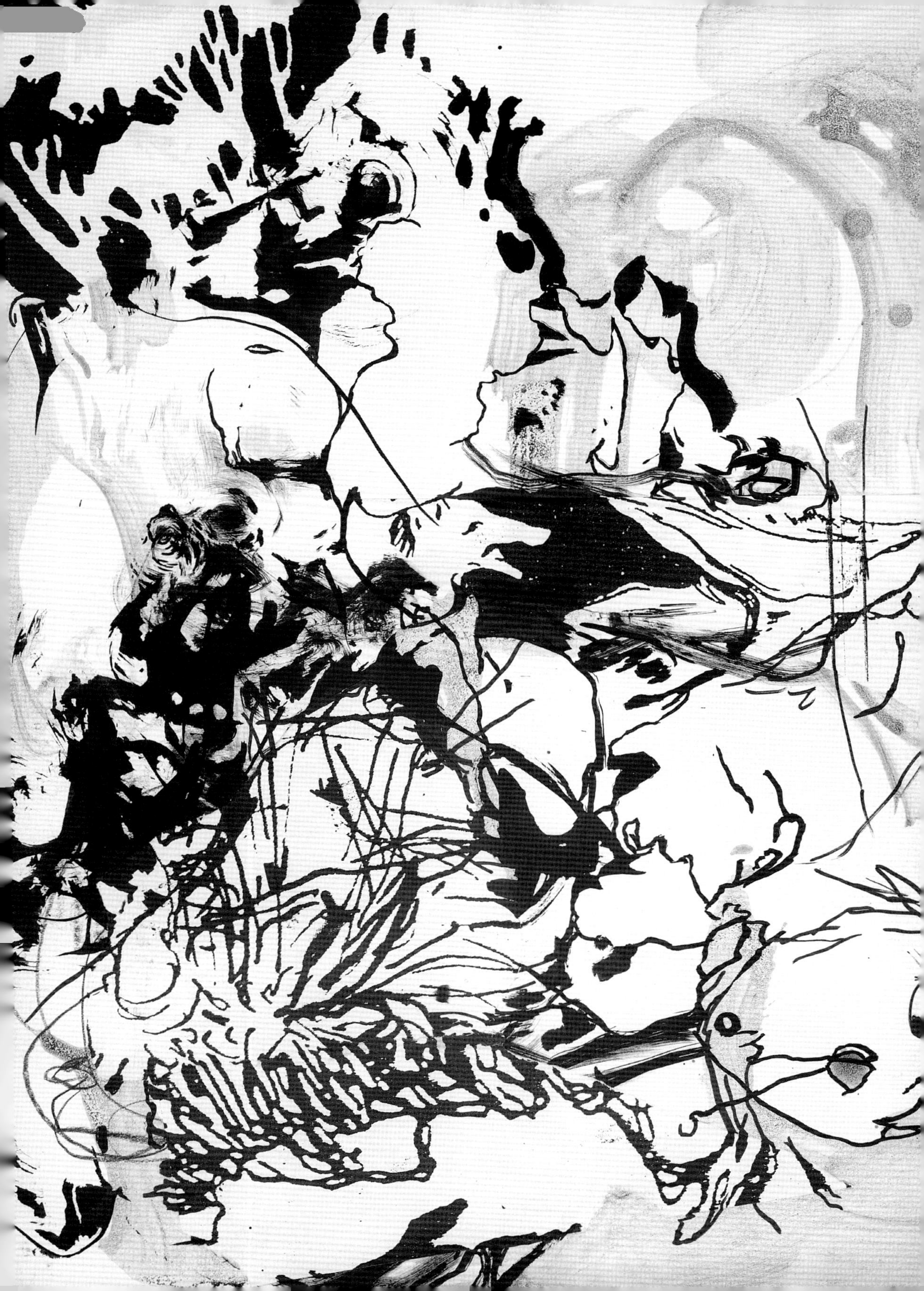

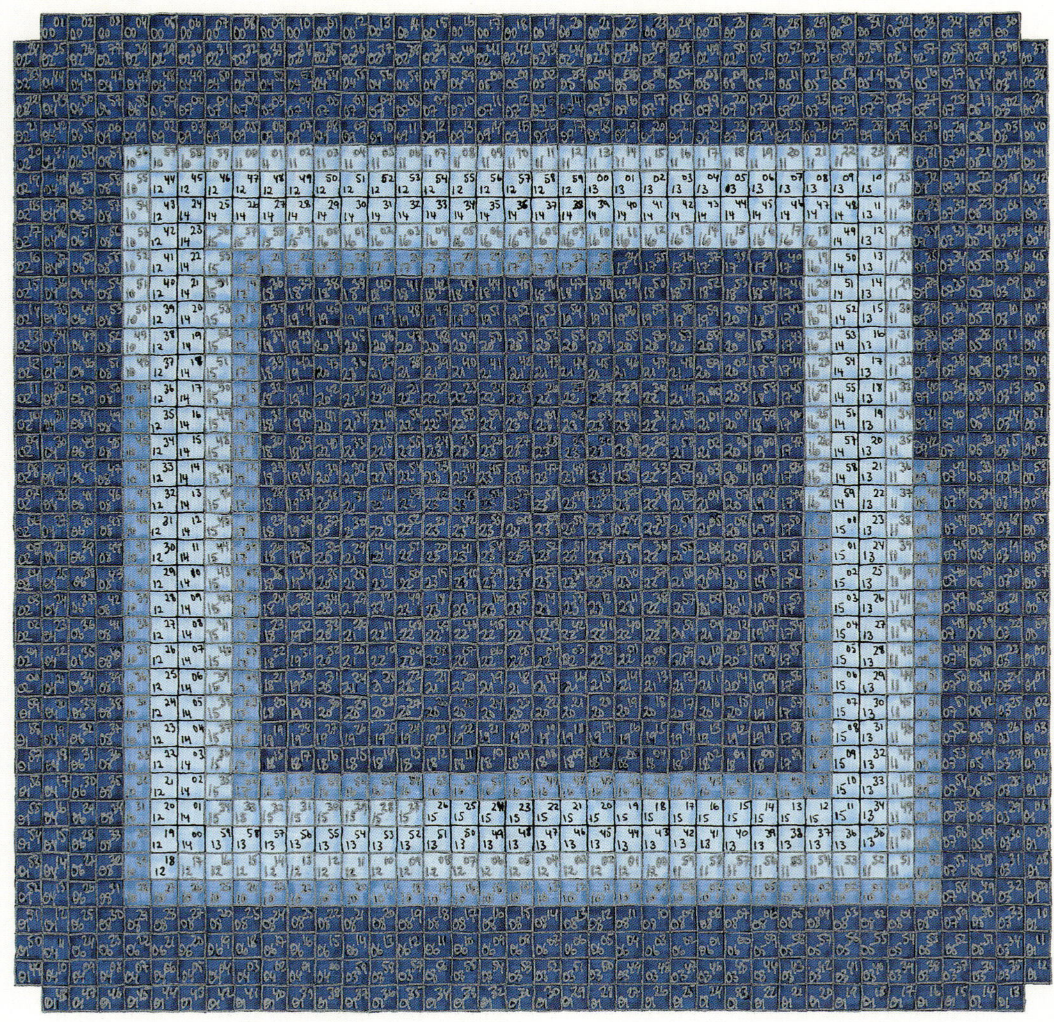

BORG 21°W 64°N
18.01.2003

BIRTING · DAYBREAK · TAGESANBRUCH   09:43 – 10:47

SOLRIS · SUNRISE · SONNENAUFGANG   10:48 – 16:28

SOLARLAG · SUNSET · SONNENUNTERGANG 16: 29 – 17:33

MYRKUR · DARKNESS · FINSTERNIS   17:34 – 09:42

TUNGLSKIN · MOONSHINE · MONDSCHEIN   15:27 – 02:17

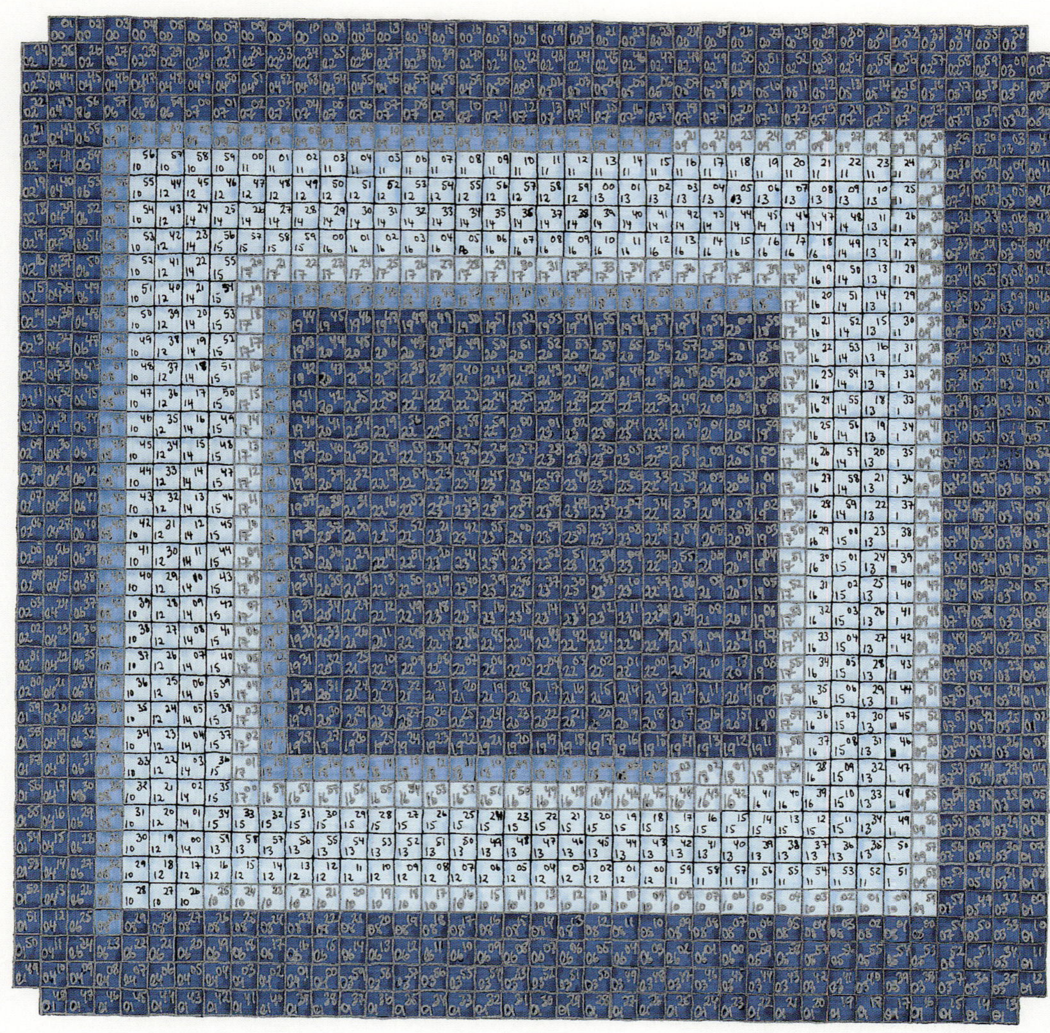

BORG 21°W 64°N
16.02.2003

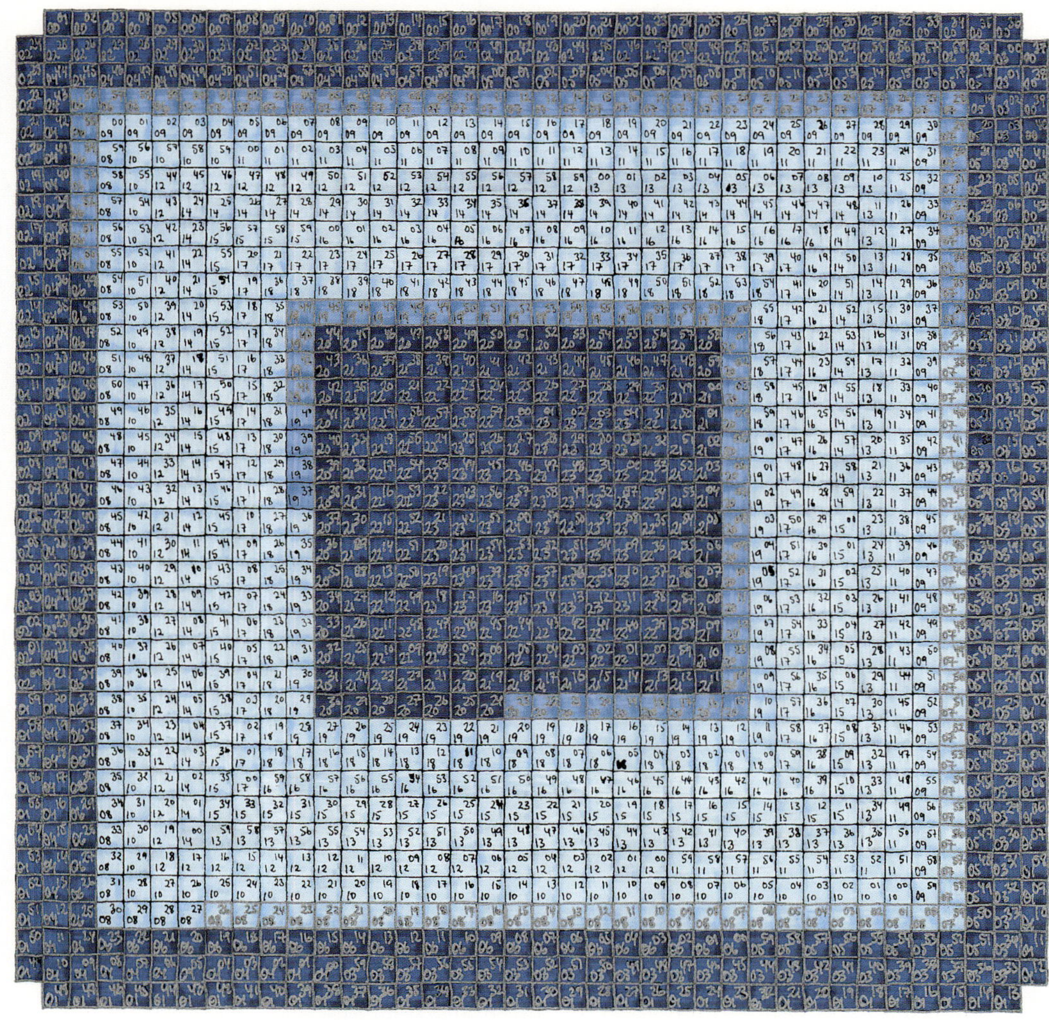

BIRTING · DAYBREAK · TAGESANBRUCH   06:50 – 07:36

SOLRIS · SUNRISE · SONNENAUFGANG   07:37 – 19:36

SOLARLAG · SUNSET · SONNENUNTERGANG   19:37 – 20:24

MYRKUR · DARKNESS · FINSTERNIS   20:24 – 06:49

TUNGLSKIN · MOONSHINE · MONDSCHINE   19:41 – 08:26

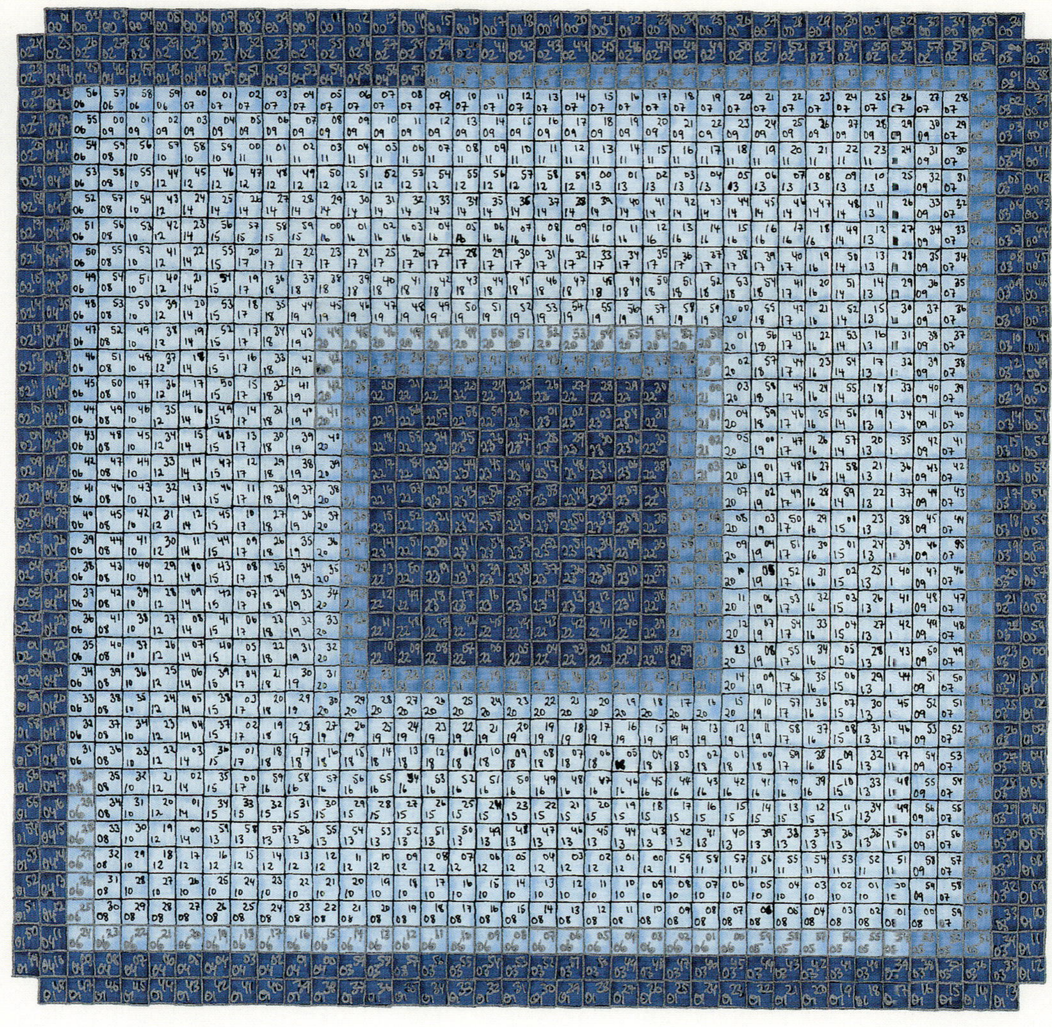

BIRTING · DAYBREAK · TAGESANBRUCH   04:58 – 05:53

SOLRIS · SUNRISE · SONNENAUFGANG   05:54 – 21:03

SOLARLAG · SUNSET · SONNENUNTERGANG   21:04 – 21:58

MYRKUR · DARKNESS · FINSTERNIS   **21:59 – 04:57**

TUNGLSKIN · MOONSHINE · MONDSCHEIN   20:41 – 06:30

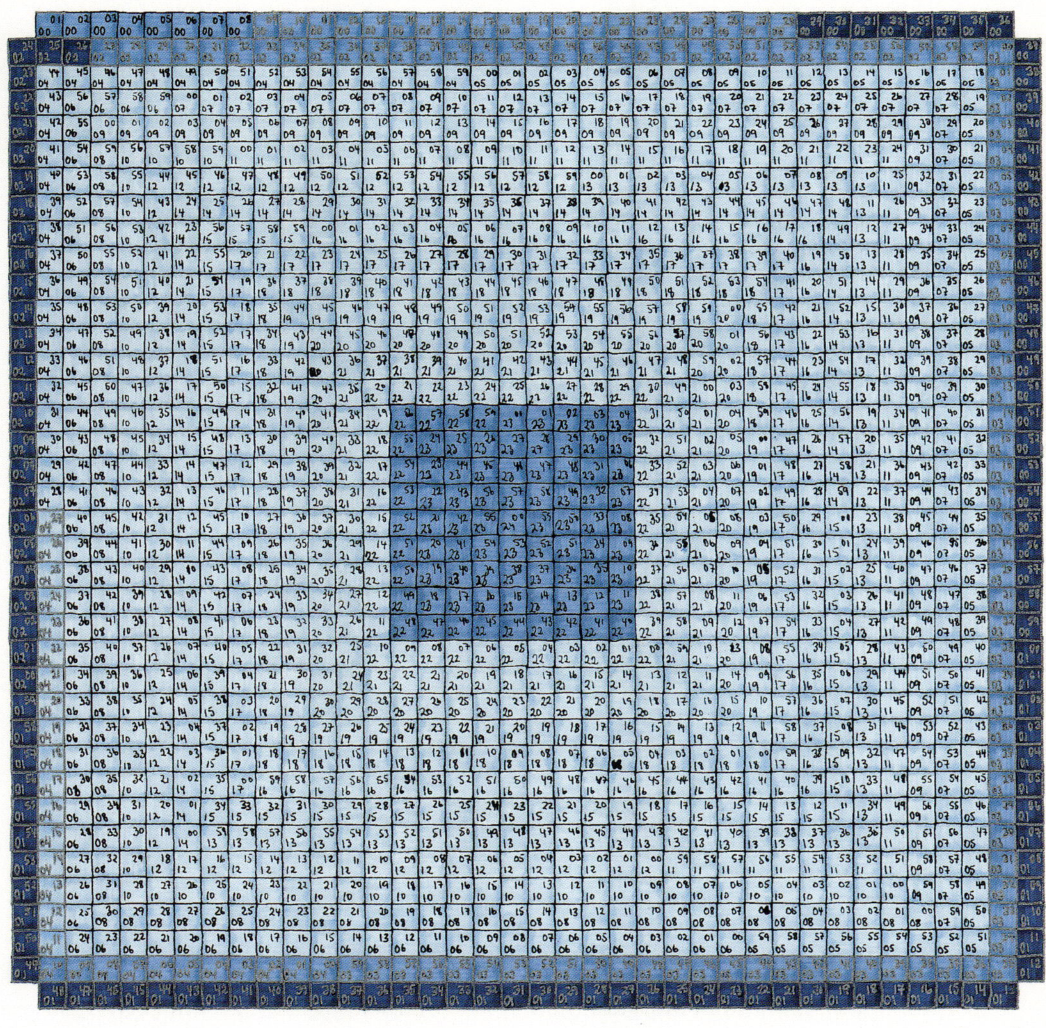

BIRTING · DAYBREAK · TAGESANBRUCH   02:27 – 04:10

SOLRIS · SUNRISE · SONNENAUFGANG   04:11 – 22:39

SOLARLAG · SUNSET · SONNENUNTERGANG   22:40 – 24:28

MYRKUR · DARKNESS · FINSTERNIS   24:29 – 02:26

TUNGLSKIN · MOONSHINE · MONDSCHEIN   24:09 – 04:27

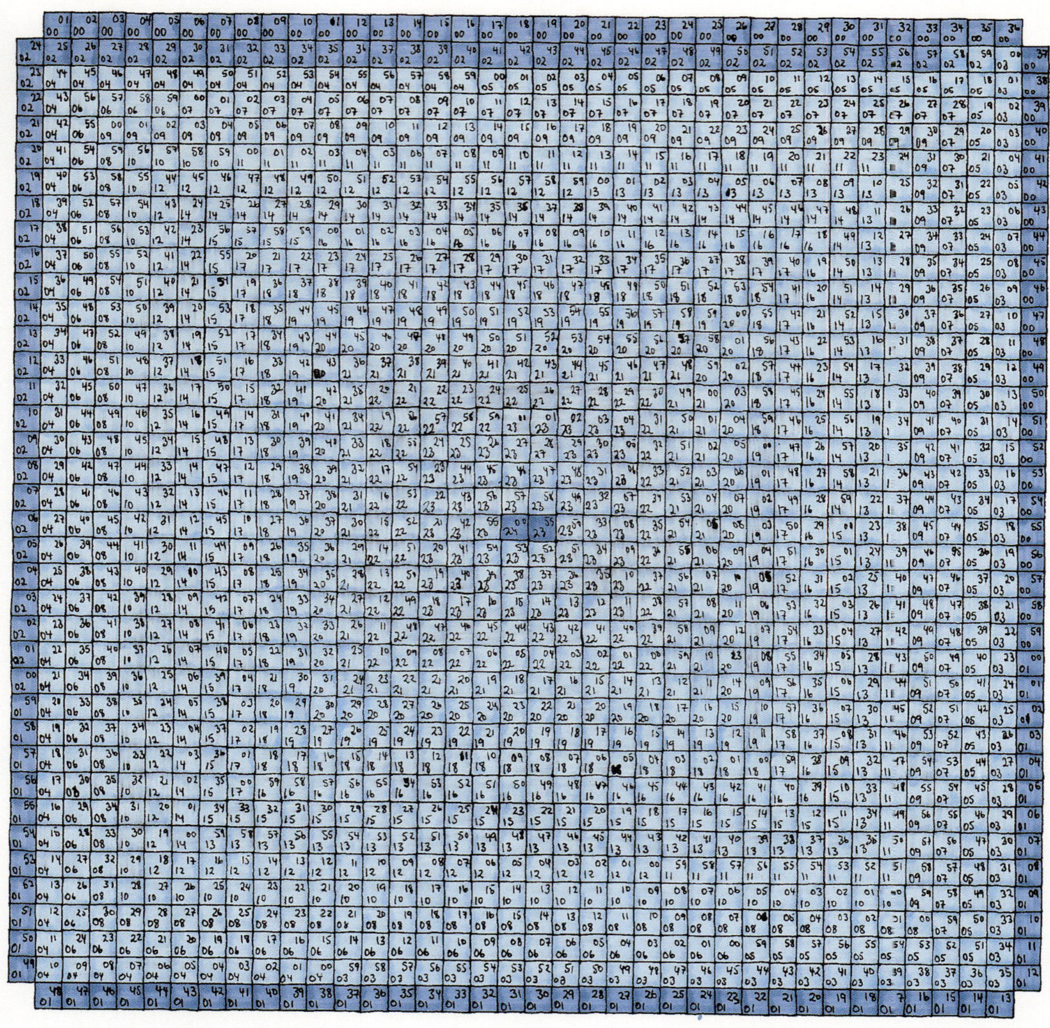

BORG 21°W 64°N
14.06.03

THE MOON IS EITHER BELOW THE HORIZON, OR, IF ABOVE, TOO CLOSE TO THE SUN TO BE VISIBLE IN THE SUN'S GLARE.

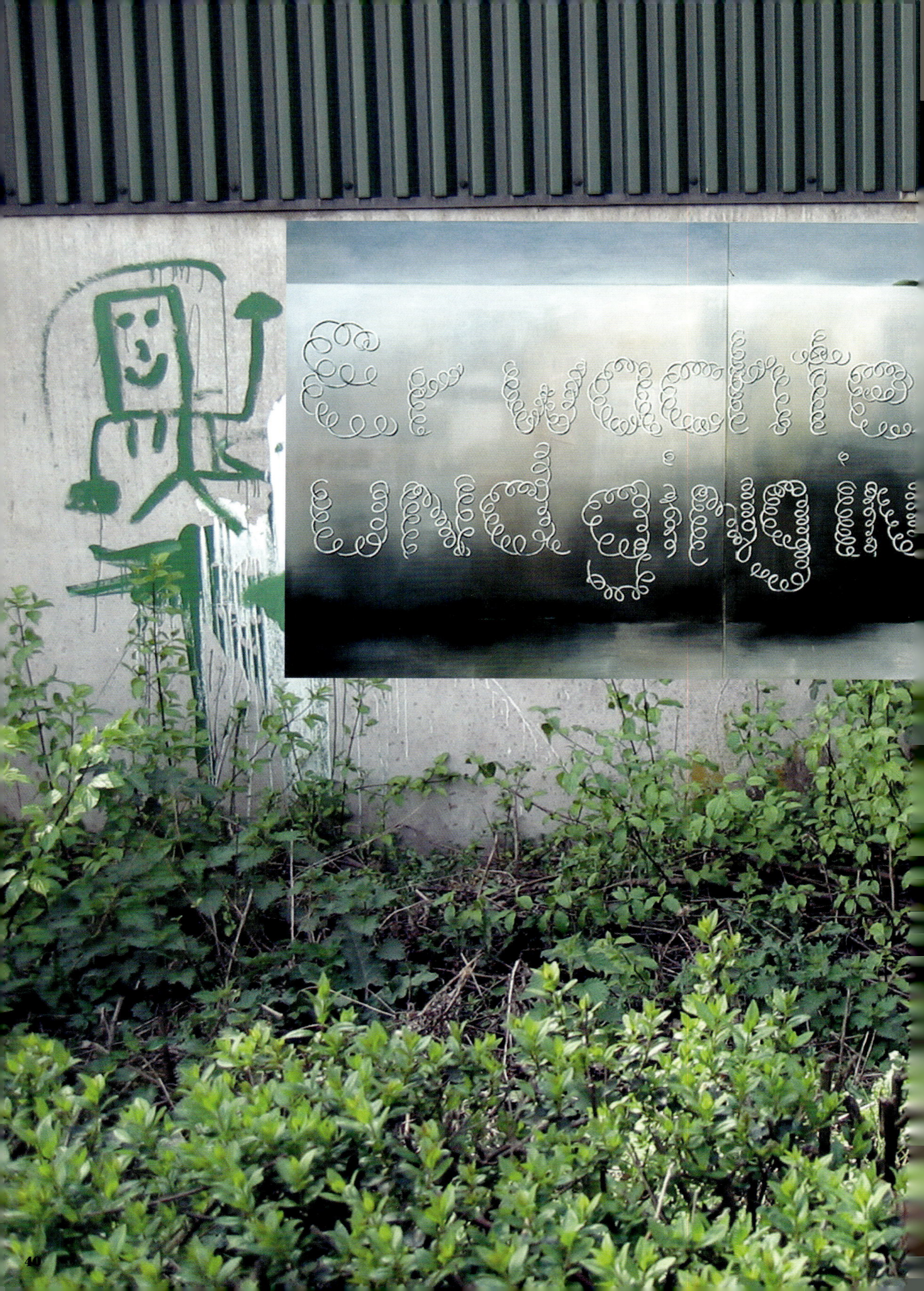

Er wachte
und singt

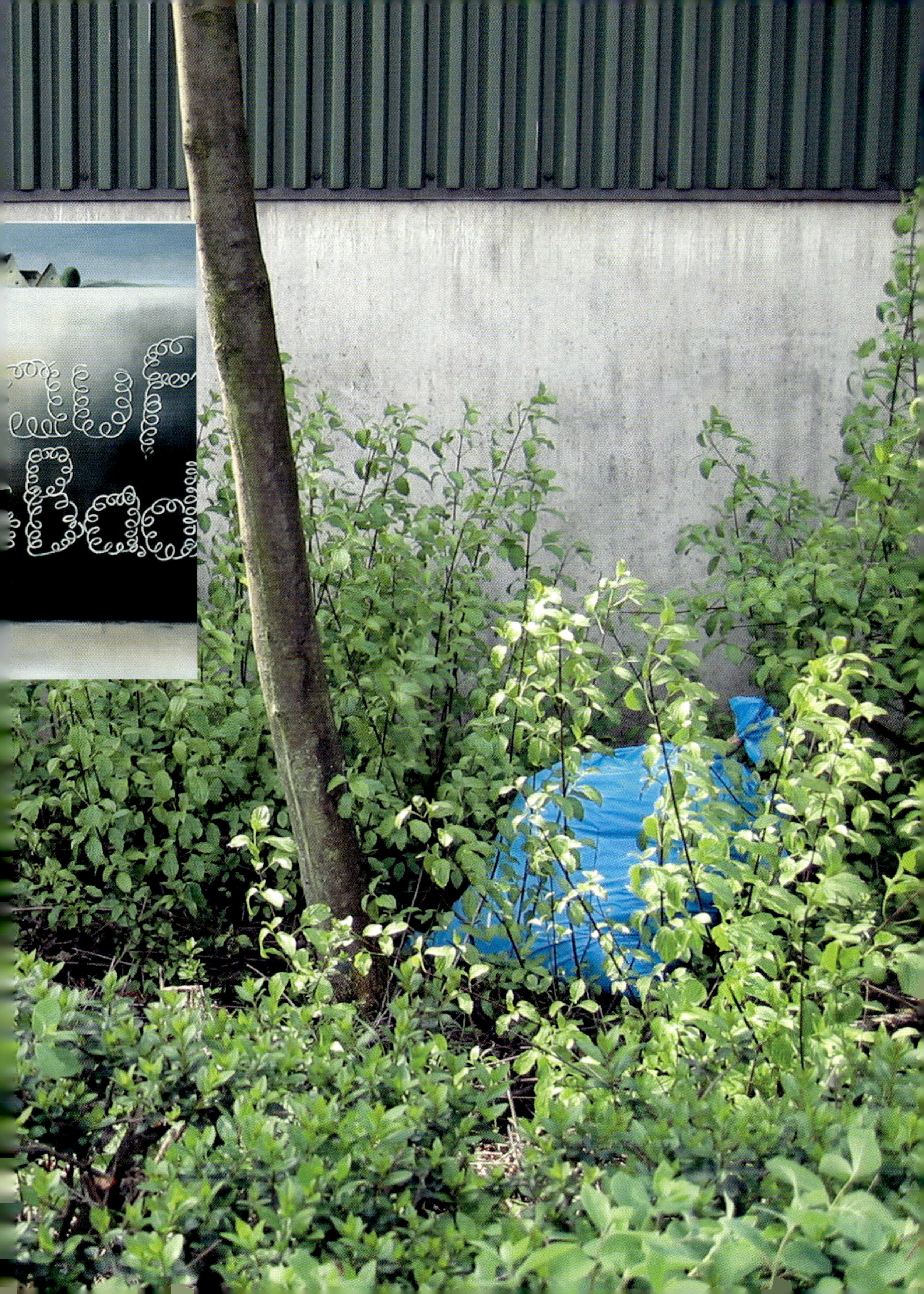

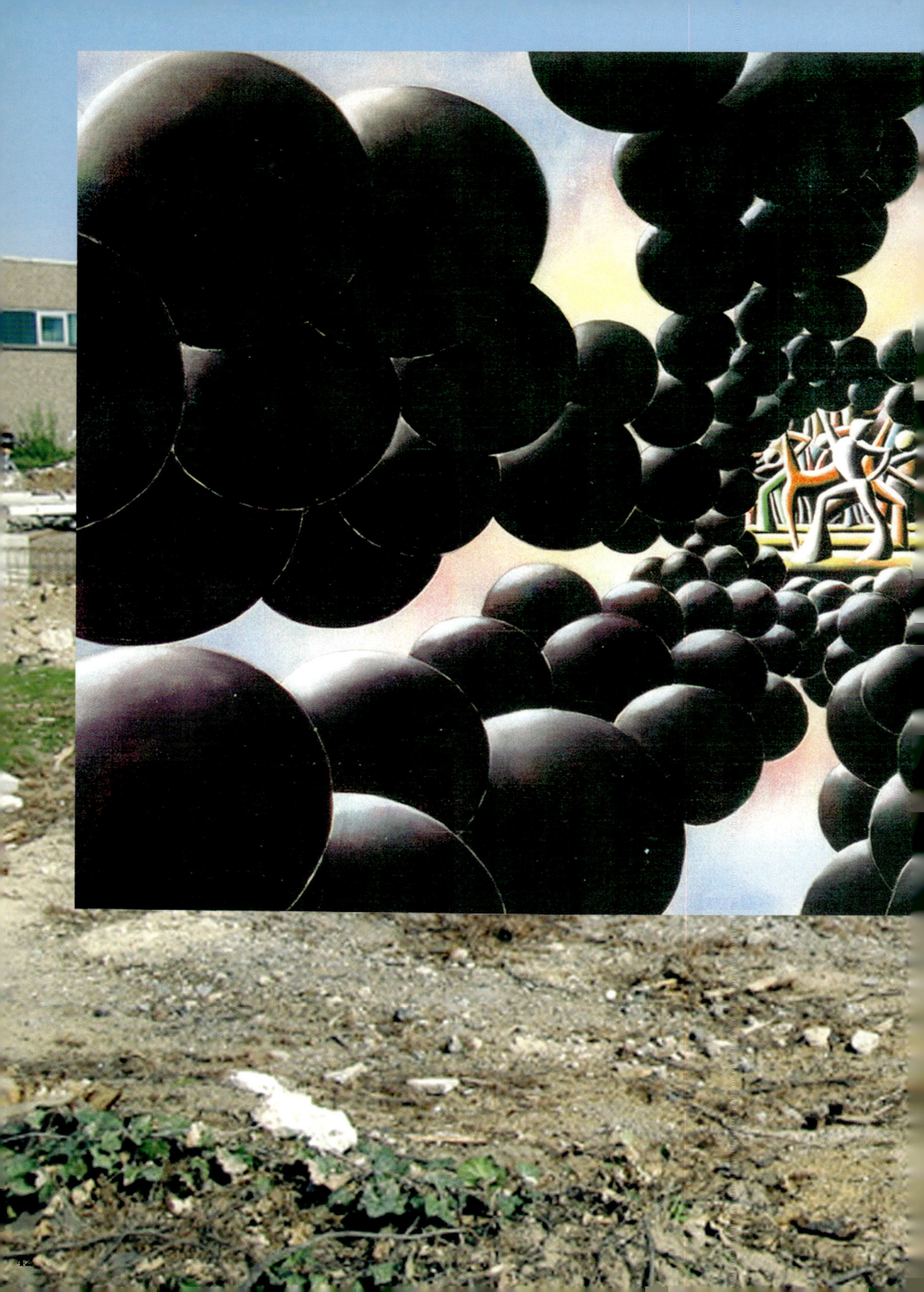

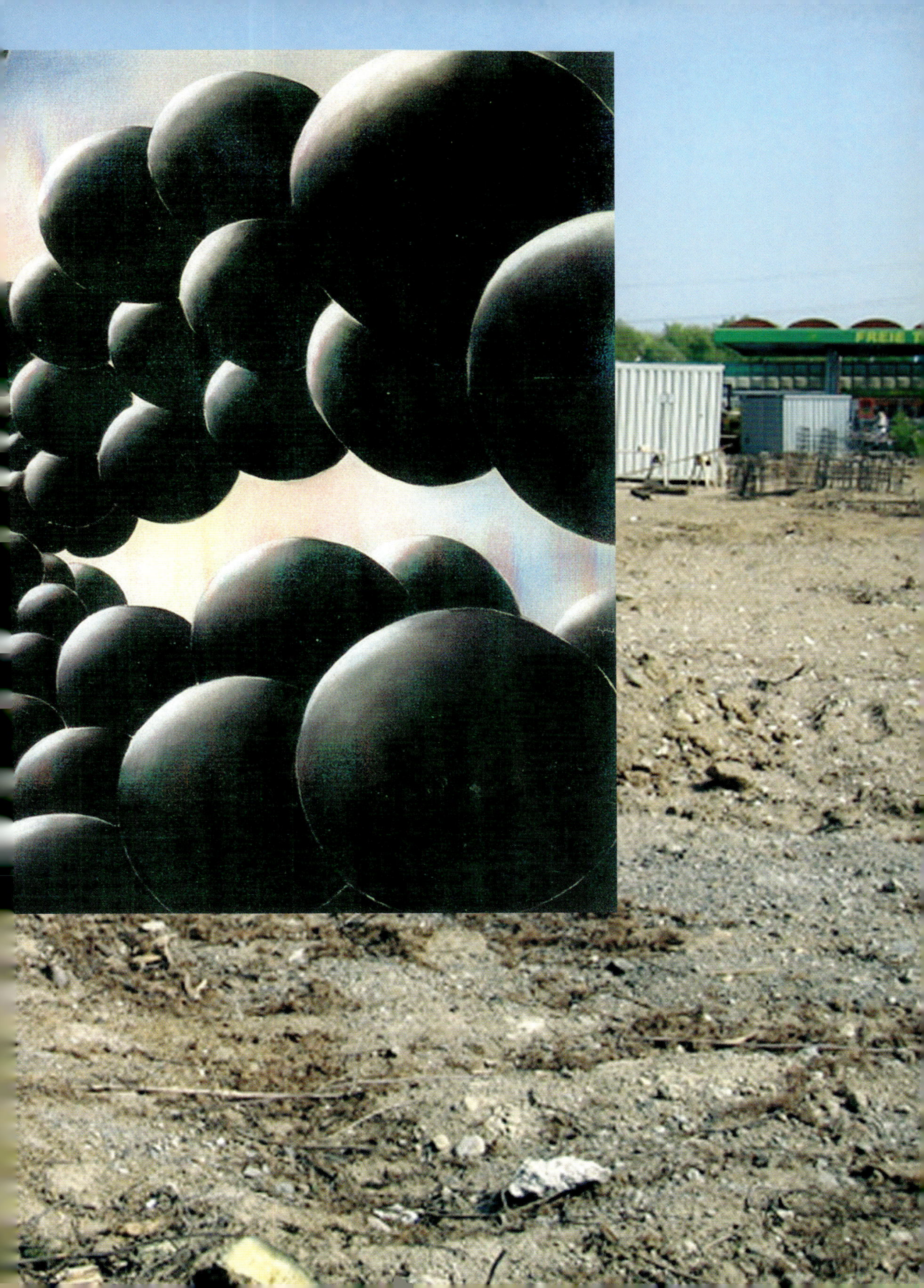

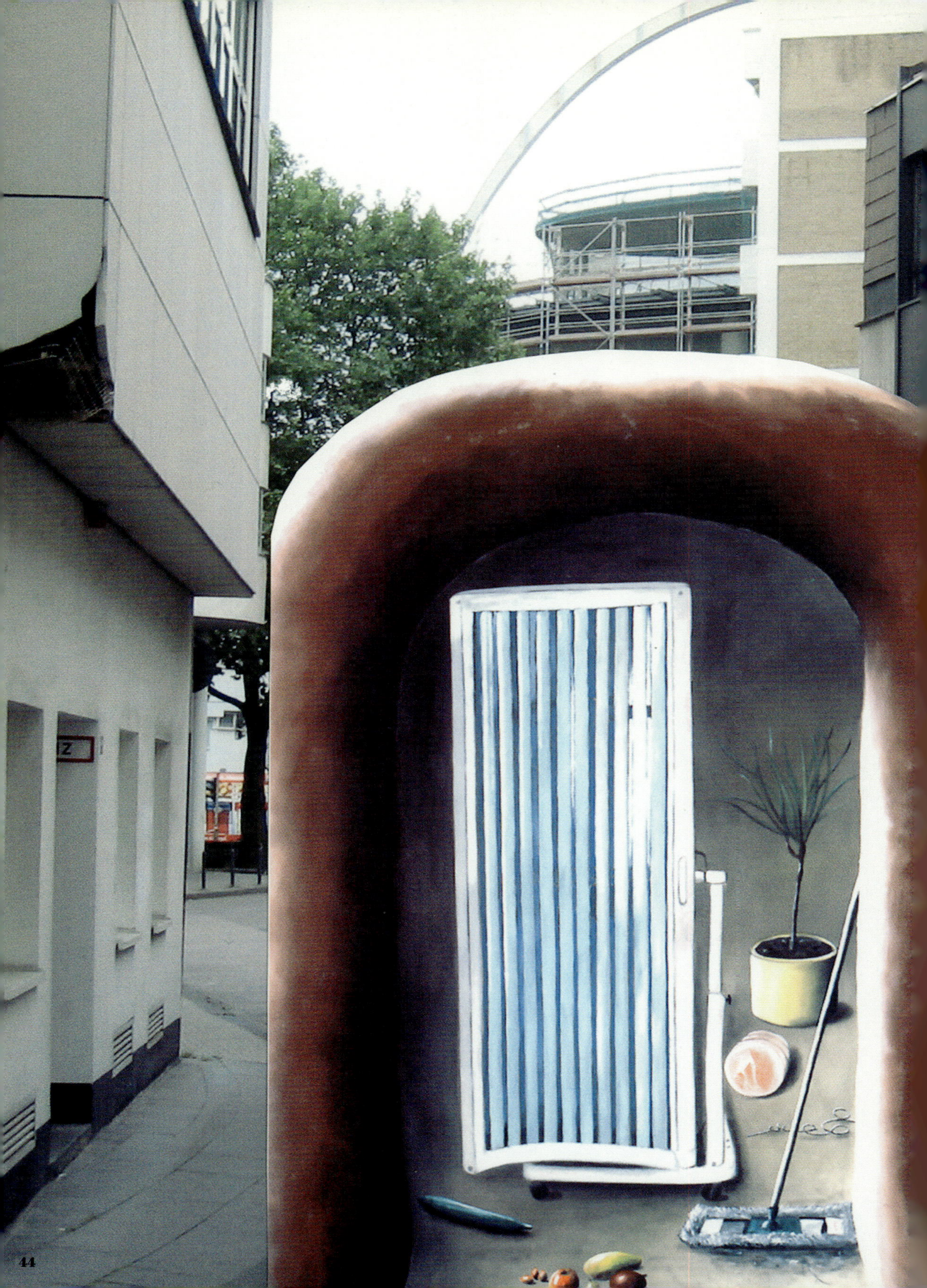

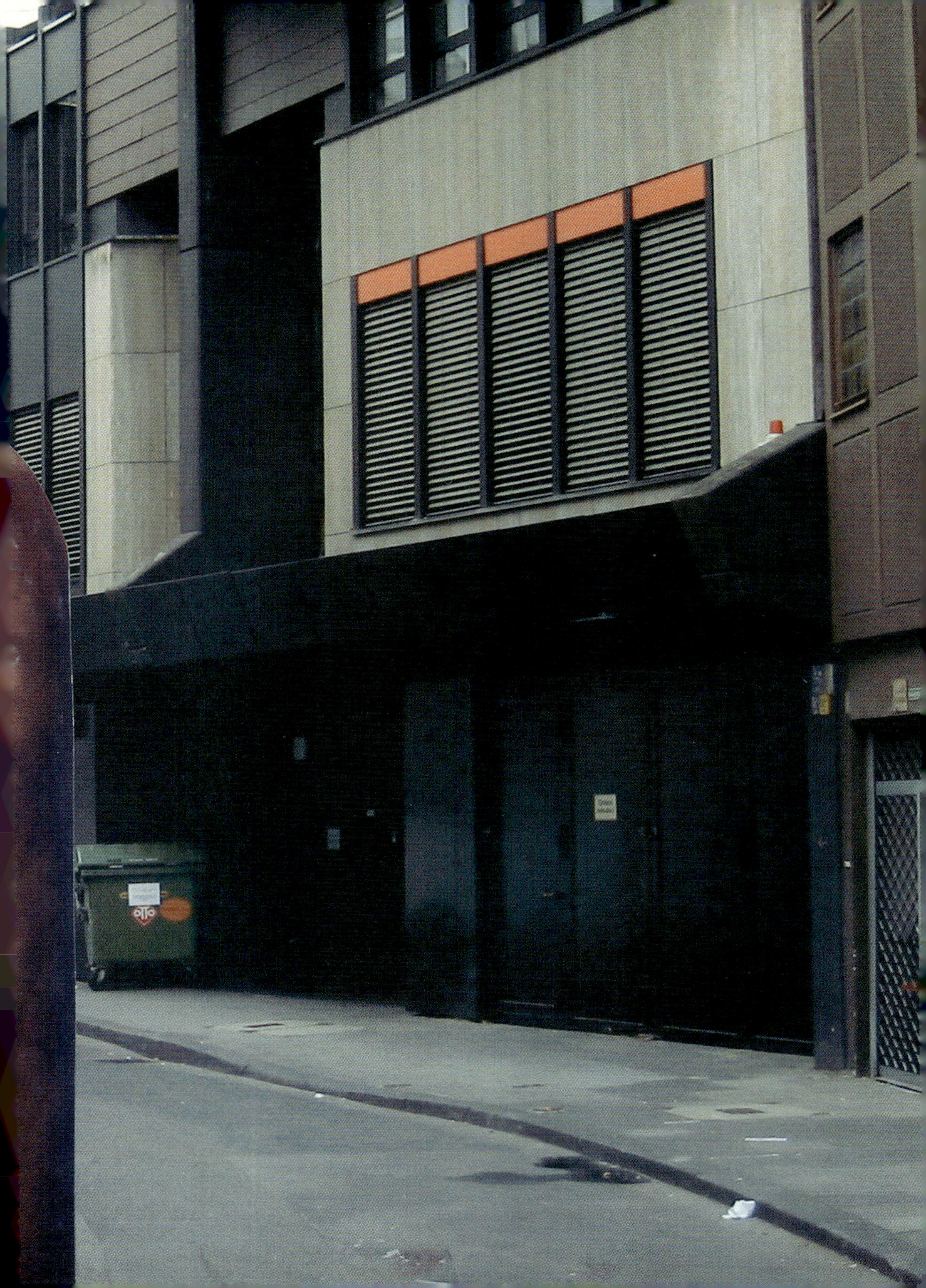

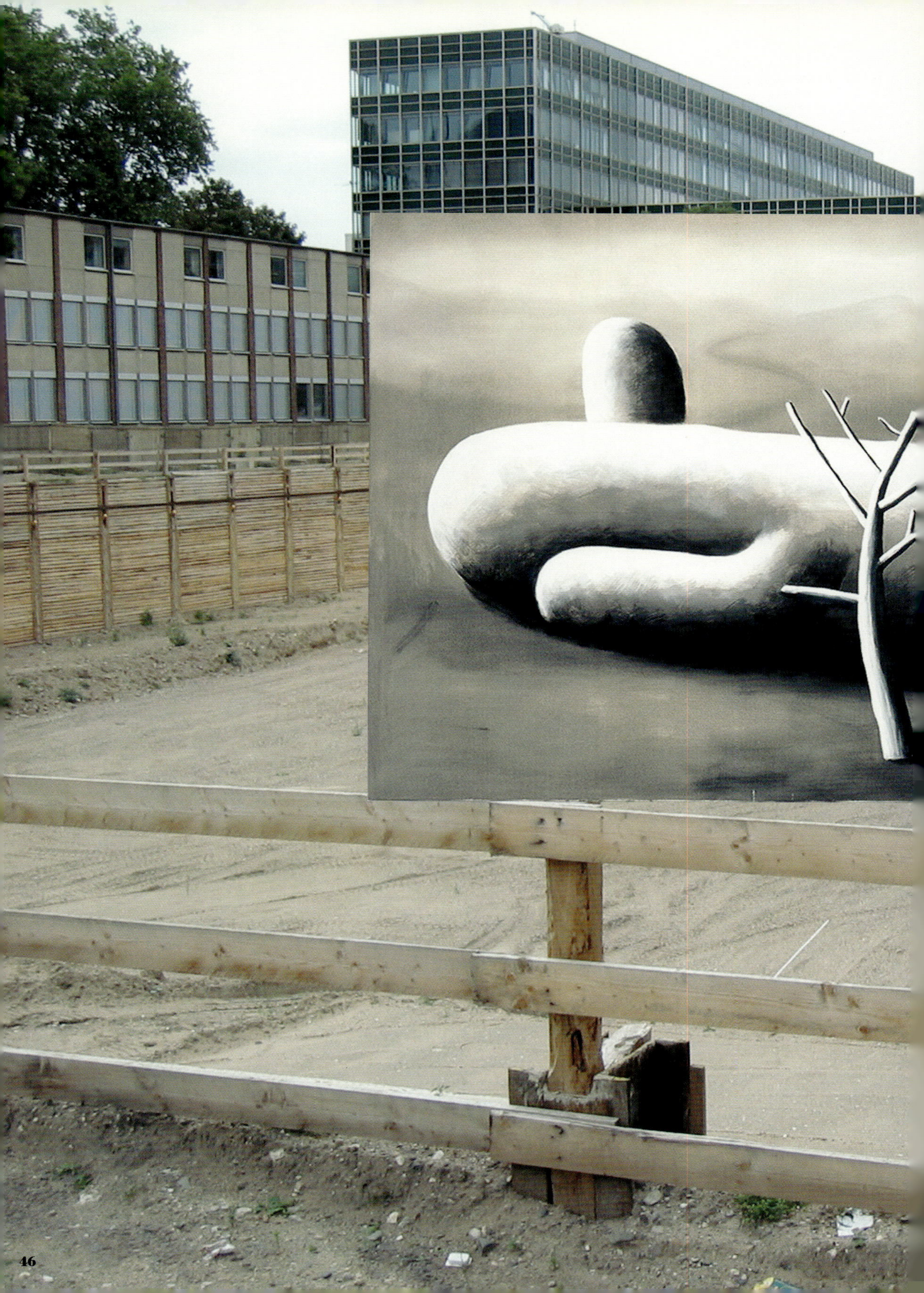

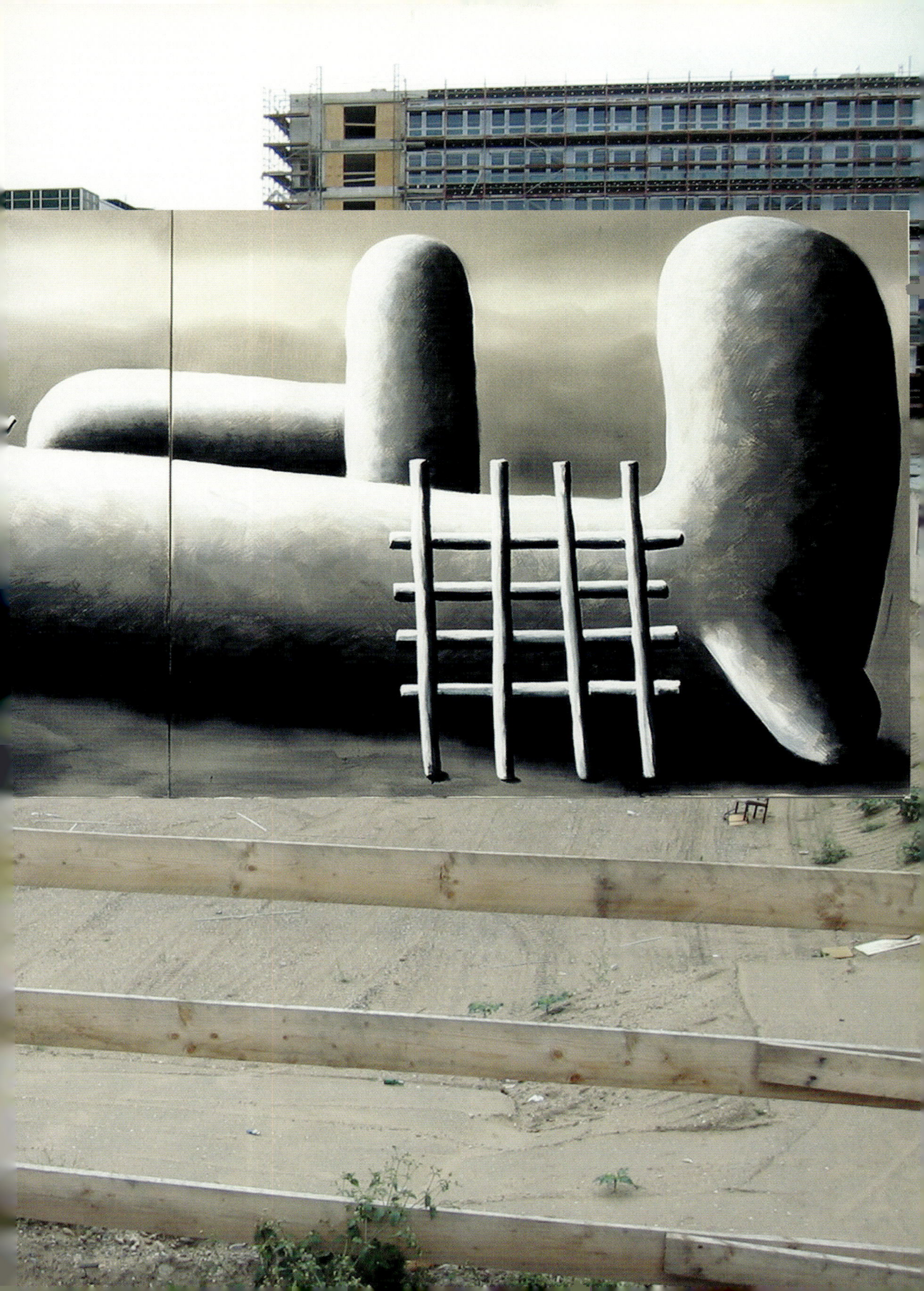

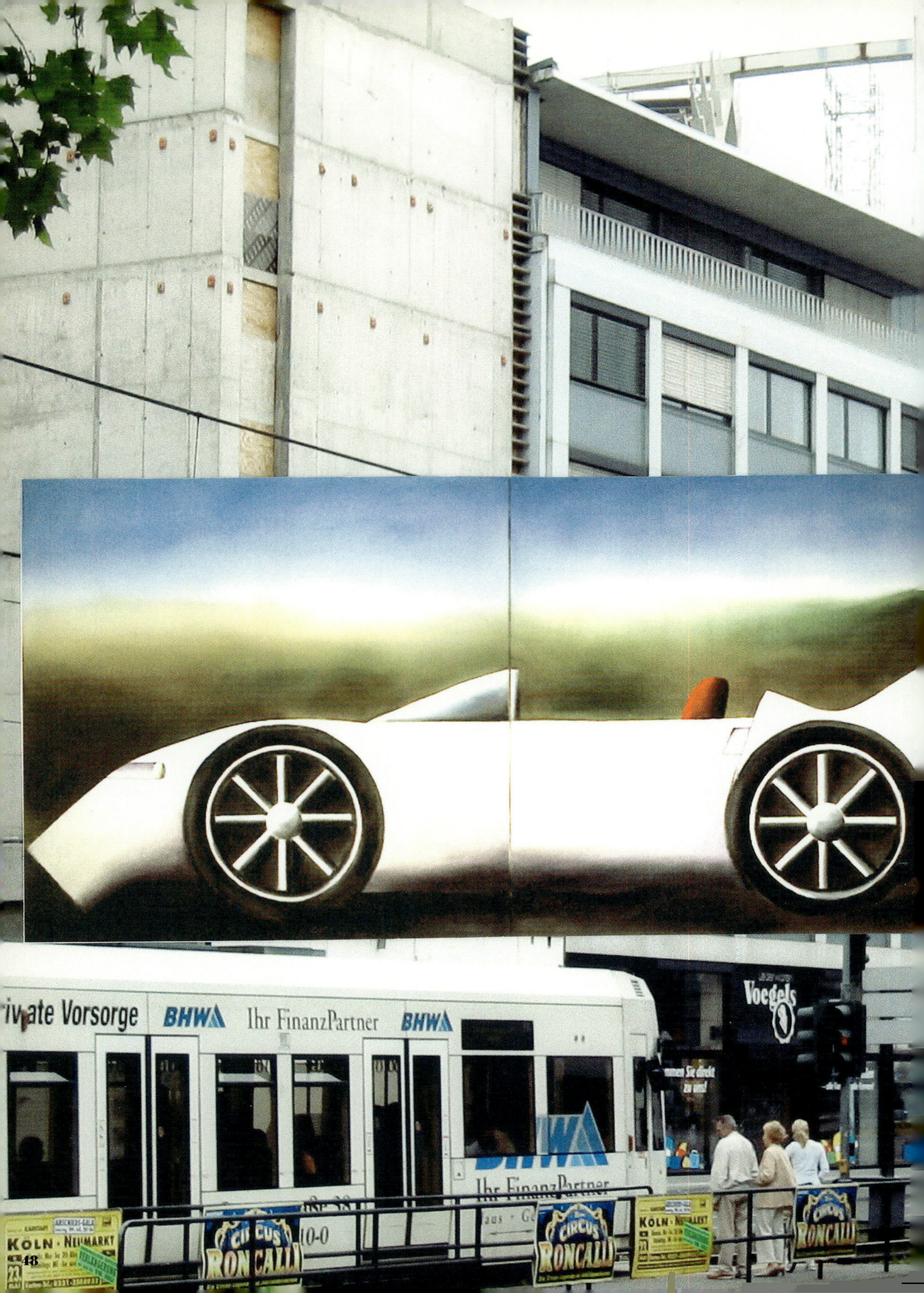

ivate Vorsorge BHW Ihr FinanzPartner BHW
Voegels
BHW
Ihr FinanzPartner
KÖLN · NEUMARKT
CIRCUS RONCALLI
KÖLN · NEUMARKT
CIRCUS RONCALLI

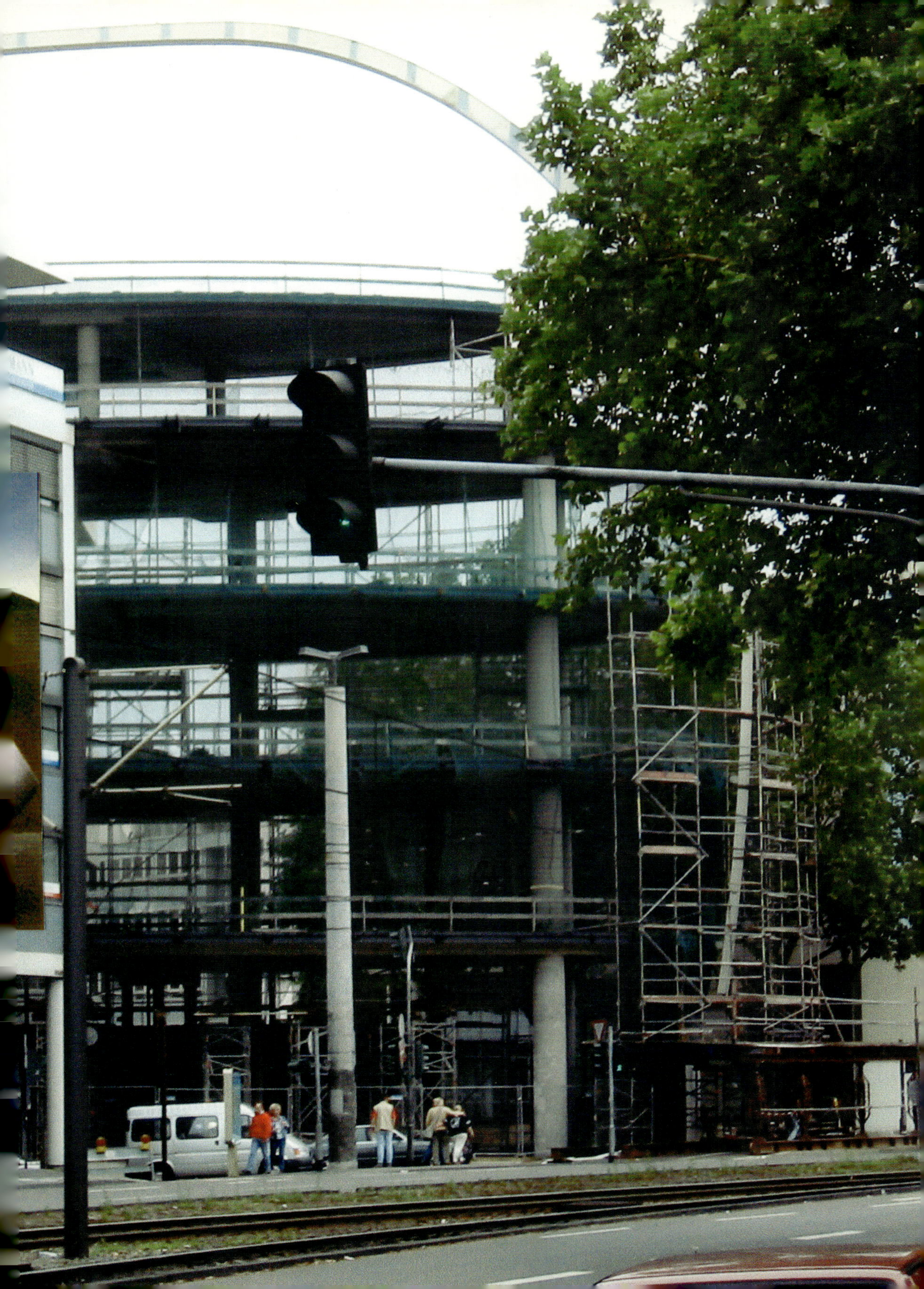

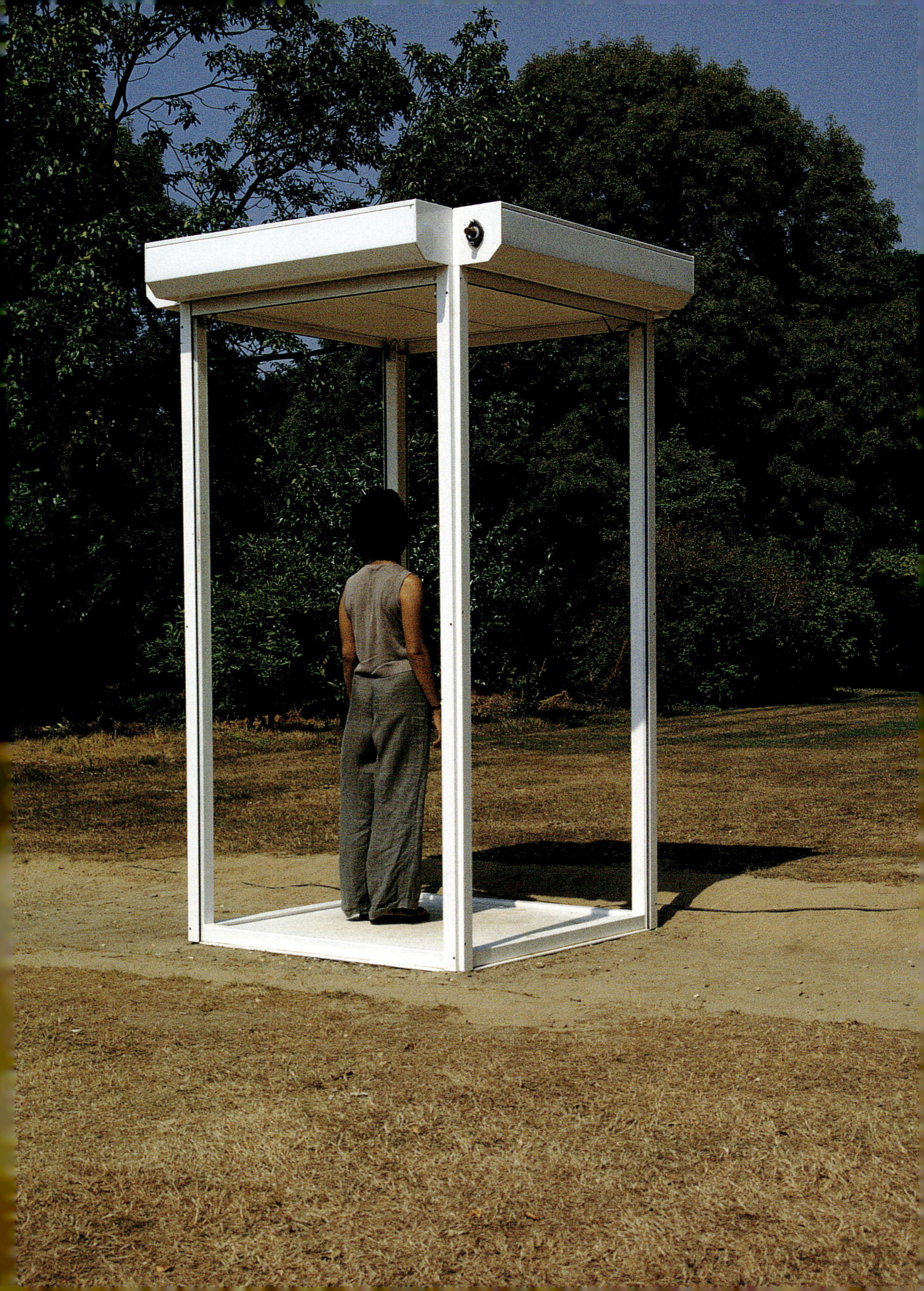

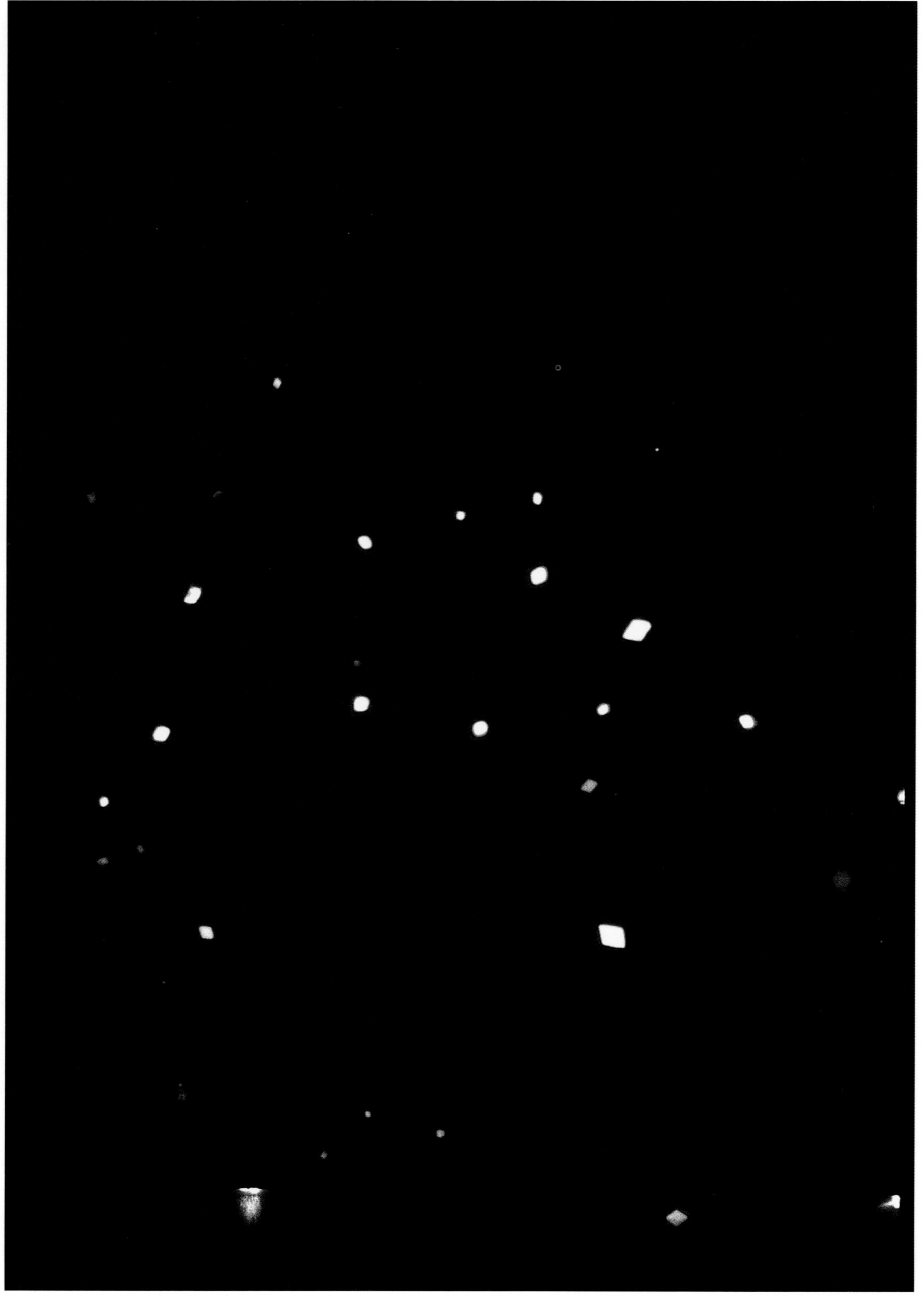

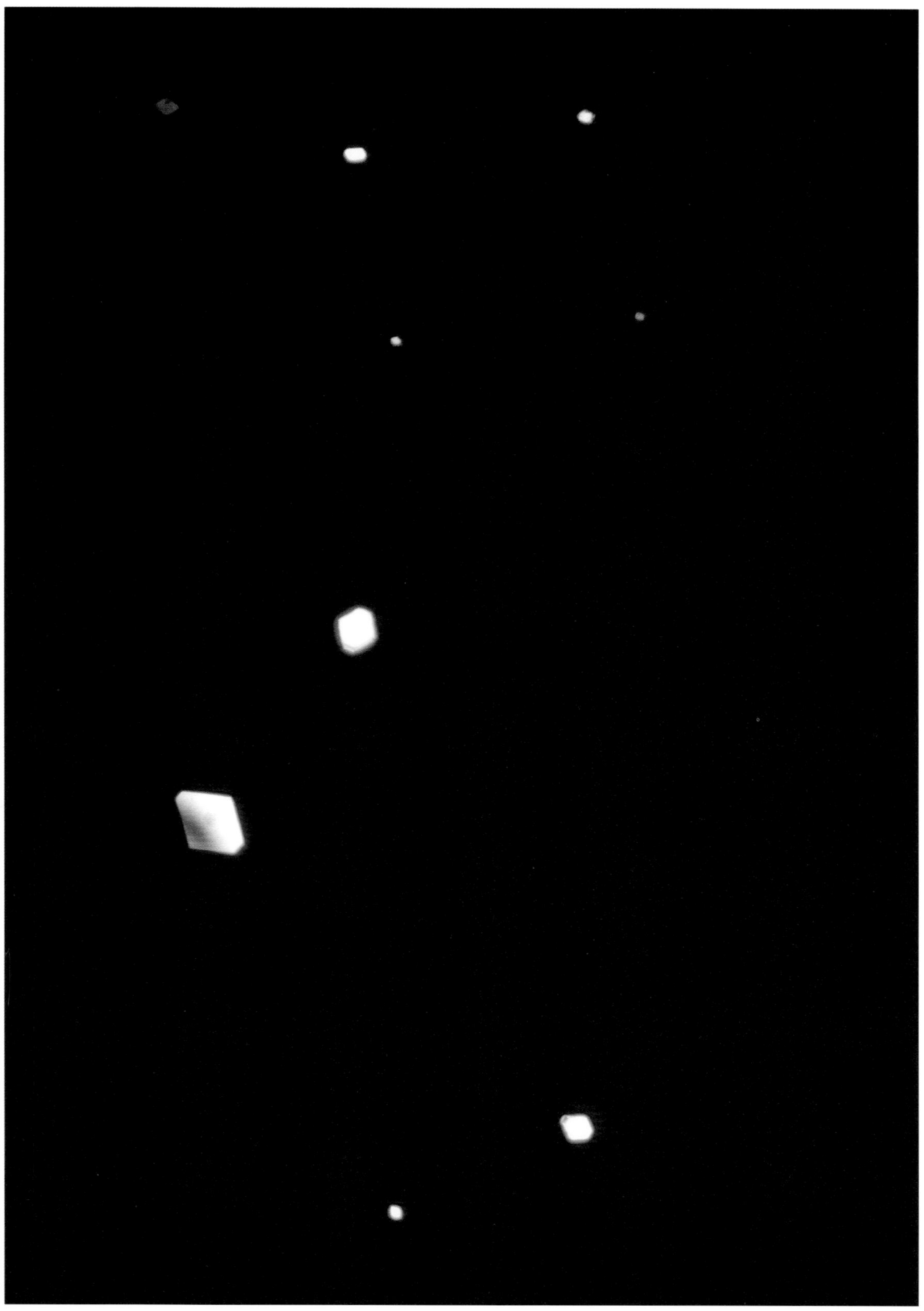

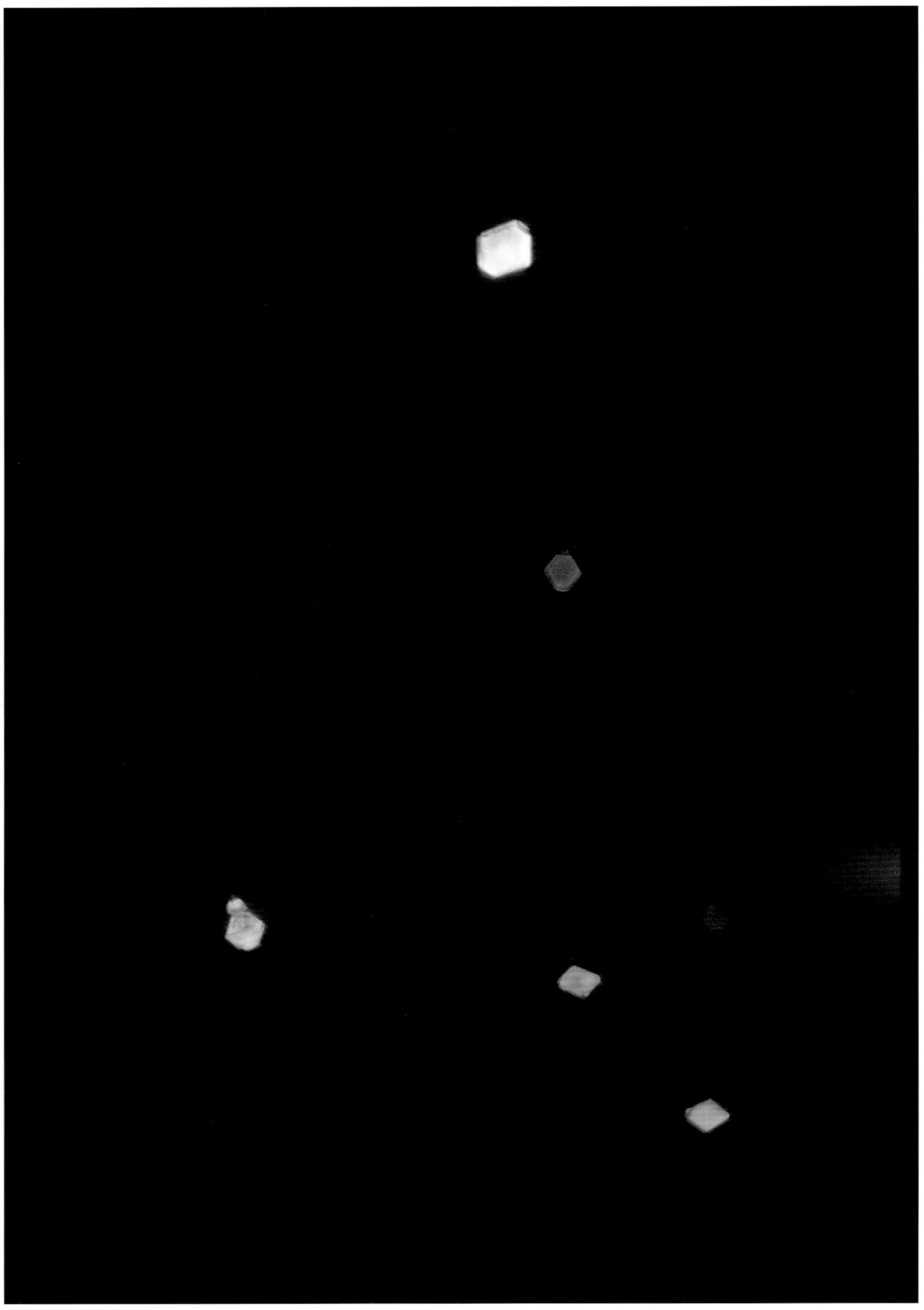

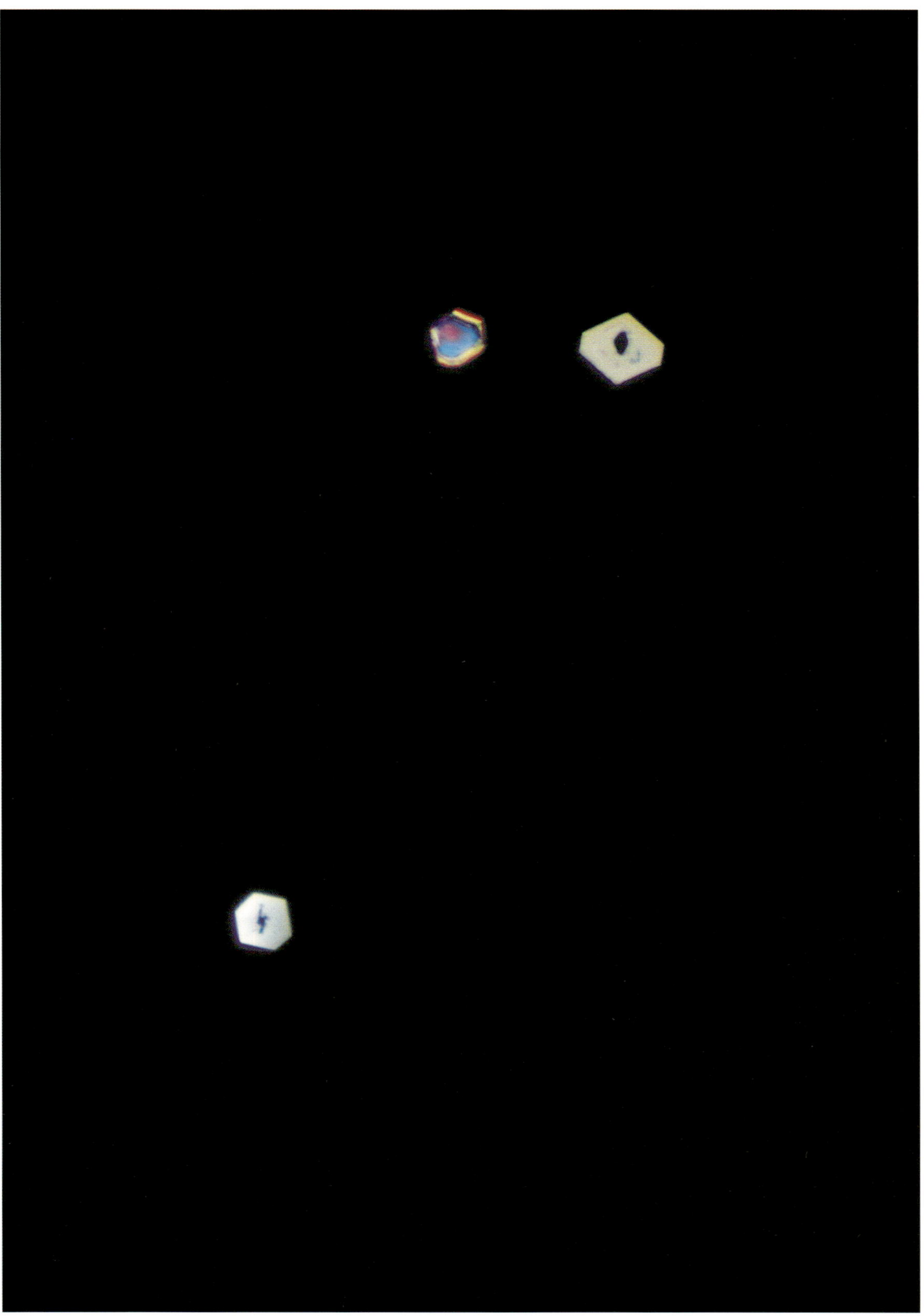

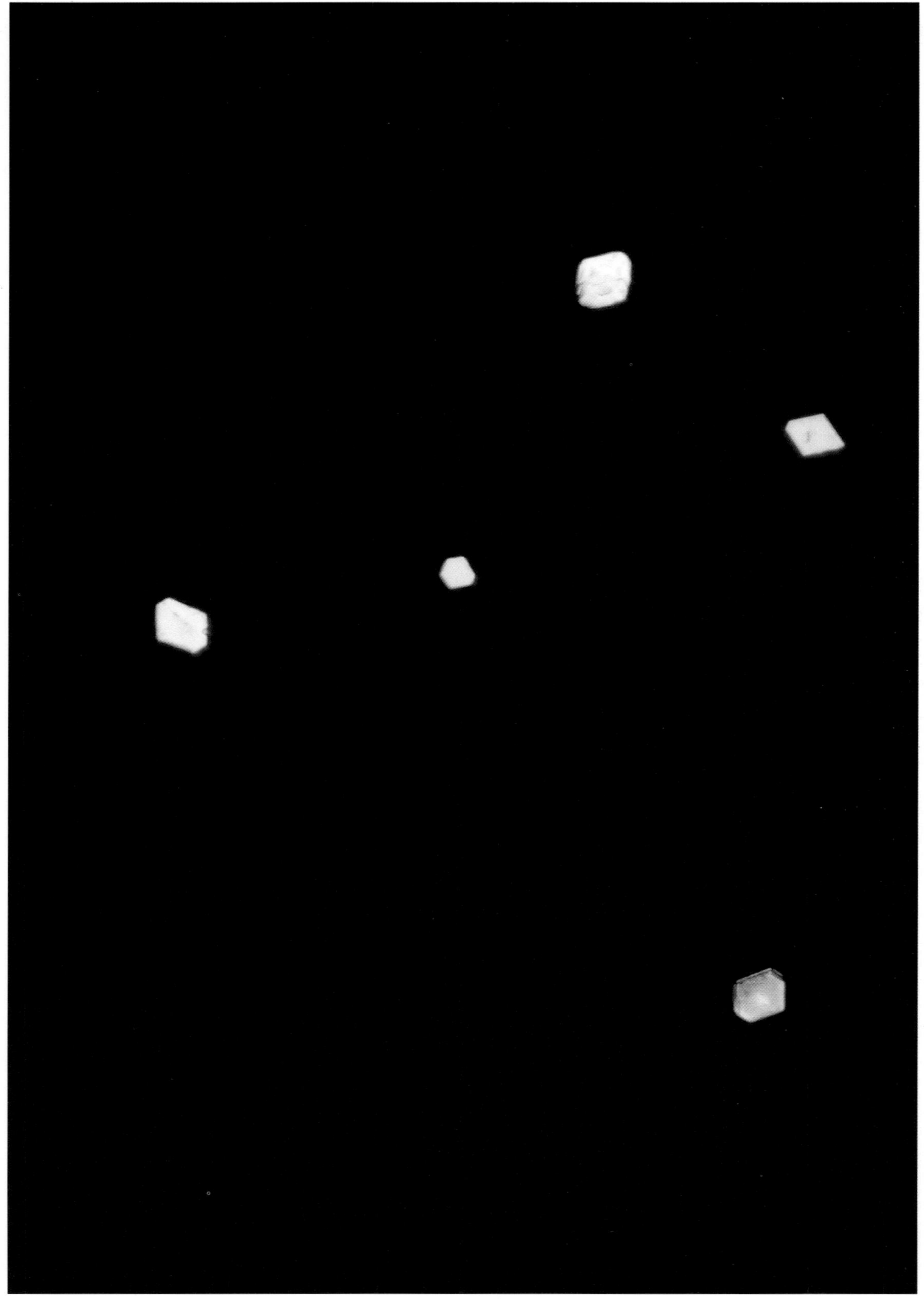

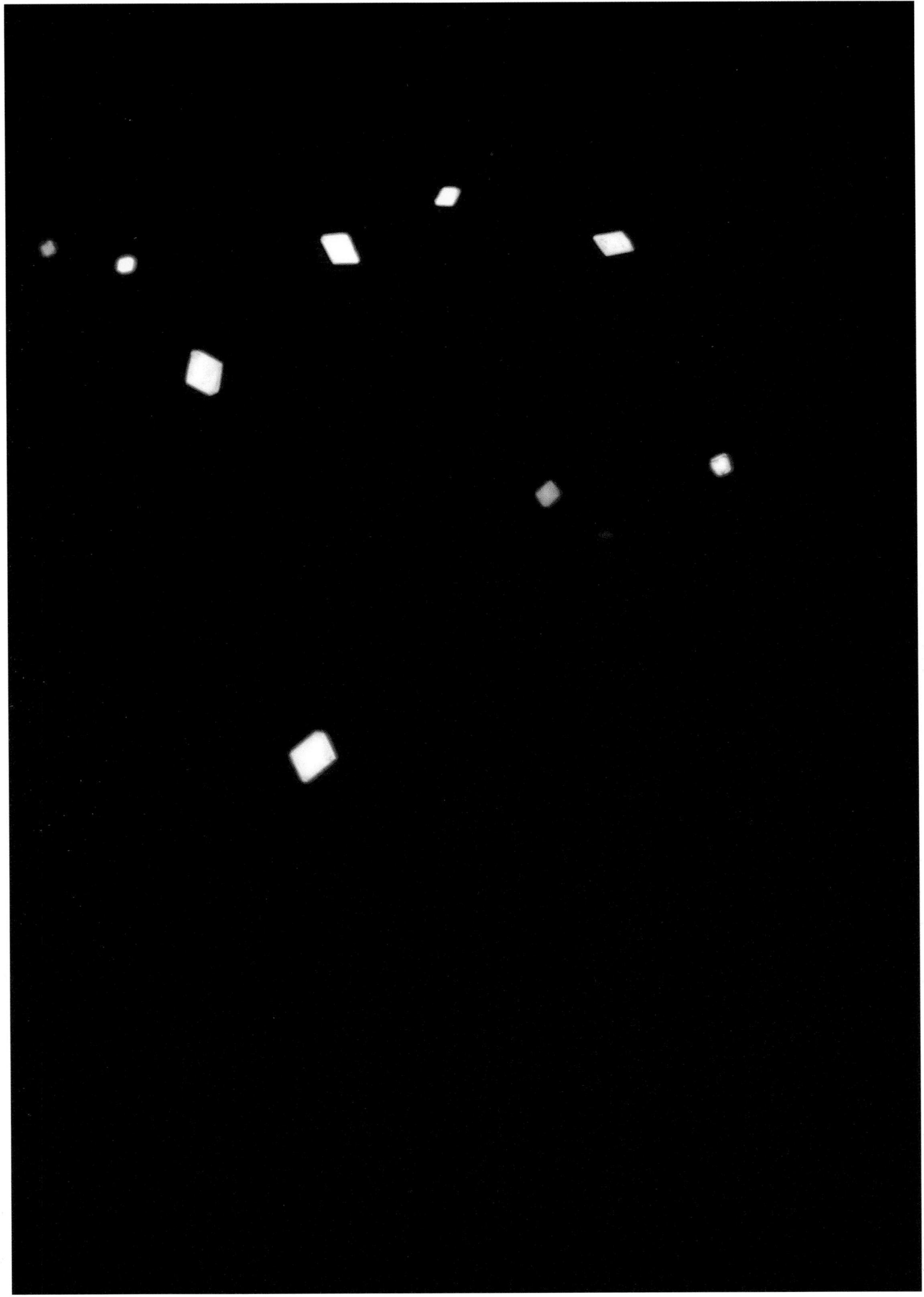

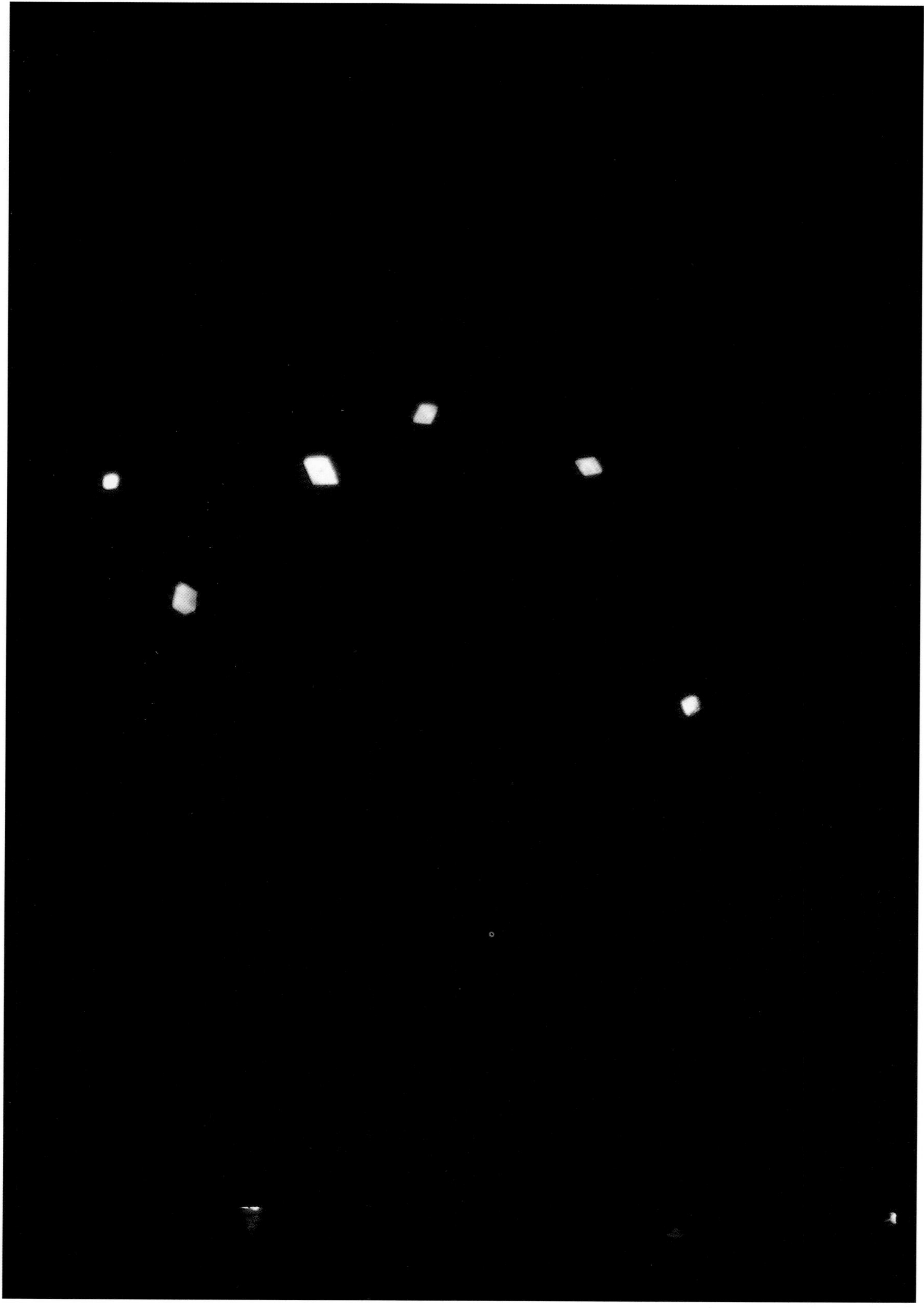

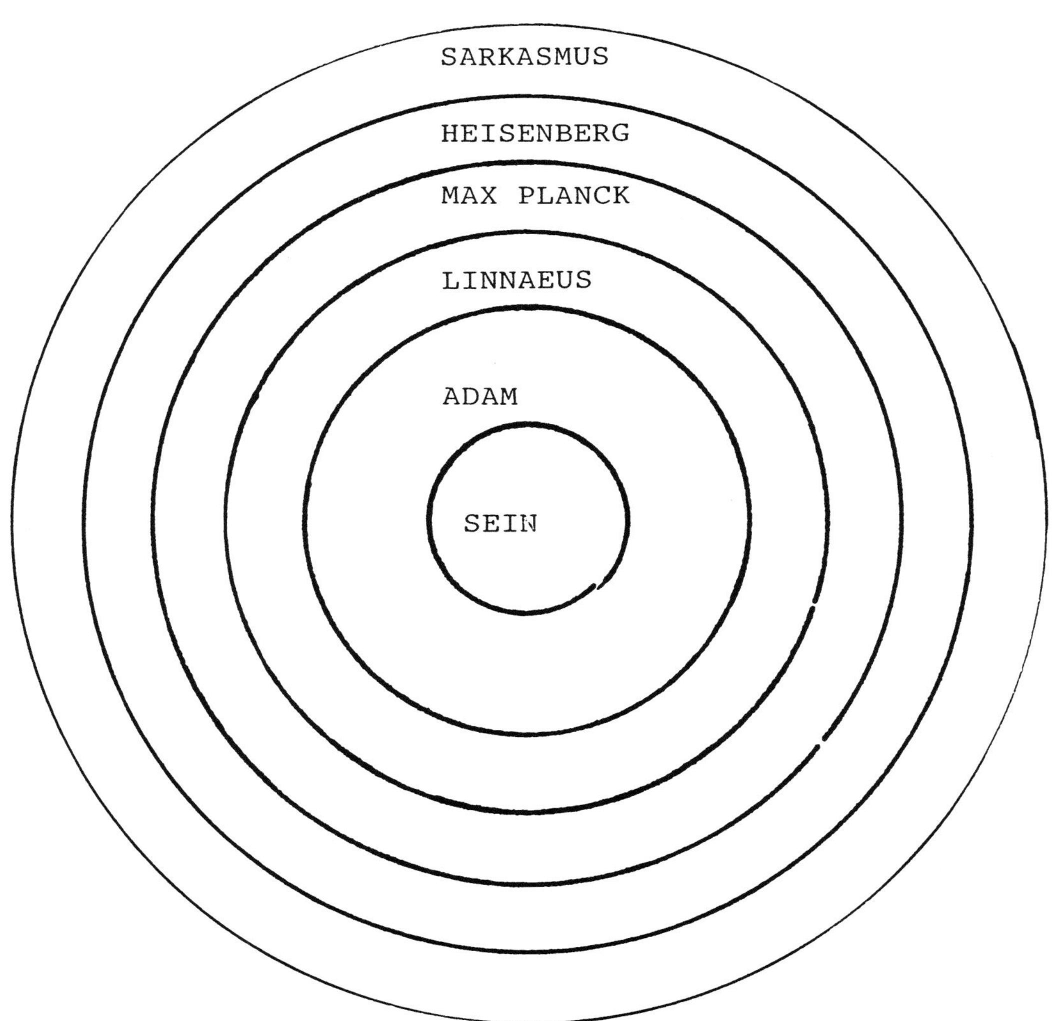

SARKASMUS
HEISENBERG
MAX PLANCK
LINNAEUS
ADAM
SEIN

<u>Objective Truth.</u> Is there access to objective truth?
Kant says, No. We live in and operate by means of the
minds and bodies given to us. This is our only vehicle
for understanding a/d knowing. But single cells can do
better than that. They can reproduce themselves, but
the product is not always an exact copy of the original.
Assume there are lots of copies and copies of copies.
The survival rate is uneven because the copies are not
always perfect copies. Some copies survive to reproduce,
some do not. This is not a matter of chance; survival
depends on how they cope with the objective facts of
their environment. This may not be understanding the
way we think of it but it underwrites an objective truth.
We call it evolution.

We can only make guesses about how long it has taken
for us to become humans. There is some help from carbon
dating which we can apply to found things(fossilized skulls)
from some bodies who look as if they might be related to us.
There is general agreement that these embody steps on the
way to our present/"human" selves even when some of those
could be false starts that did not survive to our own time.
These(skulls) are things that occupy space and have consid-
erable
~~oral~~ survival potential.

So much for the "physical" , which leaves a residue,
but what about speech? Gone as soon as uttered, has got
to precede the arrival of writing, but leaves no trace.
Assertions via sound could go back as far as throats or
their equivalent and of course there had to be a community
of creatures: someone to bellow to. These could take the
form of questions, commands, pleadings, narratives. Laced
into all of these a Yes or a No, conceivably both.
Present or implied is the flip side of every assertion.
We think, communicate, live by the Yes/No pair. And we
pass it down through time. We know this to be so; we
just don't know when(it first got said). Did Yes/No come
before us? I think not. Will it last forever? I think so.

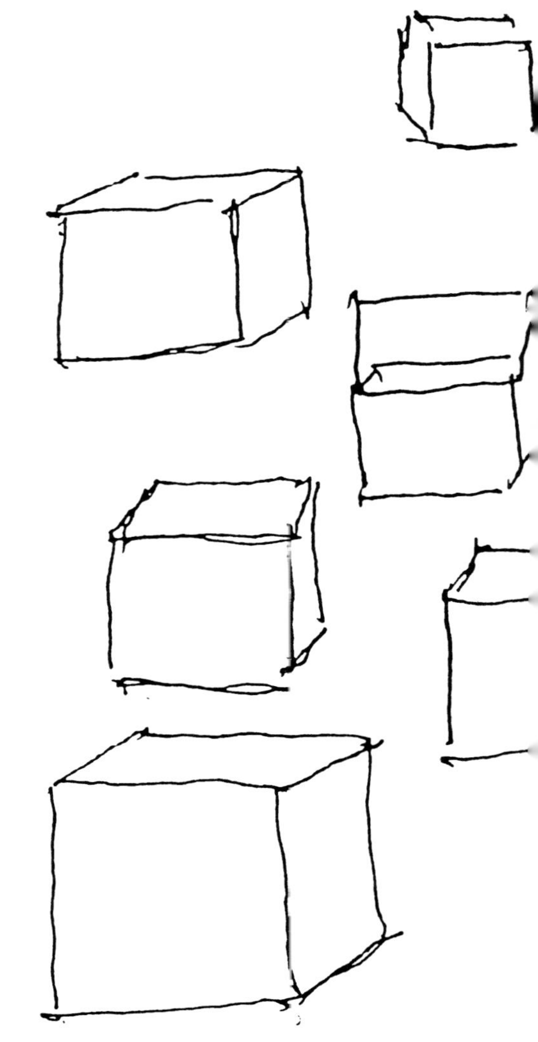

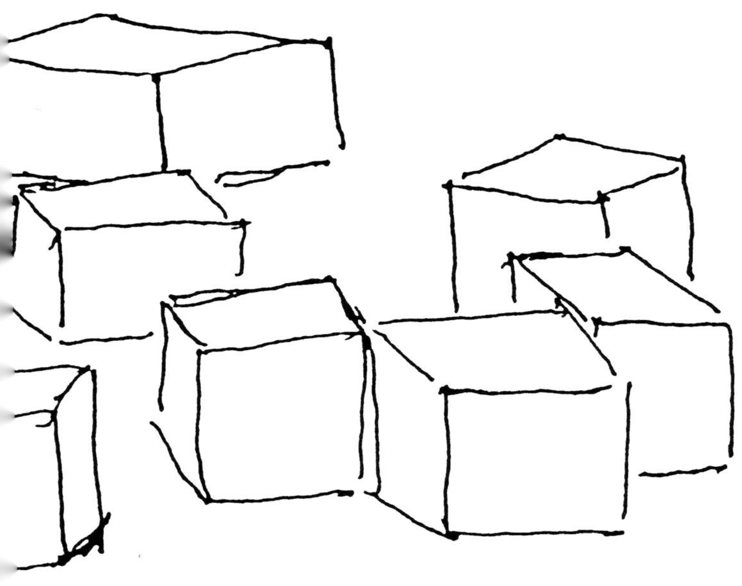

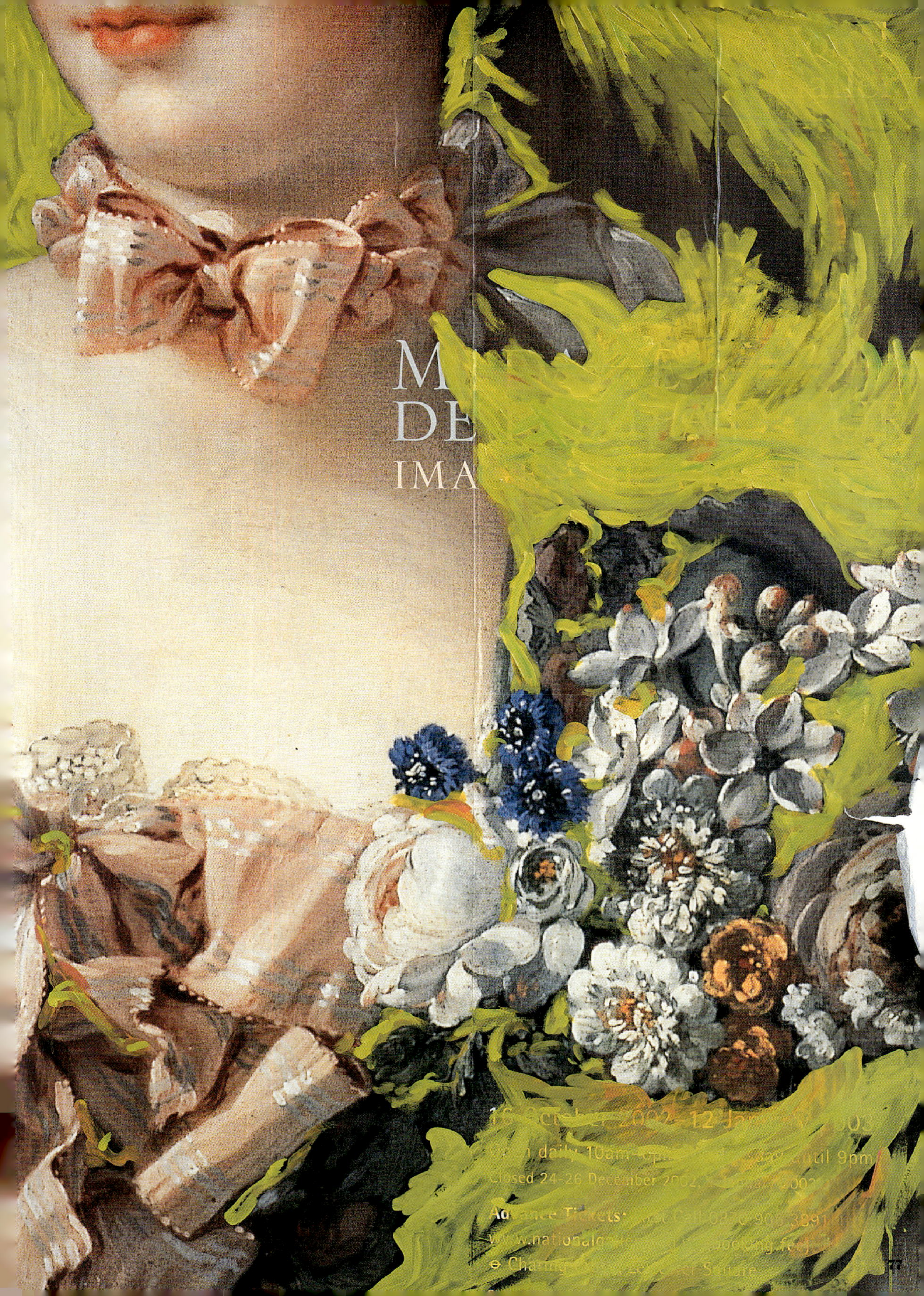
M
DE
IMA
16 October 2002 - 12 January 2003
Open daily 10am-6pm, Wednesday until 9pm
Closed 24-26 December 2002, 1 January 2003
Advance Tickets: First Call 0870 906 3891
www.nationalgallery.org.uk (booking fee)
⊖ Charing Cross/Leicester Square

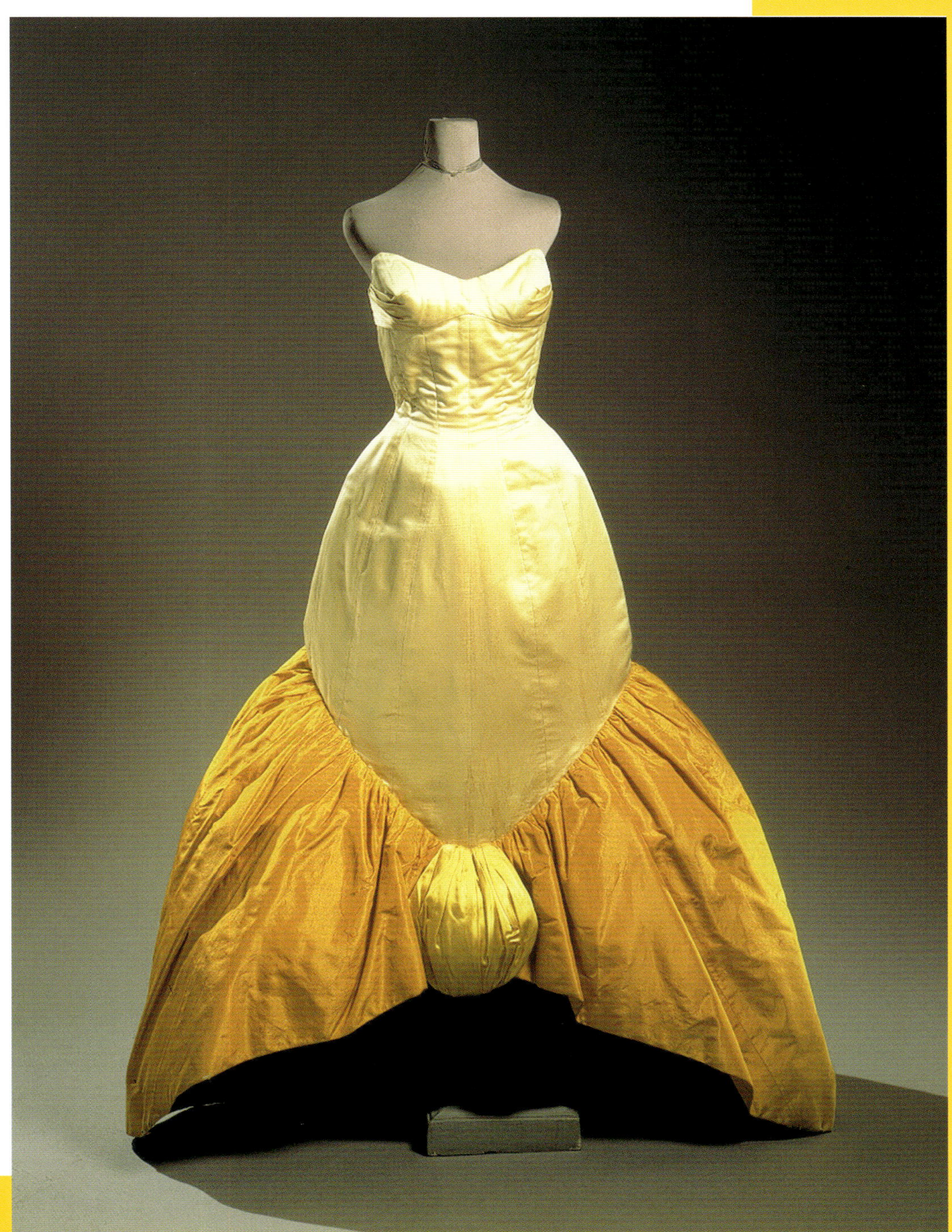

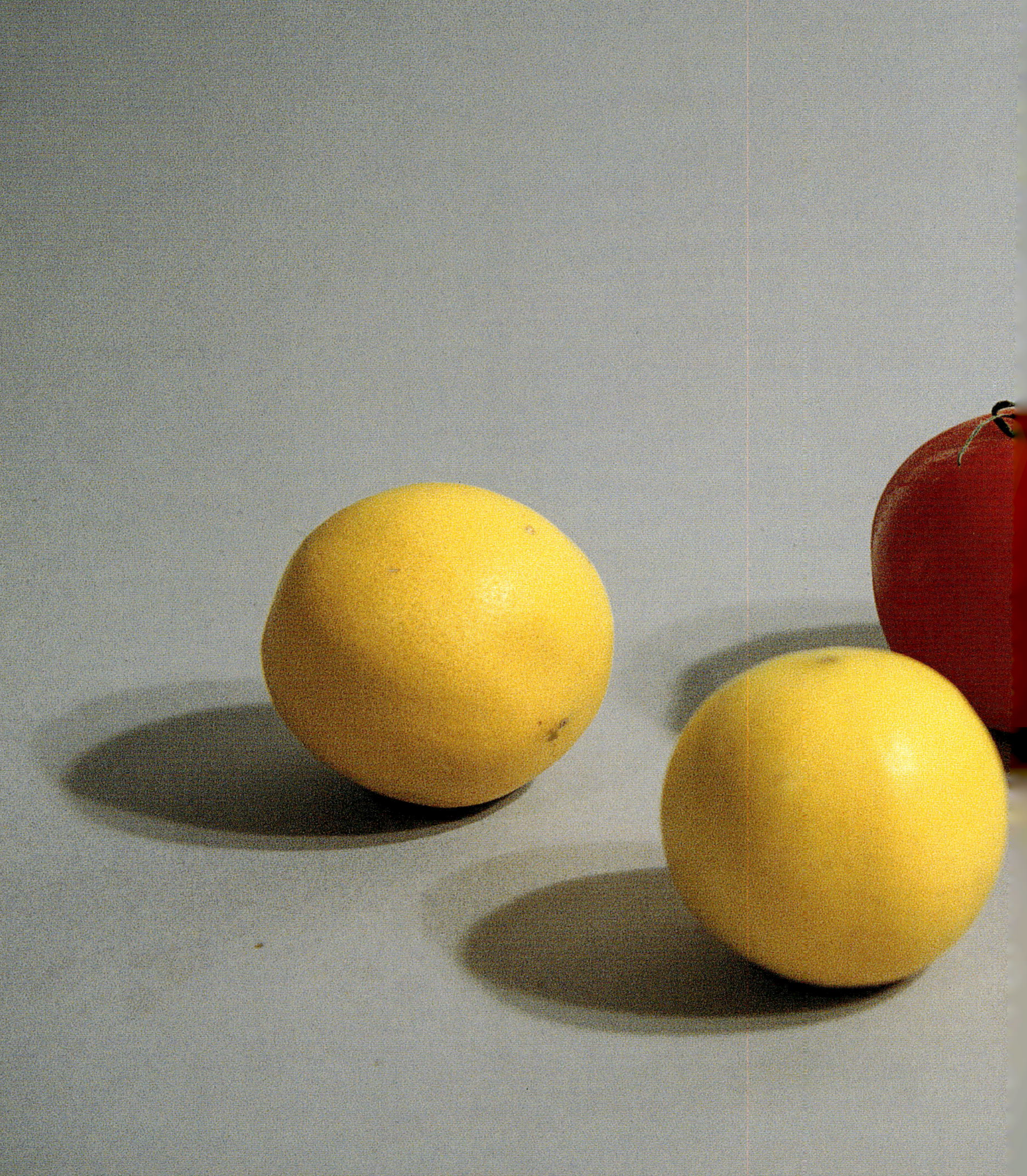

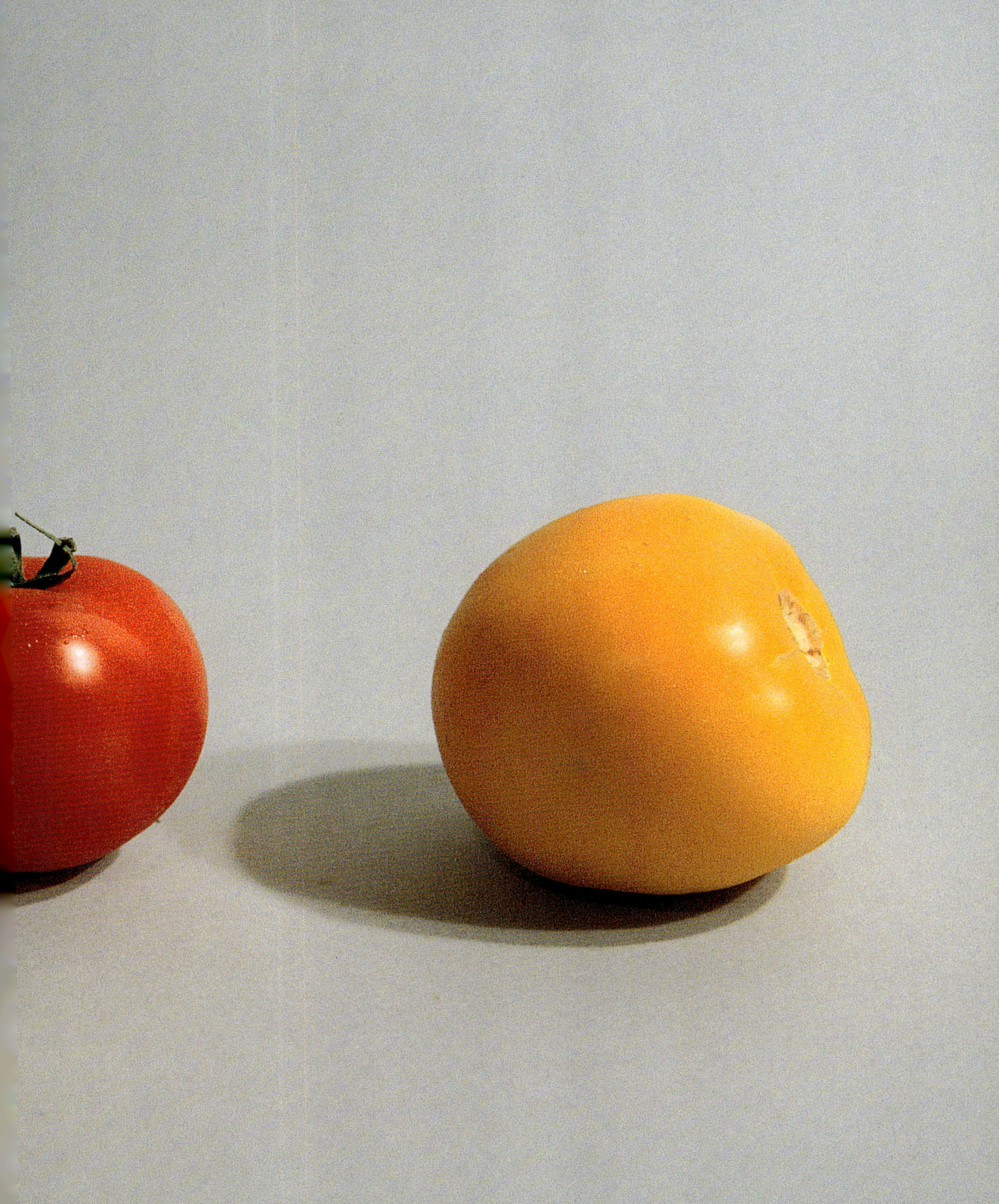

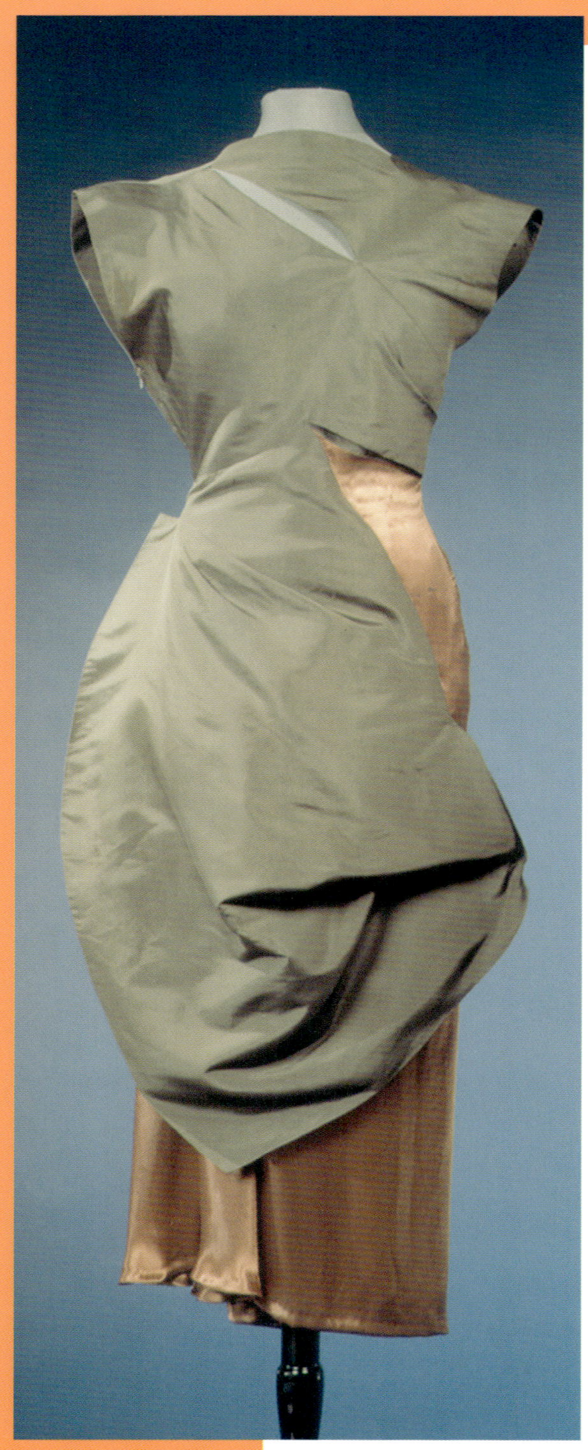

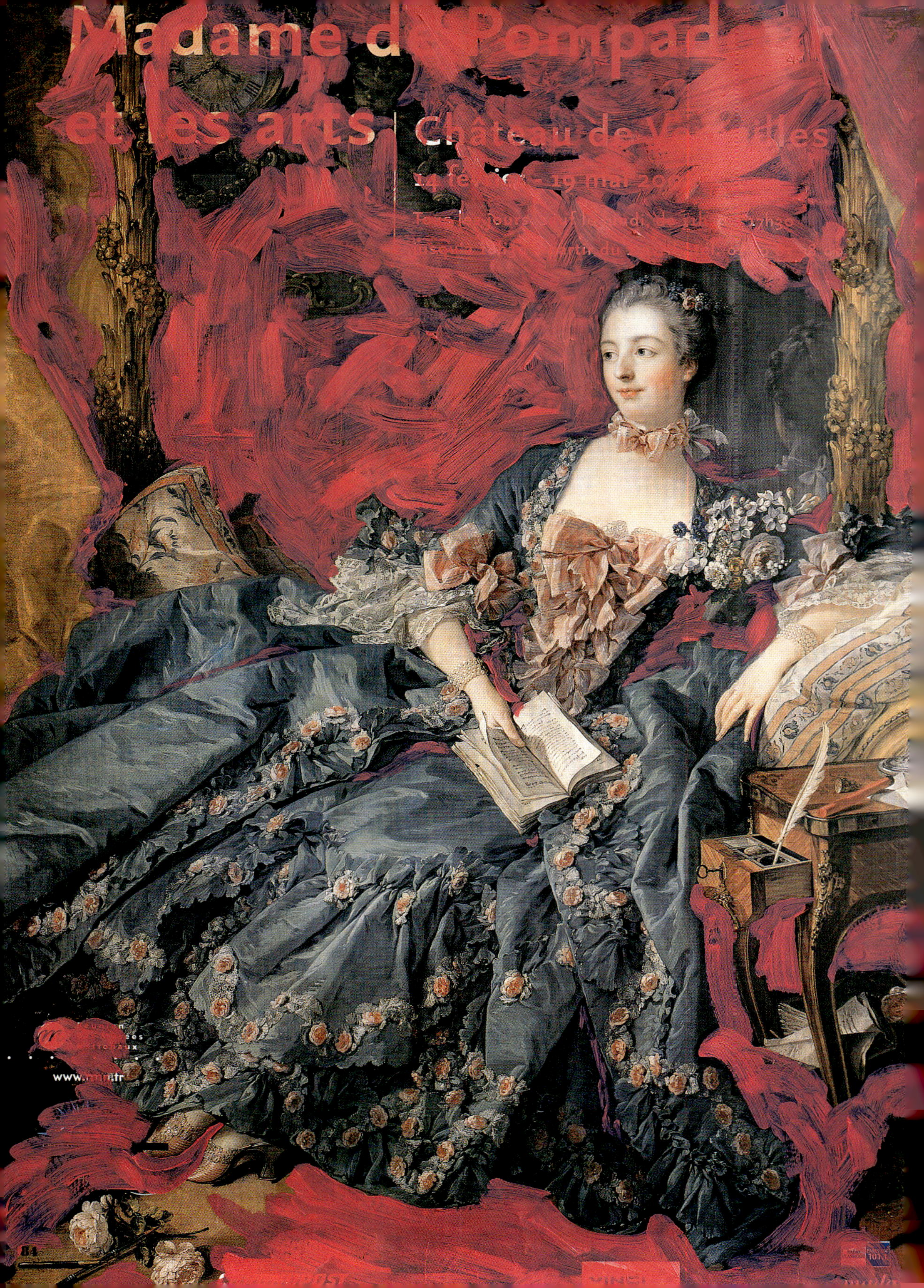

Madame de Pompadour
et les arts | Château de Versailles
14 février – 19 mai 20
www.rmn.fr
84

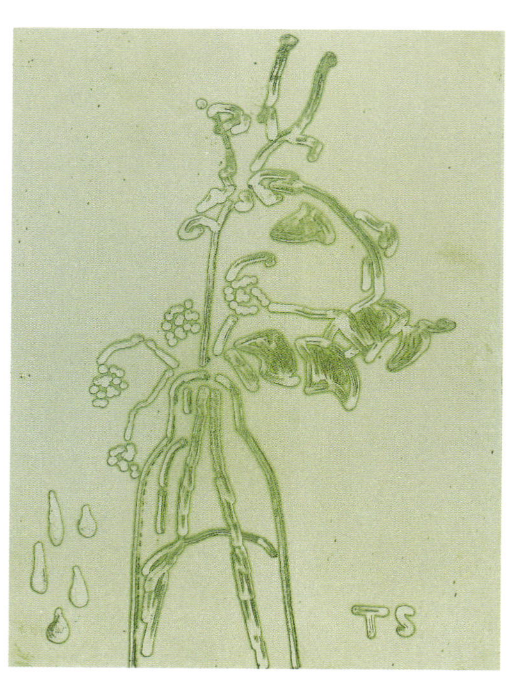
TS

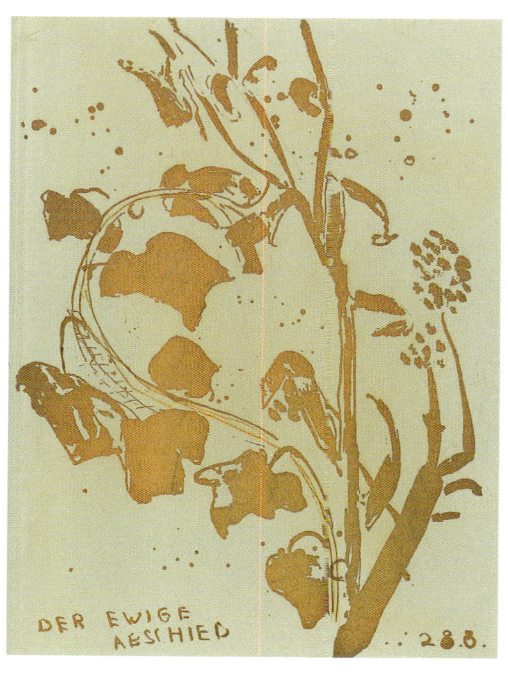
DER EWIGE
ABSCHIED
28.8.

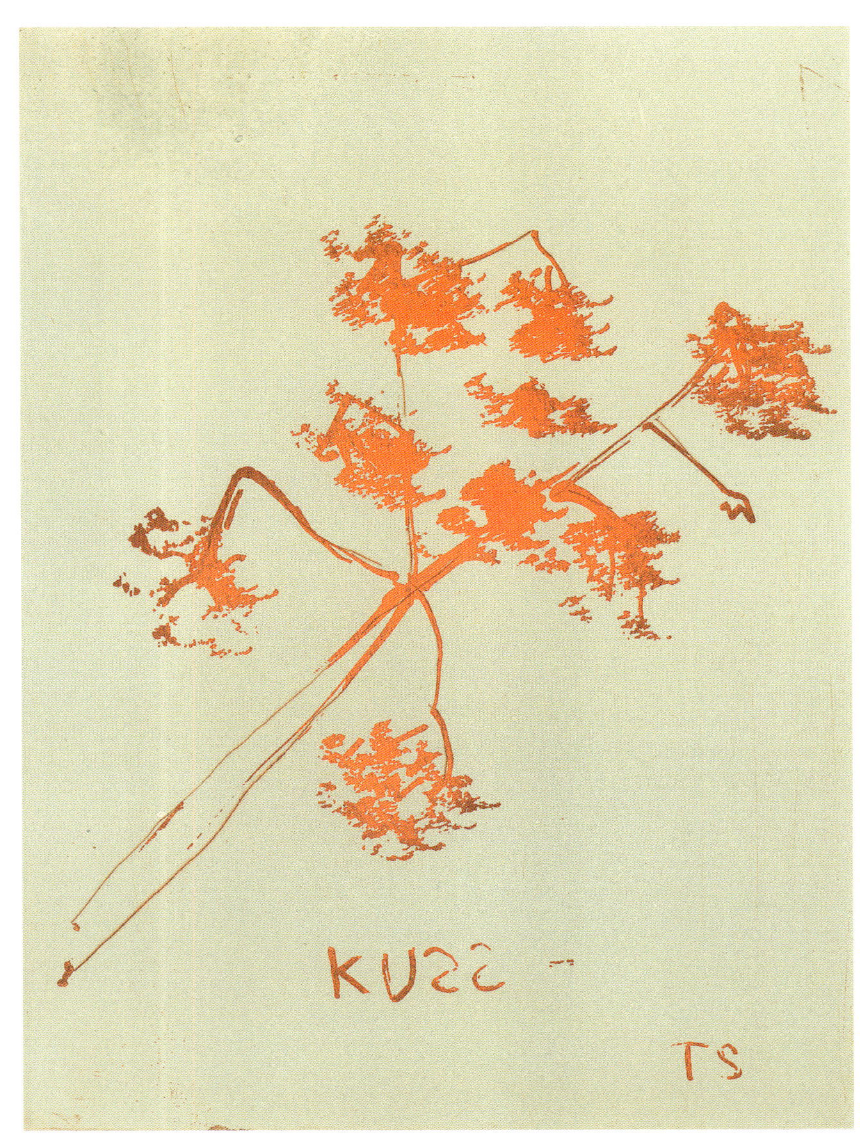
KUŽĉ -
TS

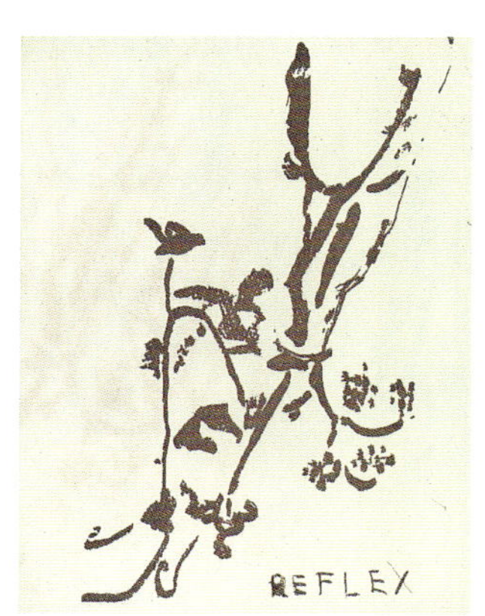
REFLEX

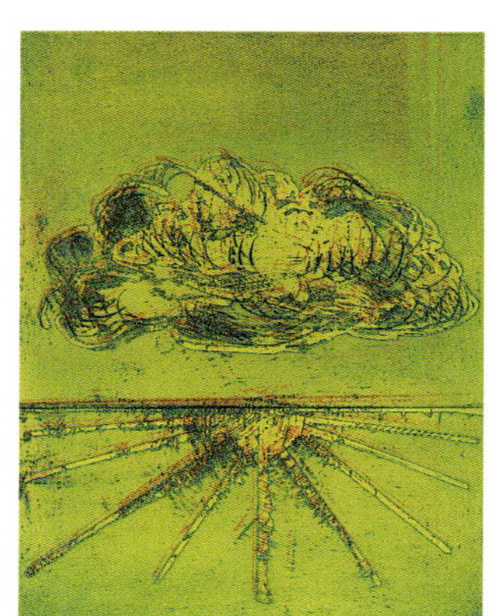

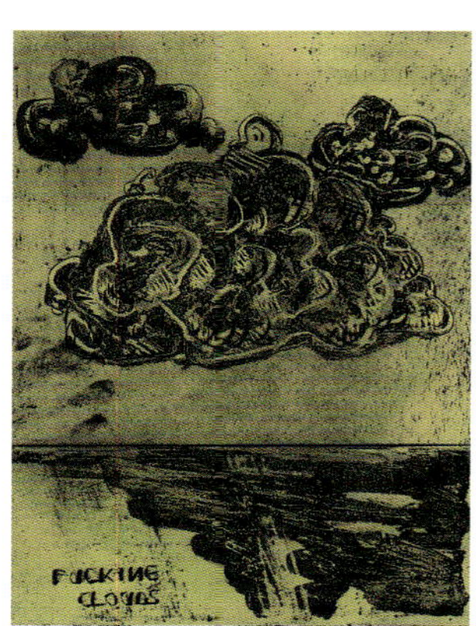
FUCKING
CLOUDS

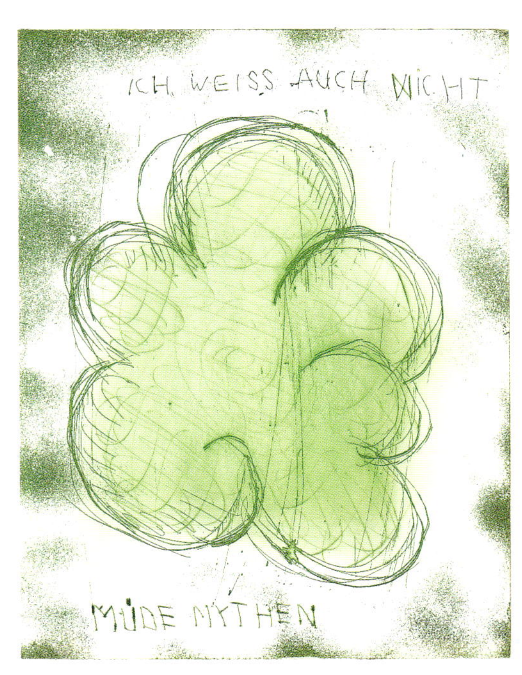
ICH WEISS AUCH NICHT
MÜDE MYTHEN

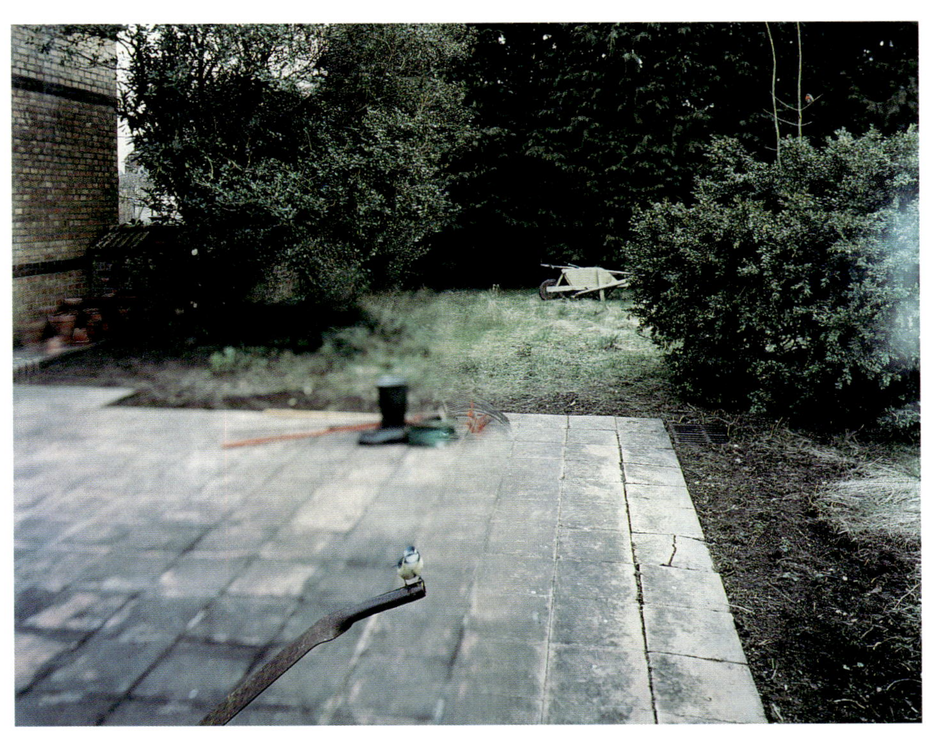

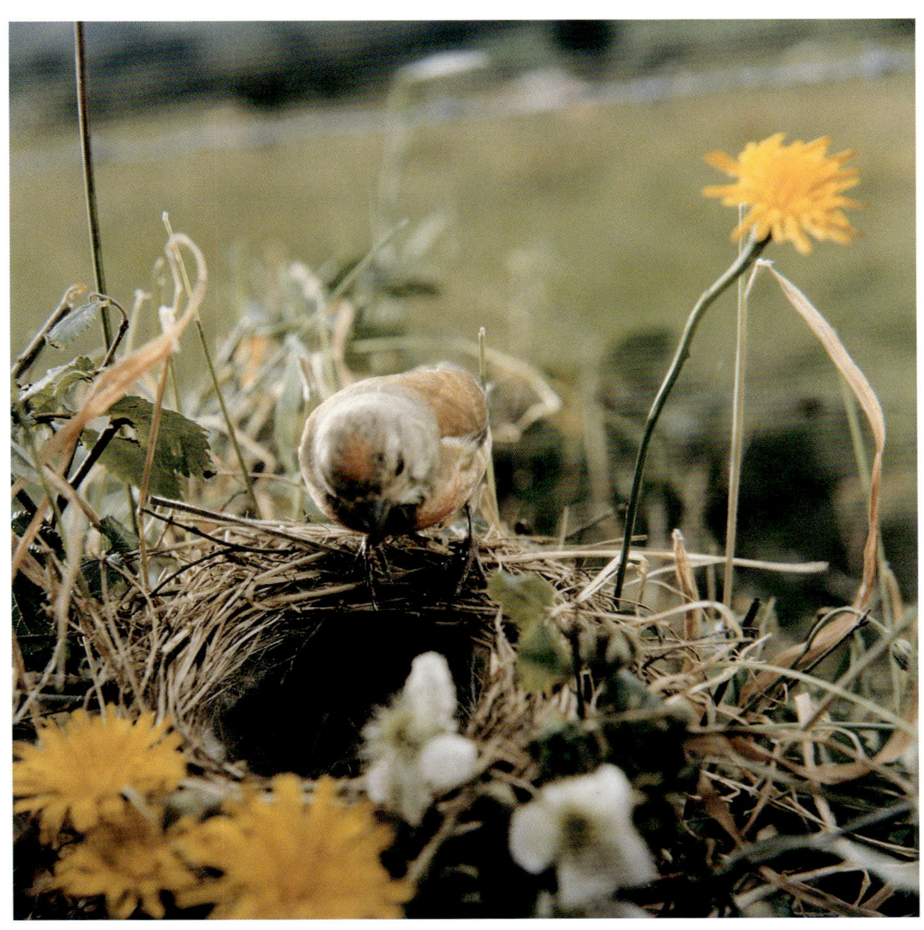

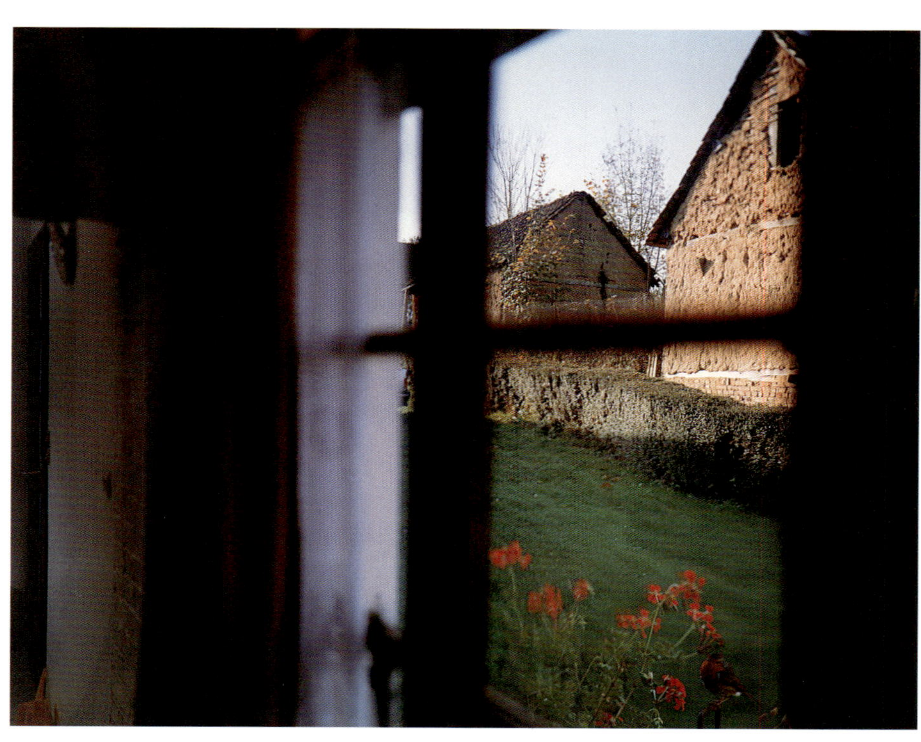

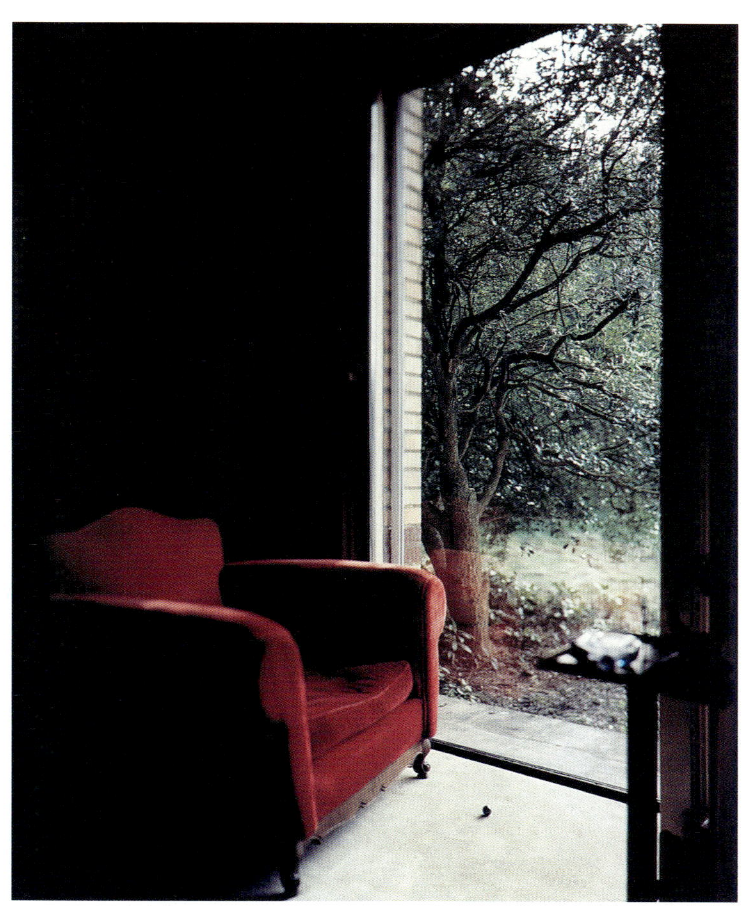

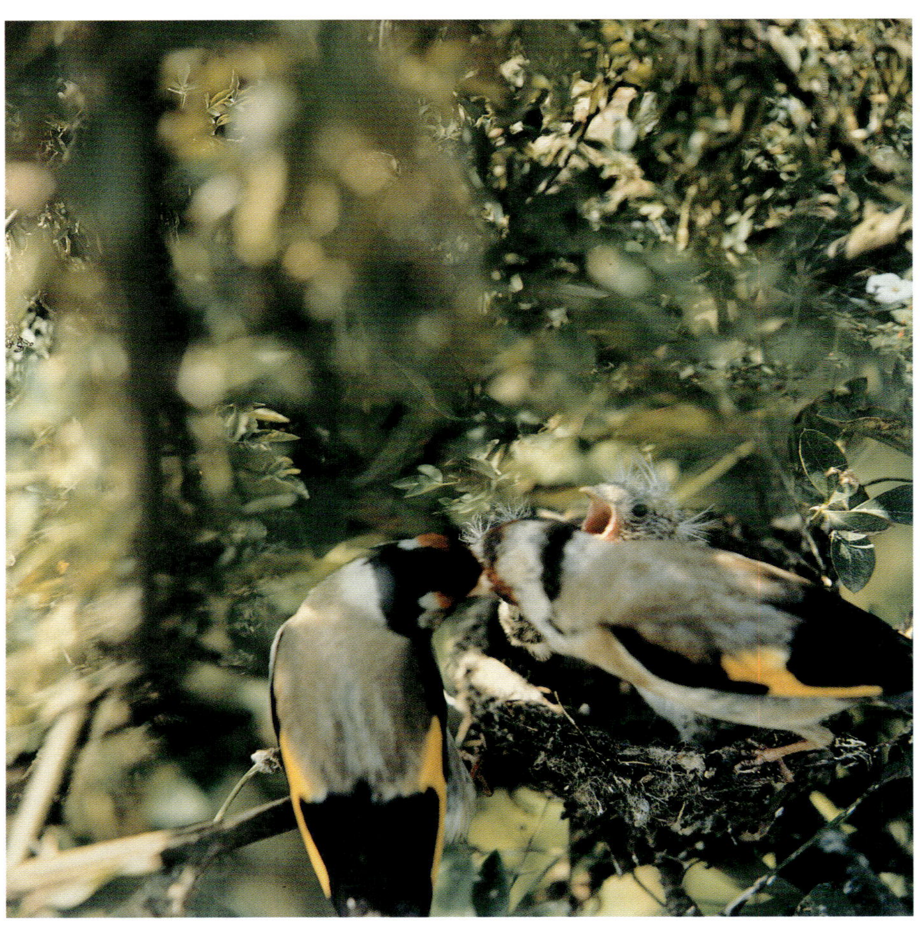

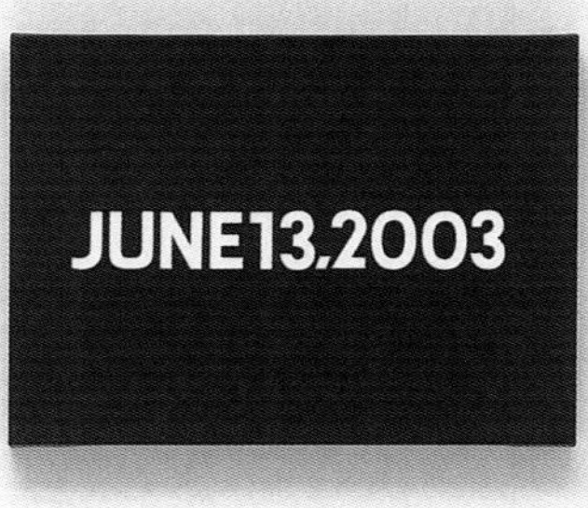
JUNE13,2003

JUNE25.2003

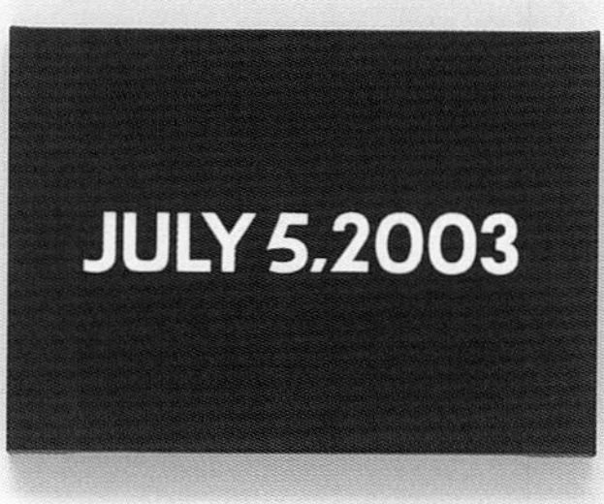JULY 5,2003

JULY18.2003

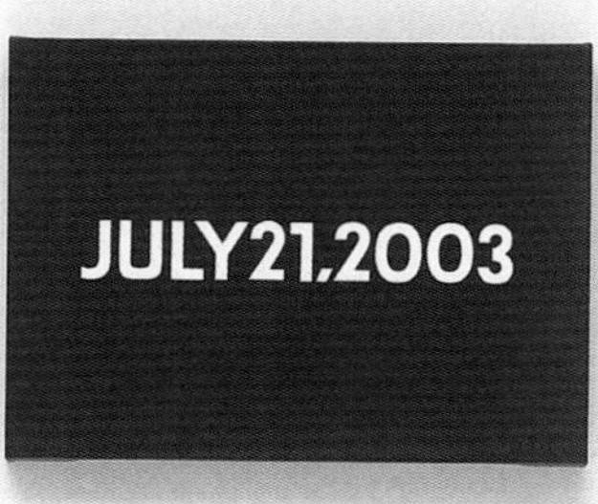
JULY21,2003

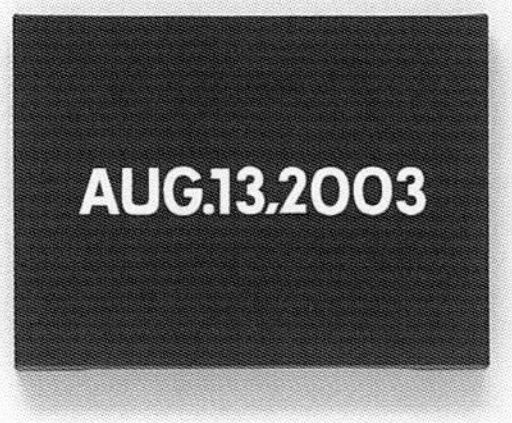

AUG.13.2003

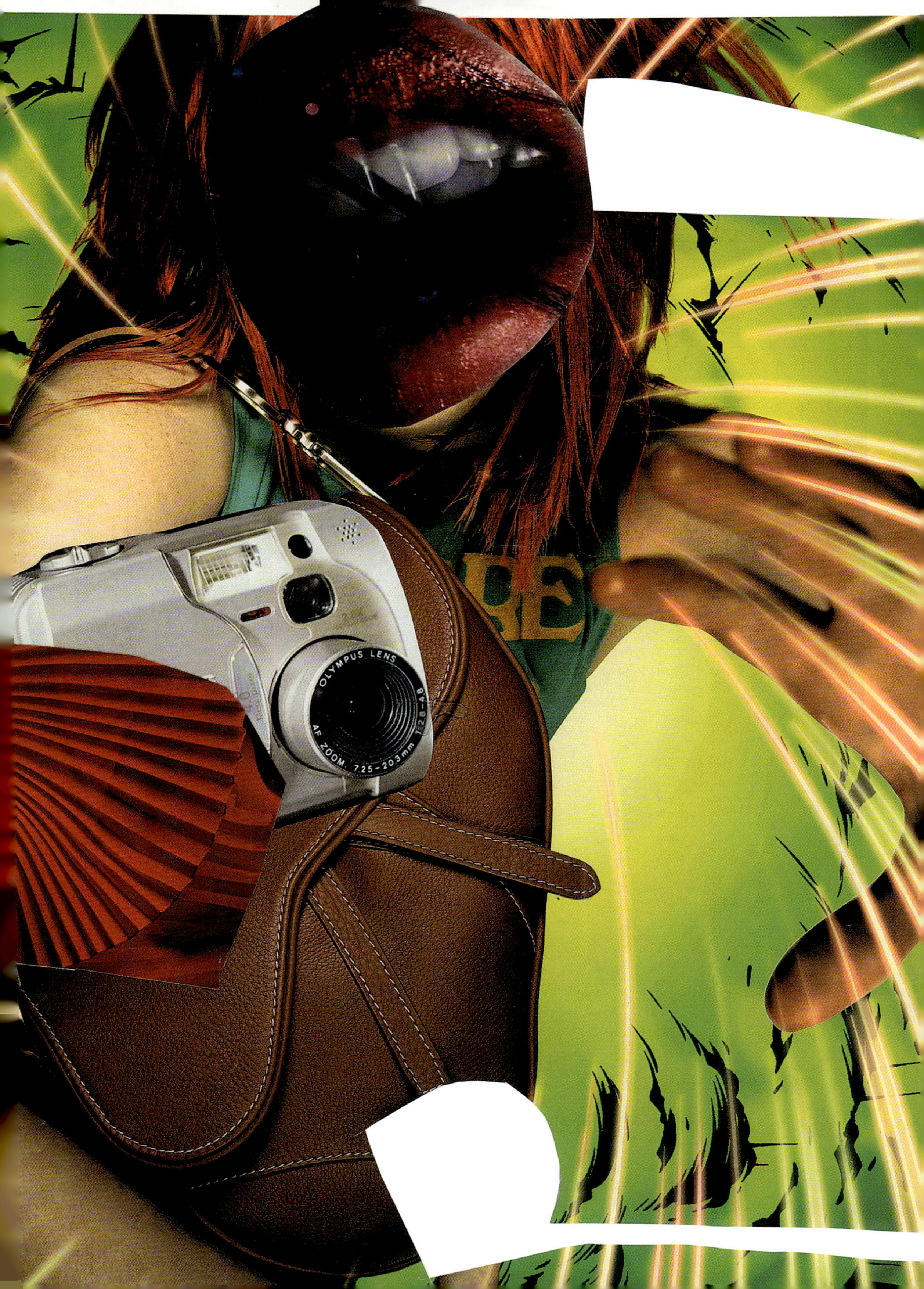

OLYMPUS LENS
AF ZOOM 7.25-20.3 mm
1:2.8-4.8
RE

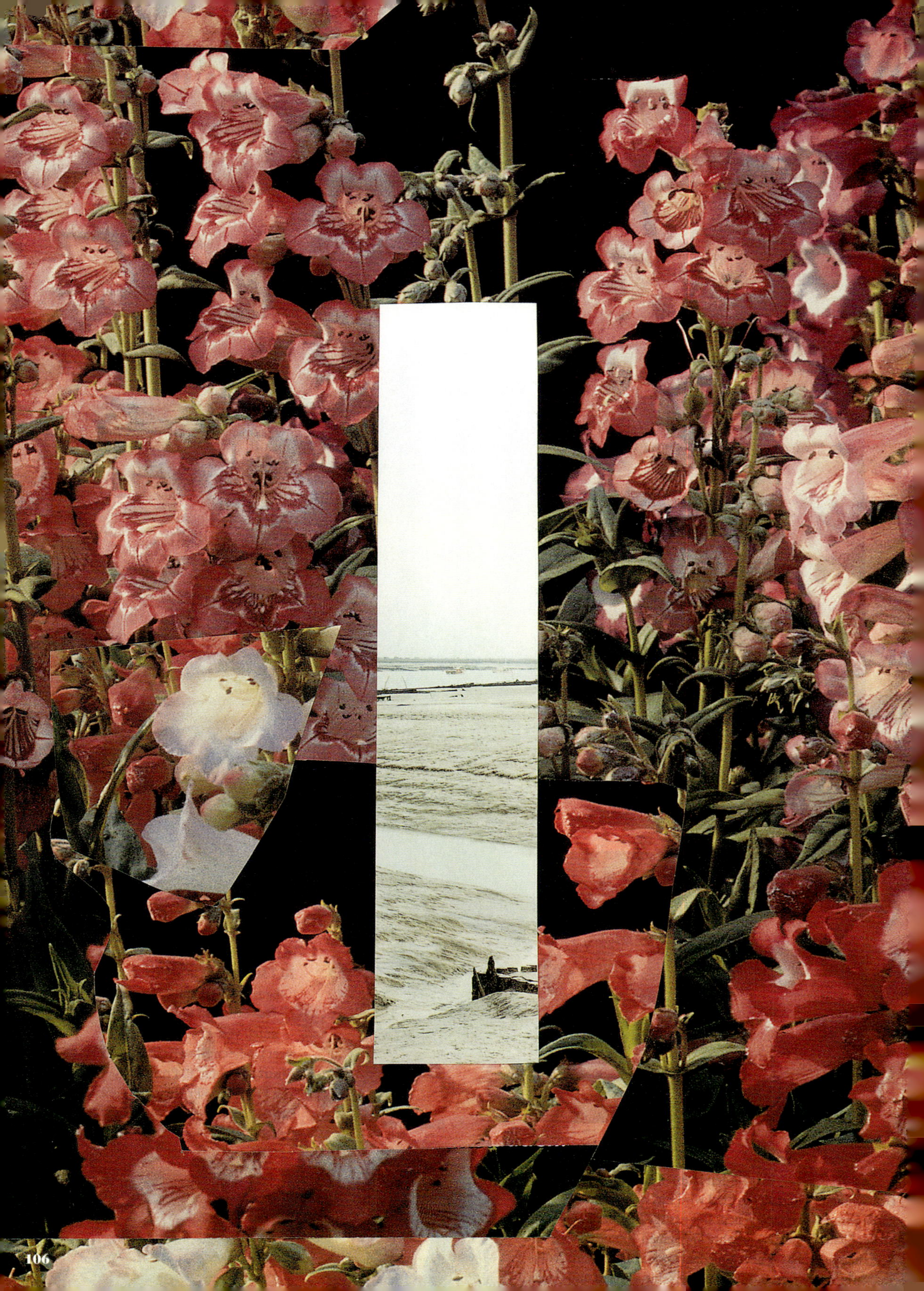

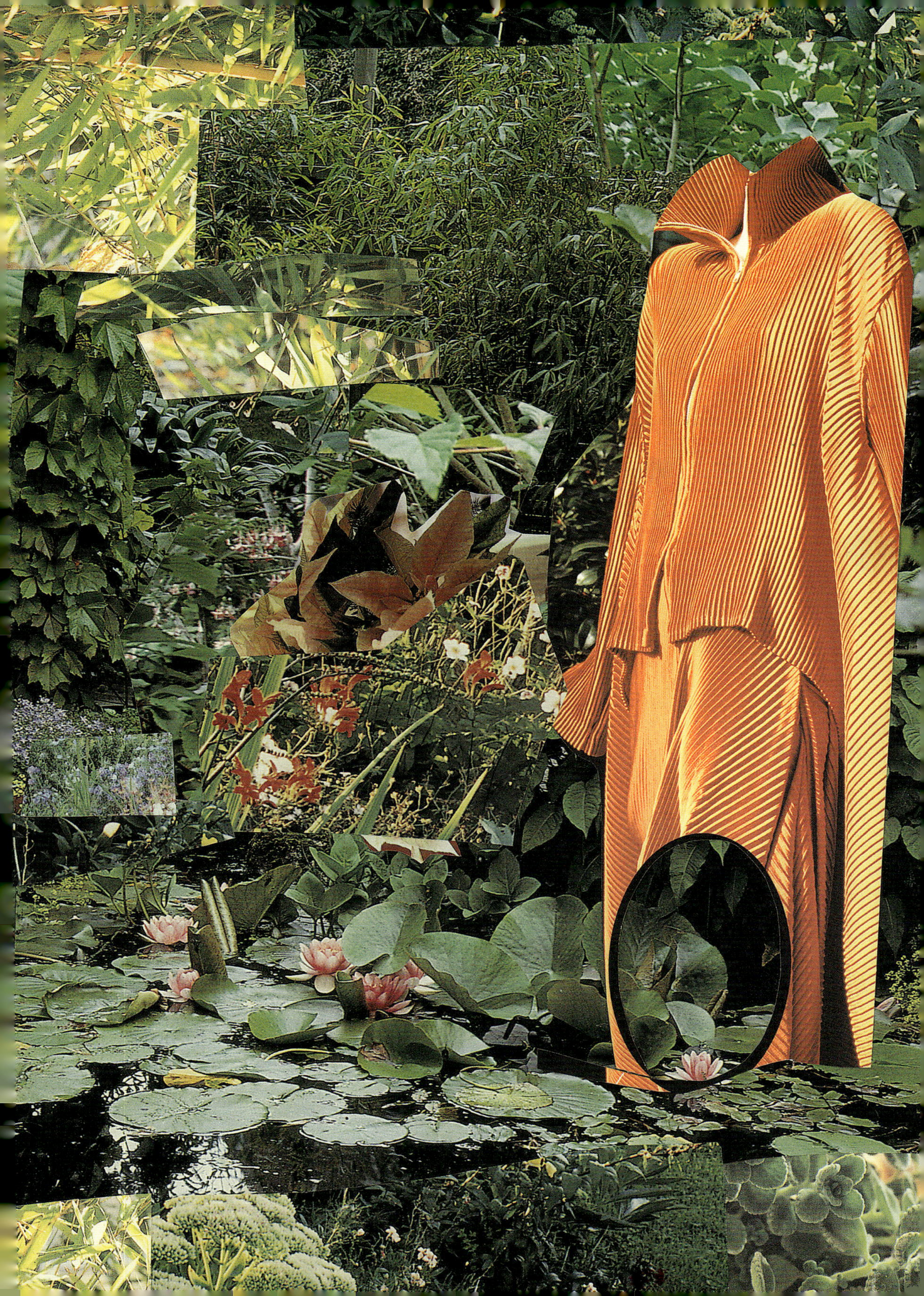

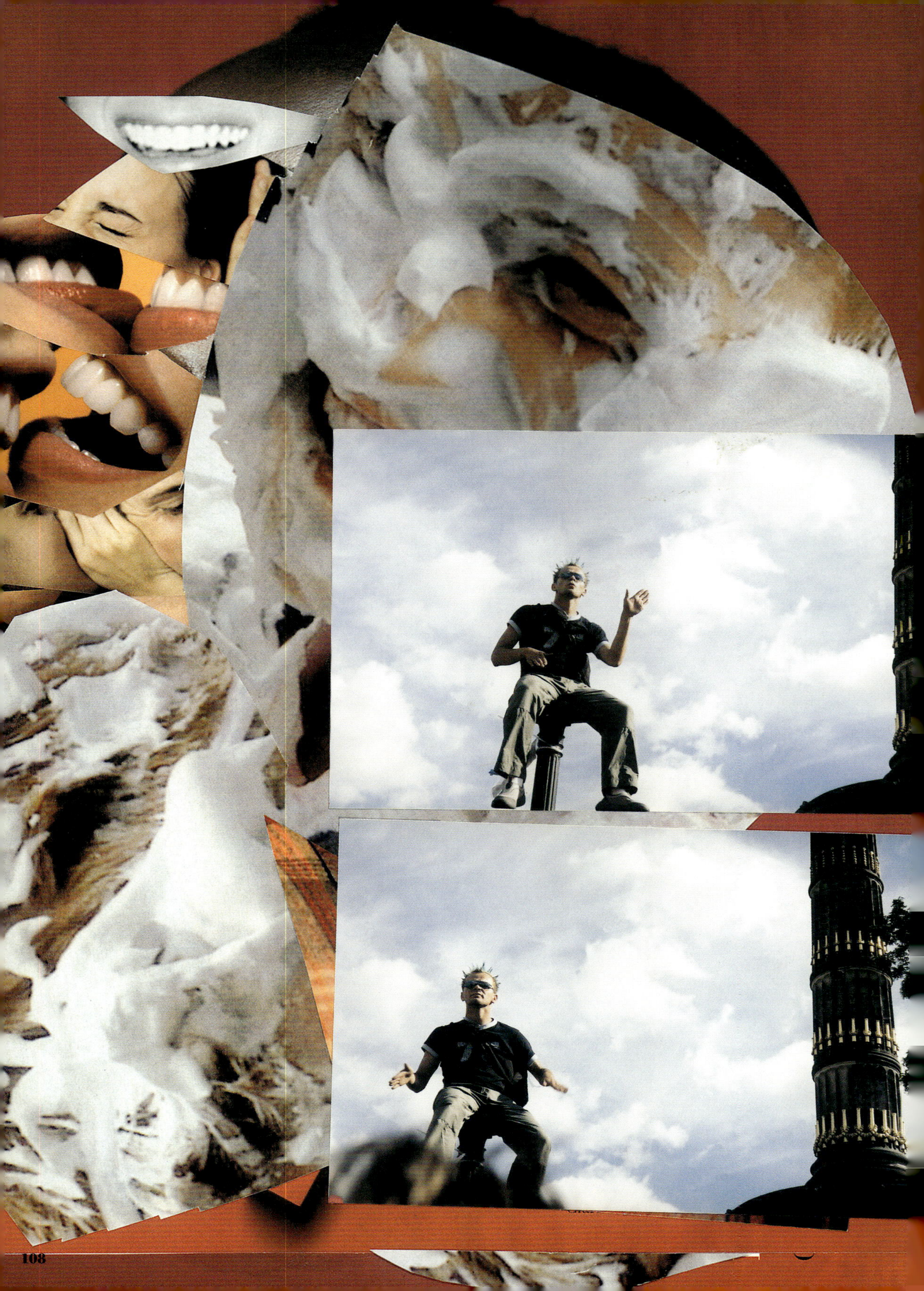

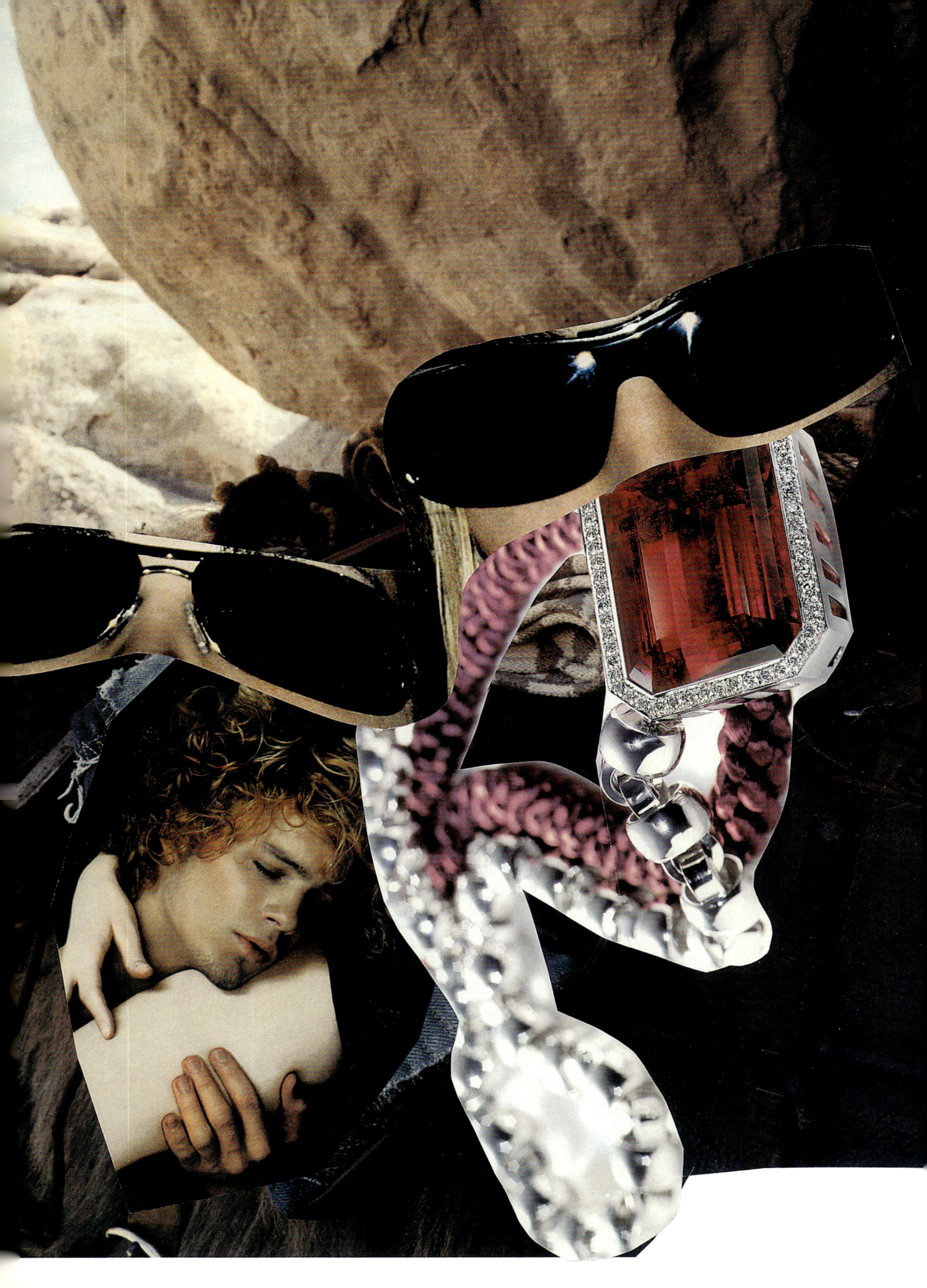

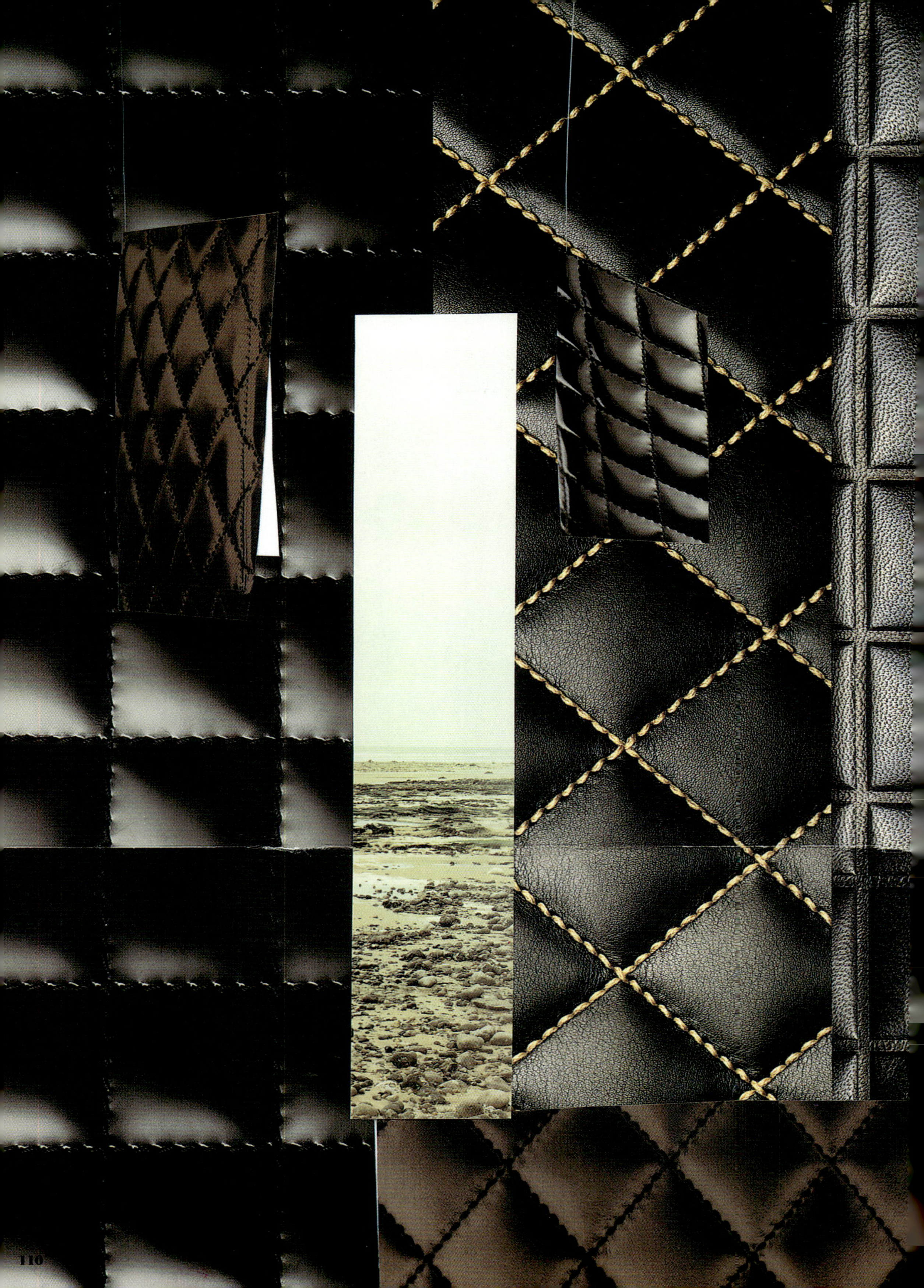

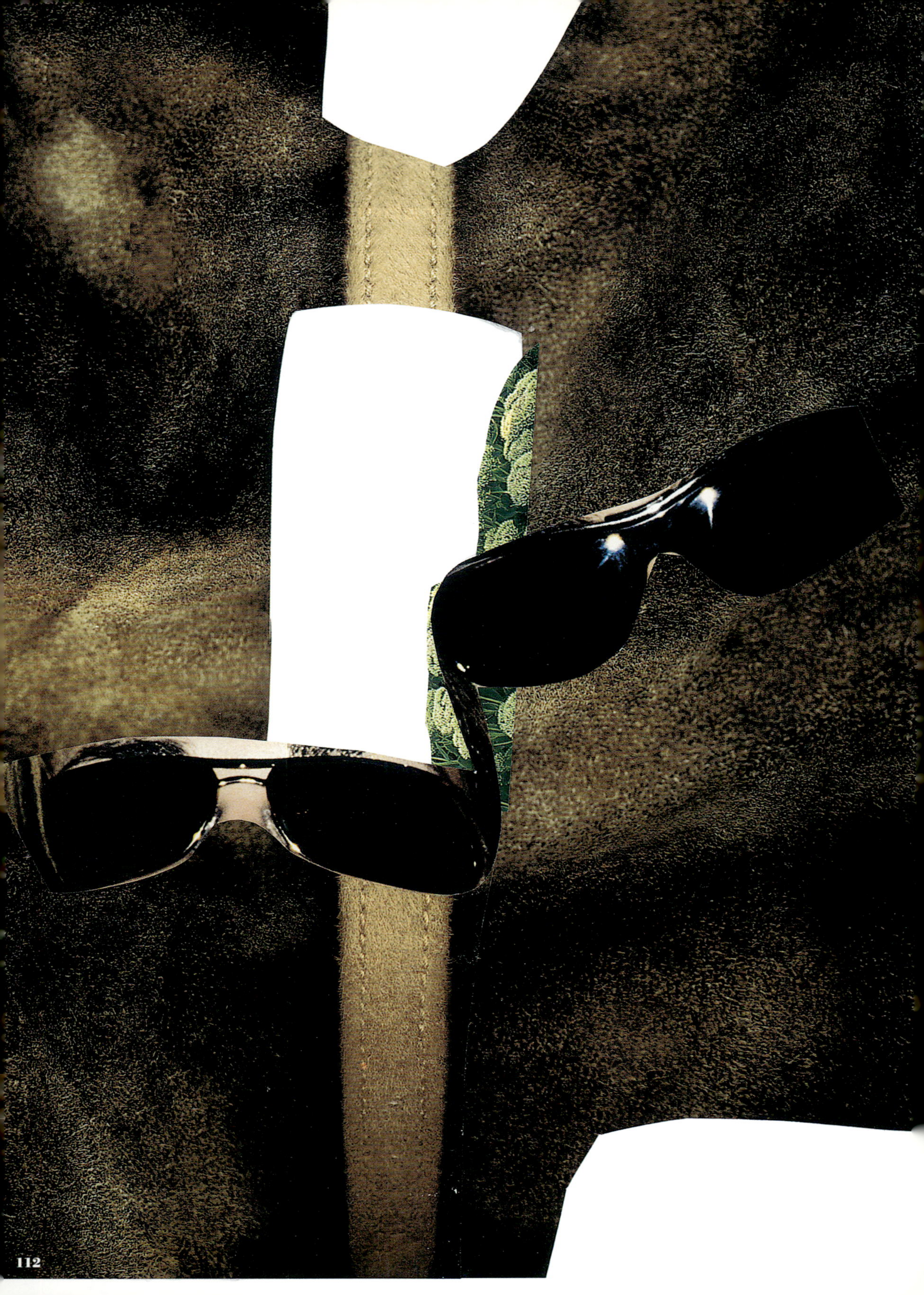

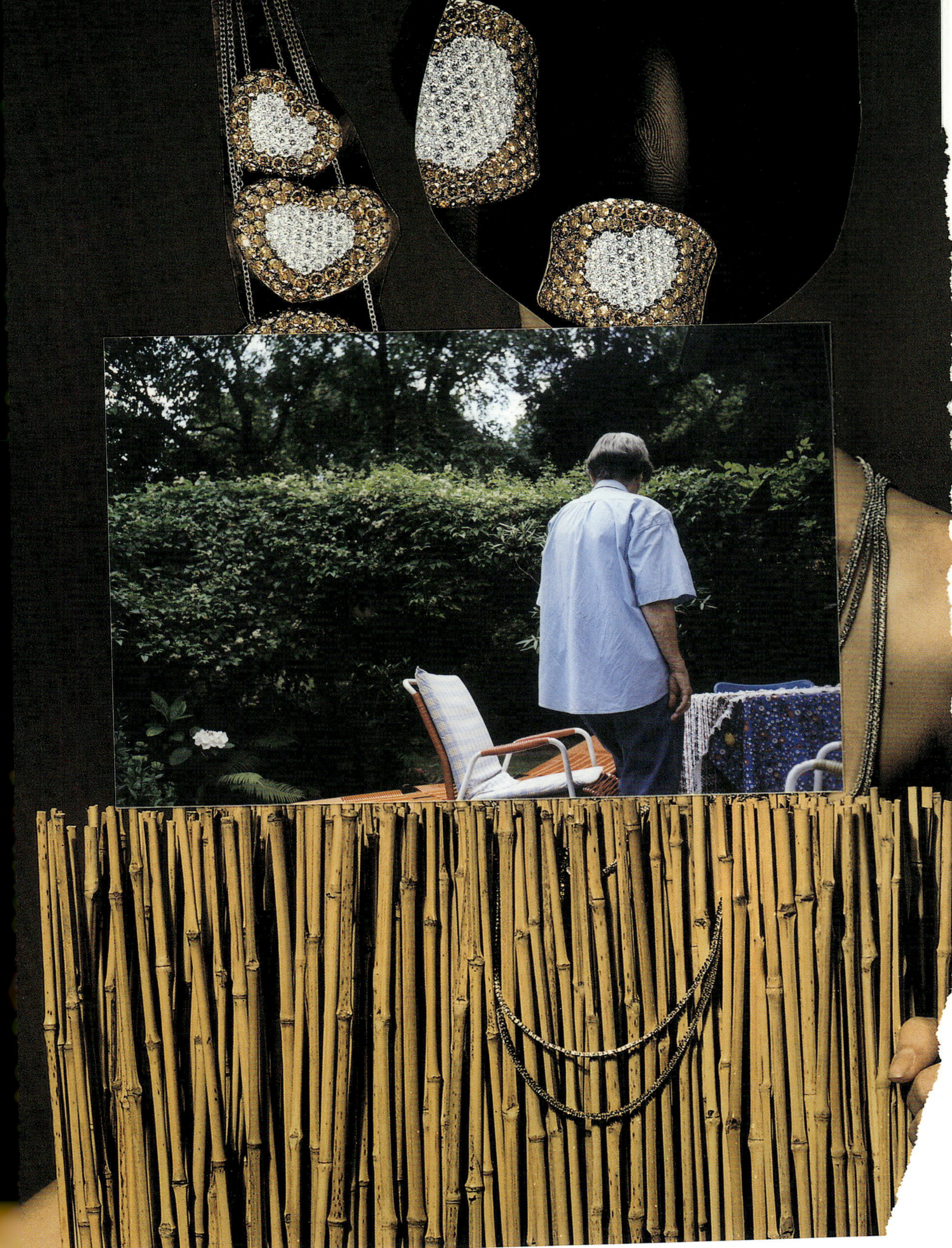

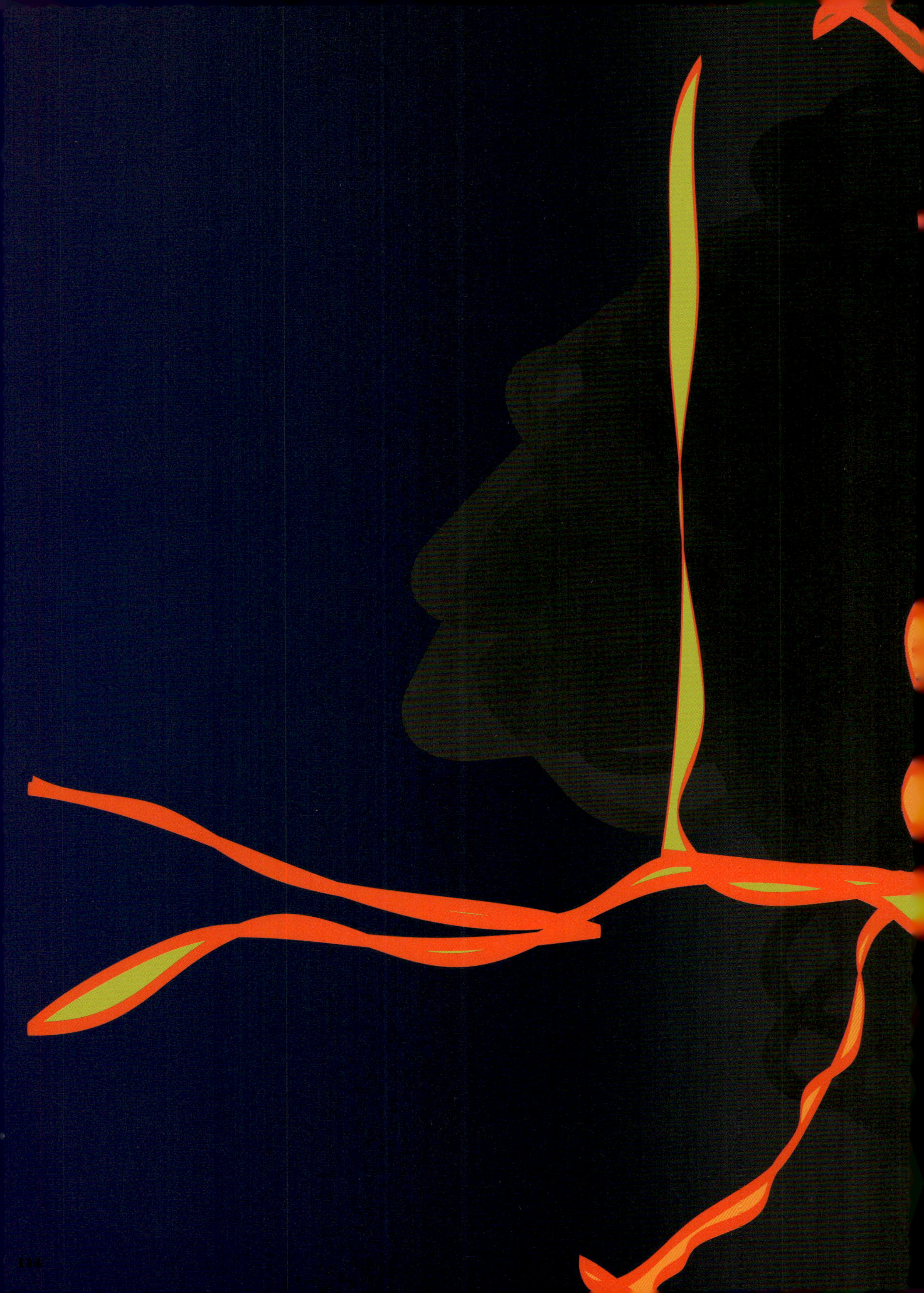

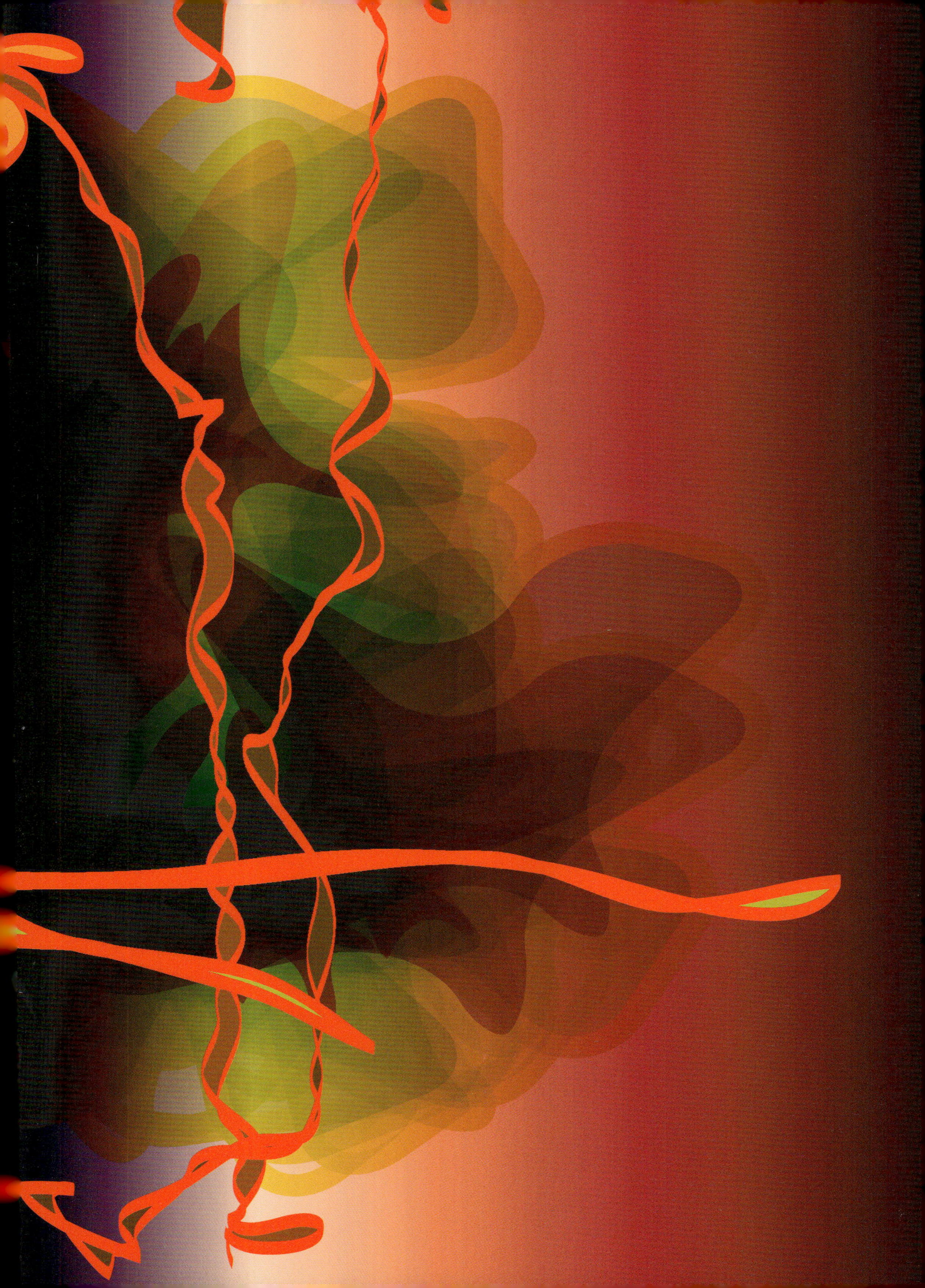

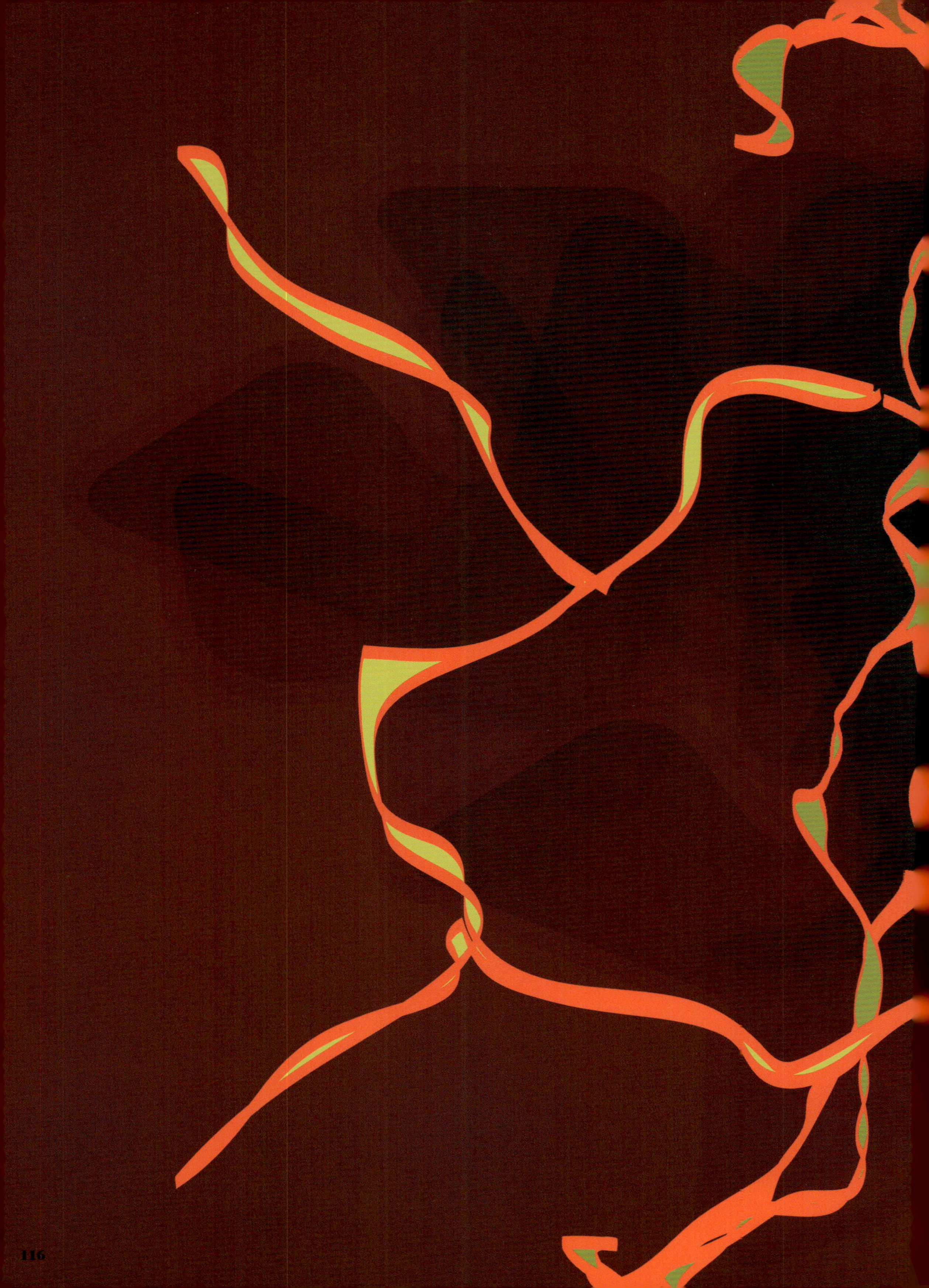

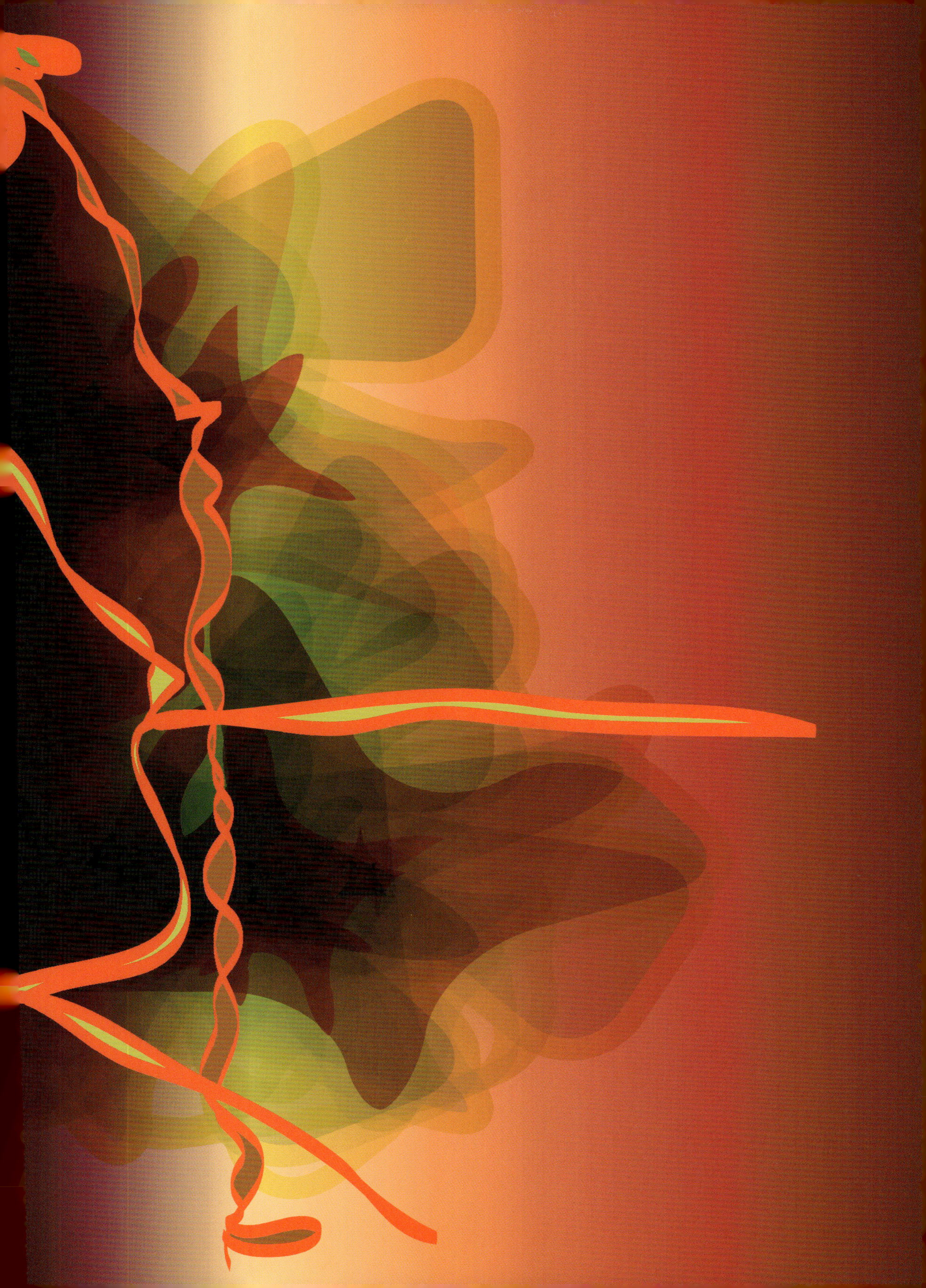

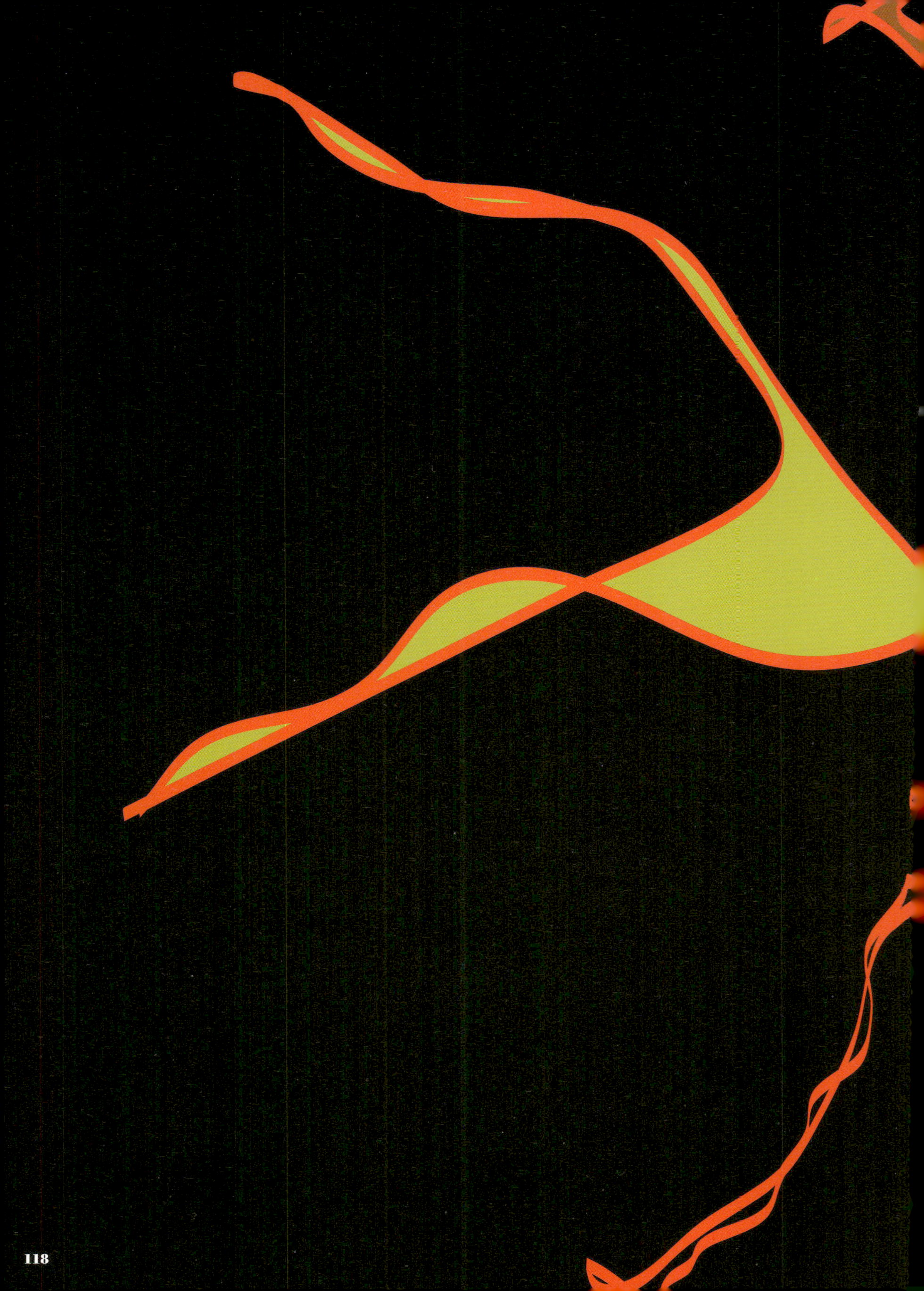

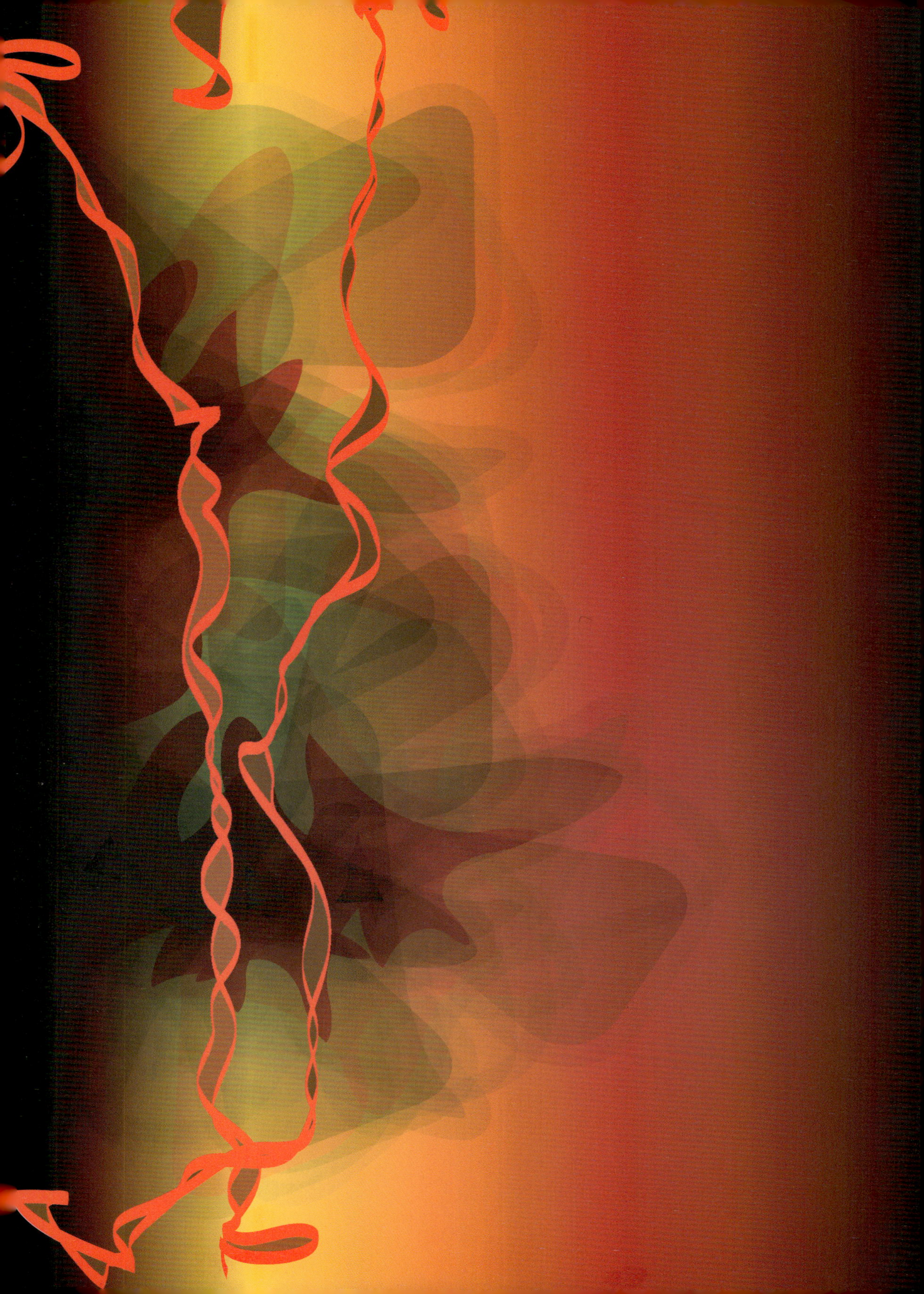

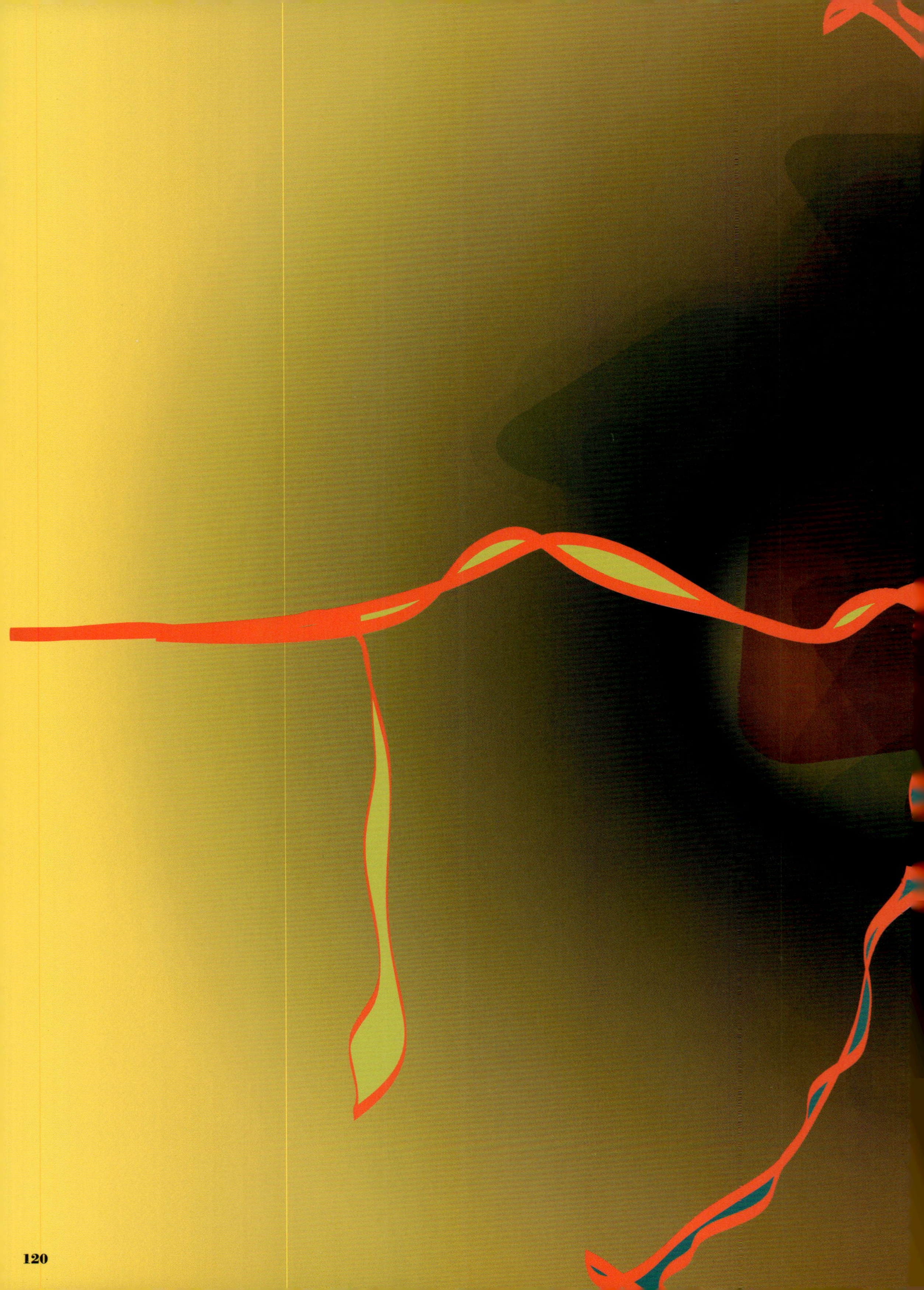

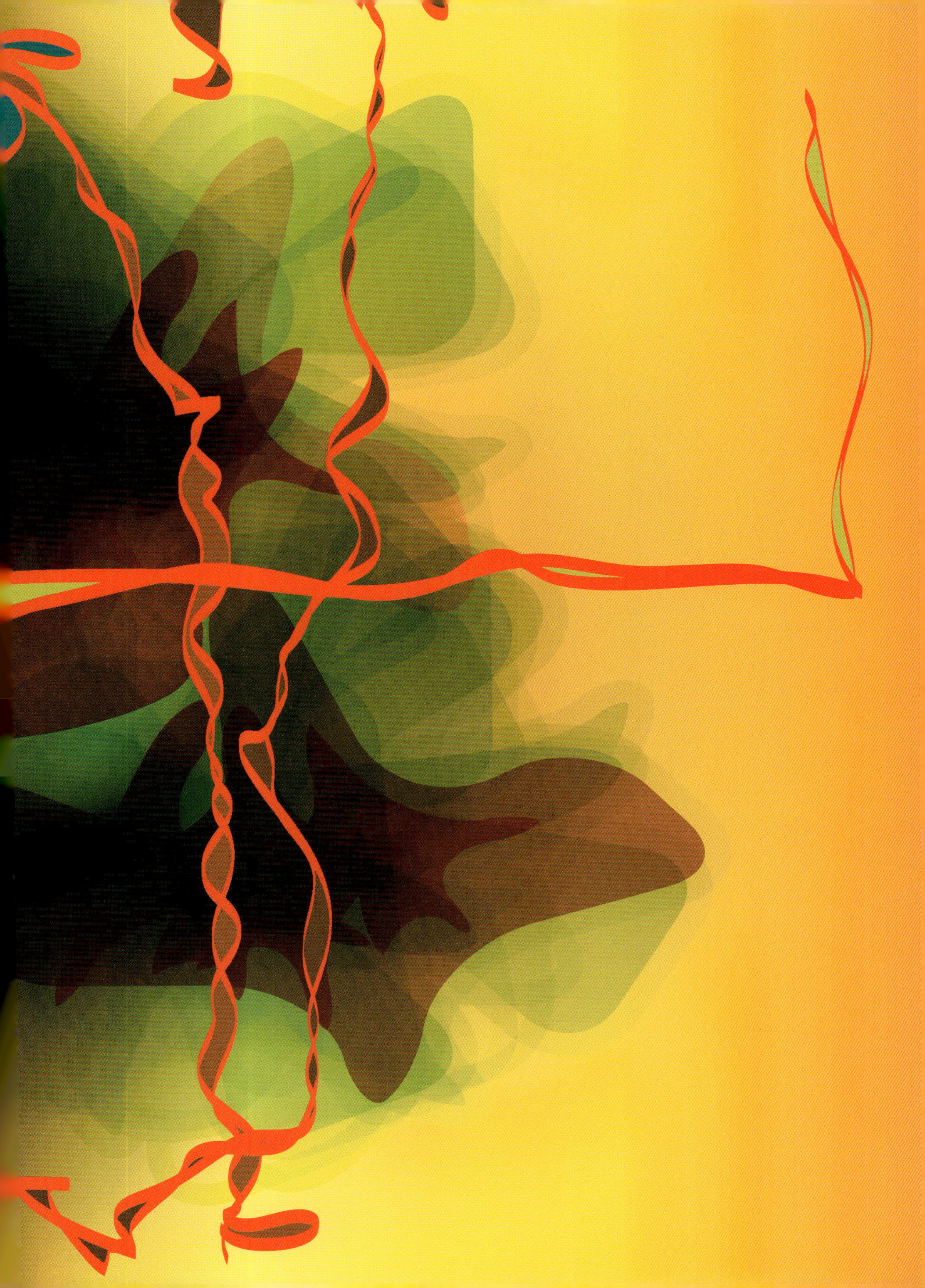

... Wir haben nun ein kleines Verzeichnis der „Zellen" aufgestellt, die der Künstler im Laufe der Menschheitsgeschichte nach und nach geschaffen hat. Wir haben von der Zelle der Materie gesprochen, von der (für alle menschlichen Vorgänge fundamentalen) Zelle der Lust, von der Fähigkeit, die Bilder zu verändern, also der „Fähigkeit zum Bild", von der Fähigkeit, sich selbst „wiederherzustellen" (und also nicht nur das, was außerhalb unserer selbst ist), sodann von der Fähigkeit, „sein eigenes Bild" zu sein. Um es zusammenzufassen: Der Mensch fühlt sich fähig, sowohl sich selbst, als auch kraft seiner Intelligenz ein Bewusstsein seiner selbst und all dessen, was außerhalb seiner selbst ist, herzustellen. Daraus lässt sich ein weiterer Schluß ziehen: indem er außerhalb seiner selbst etwas herstellt, erschafft der Künstler (der Mensch) sich selbst.

Eine weitere Zelle ist die Phantasie, die Herstellung einer Immaterialität: einer Natur, die real ist, auch wenn sie nicht alle Eigenschaften und materiellen Komponenten der Natur im allgemeinen Sinne besitzt.

All diese „Zellen" finden wir in der zeitgenössischen Kunst. Was aber ist es, was sie so hinfällig macht, dass wir behaupten müssten, sie seien nicht mehr zu gebrauchen? Wir haben darüber bereits ausführlich gesprochen. Wir finden diese „Zellen" überall in der Welt: in dem, was uns als kulturelles Erbe überkommen ist, an den Orten, wo dieses Erbe sich niedergelassen hat (zum Beispiel in den Museen), wir finden sie in unserem Gedankengut, und so weiter. Aber wir können sie nicht gebrauchen. Wir begreifen die Sache etwas besser, wenn wir uns klarmachen, dass ein Ding, das nicht mehr zu gebrauchen ist, eben tot ist; es lebt nicht mehr. Es sind tote Zellen. Und wenn wir uns nun an das erinnern, was wir anfangs sagten, so müssen wir erkennen, dass diese Zellen offensichtlich deshalb abgestorben sind, weil es in der modernen Kultur zu schweren Verwundungen gekommen ist.

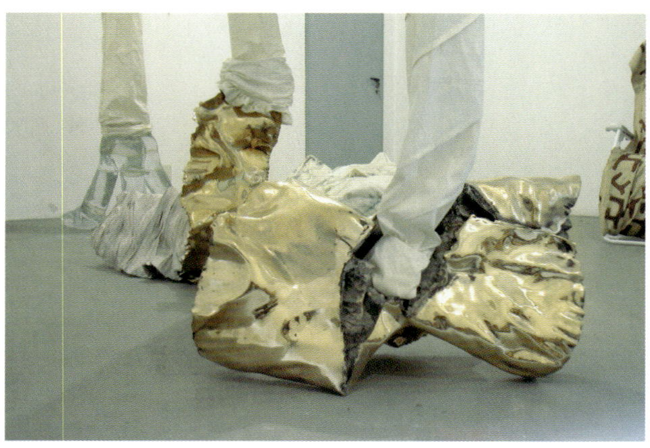

Unsere Aufgabe in der heutigen Zeit ist es, unsere Interesse und unsere Aufmerksamkeit von diesen toten Zellen abzuwenden: anstatt die Kruste zu beklagen, die sie bilden, müssen wir unter der Kruste arbeiten, denn das ist der Ort, an dem das neue Gewebe nachwächst. All die Künstler, die nach und nach die Phantasie, die Metaphysik, die Natur, die Lust, die Materie „erfunden" haben, arbeiteten unter der Kruste, die durch die Verwundungen während der schwierigen Auseinandersetzung zwischen den verschiedenen Naturen entstanden ist.

Unsere Untersuchung ist einerseits konstruktiv und vital, andererseits bedarf sie eines langen Atems. Zu Beginn sagten wir, dass dies der erste Kriegstag Eurer Generation ist: da dieser Krieg ausgebrochen ist, da die Menschheit von dieser Wunde geschlagen ist, haben wir Künstler die Aufgabe, so zu arbeiten, dass dann, wenn dieser Krieg zu Ende ist, wenn diese „Kruste" wieder aufbricht, darunter ein lebendiges, elastisches Gewebe zutage tritt, das ein neues Menschheitsbild zu geben vermag. Es wird also eine Erweiterung bedeuten. Es wird ein Schritt nach vorne sein. Damit will ich nicht behaupten, Schwierigkeiten an sich seien positiv und brächten uns weiter. Vielmehr hätte der Mensch vielleicht sehr gut in der ersten Phase weiterleben können. Doch wie immer, der Künstler ist derjenige, der die Probleme zu lösen hat, die zu seiner Zeit, in seinem Raum, in diesem Moment sonst keiner zu lösen imstande ist. Ich spreche nicht vom Künstler als einem „Ich", sondern als einem „Verhalten". Und von dem Augenblick an, in dem Ihr in diese Art des Sich-Verhaltens eintretet, steht Ihr zu dem, was geschieht, in einer besonderen Beziehung. In einer besonderen Beziehung auch in Hinsicht darauf, was Ihr erleiden werdet.

Tatsächlich befindet Ihr, befinden wir uns nicht in der Lage derer, die erleiden; als Künstler gehören wir stets zu den aktiven Individuen (soweit die Umstände es uns erlauben). Wir sind also keine Pessimisten, sondern im wesentlichen Sinn Optimisten…

Luciano Fabro

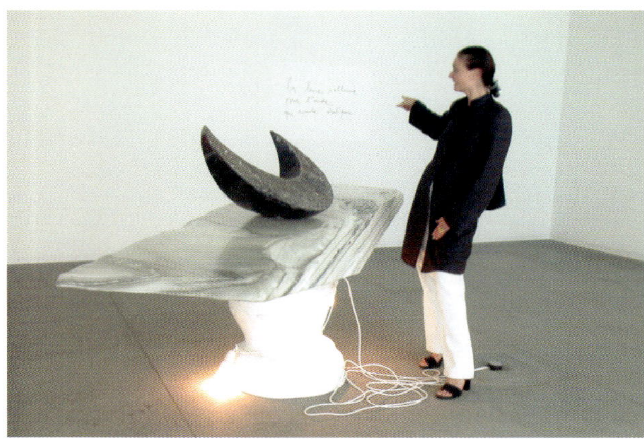

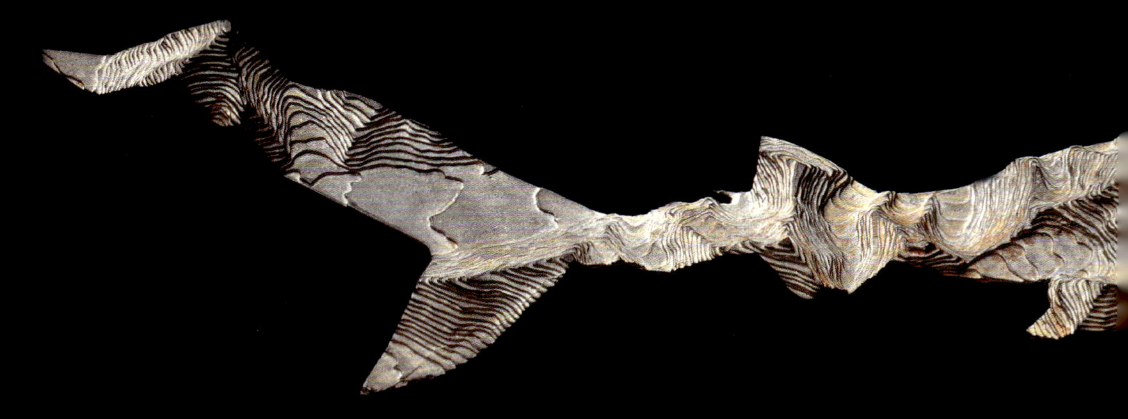

DIE FARBE DES WASSERS

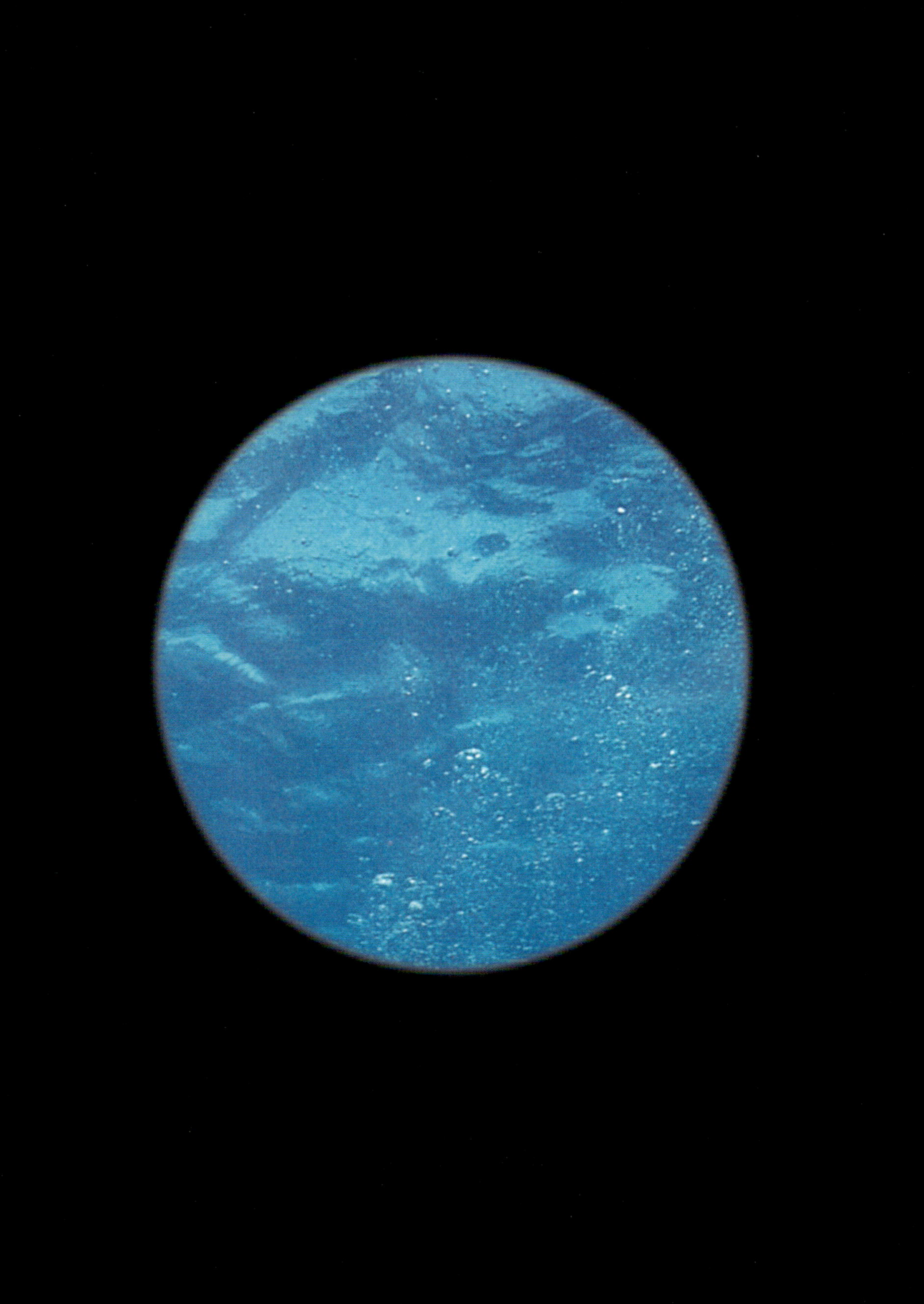

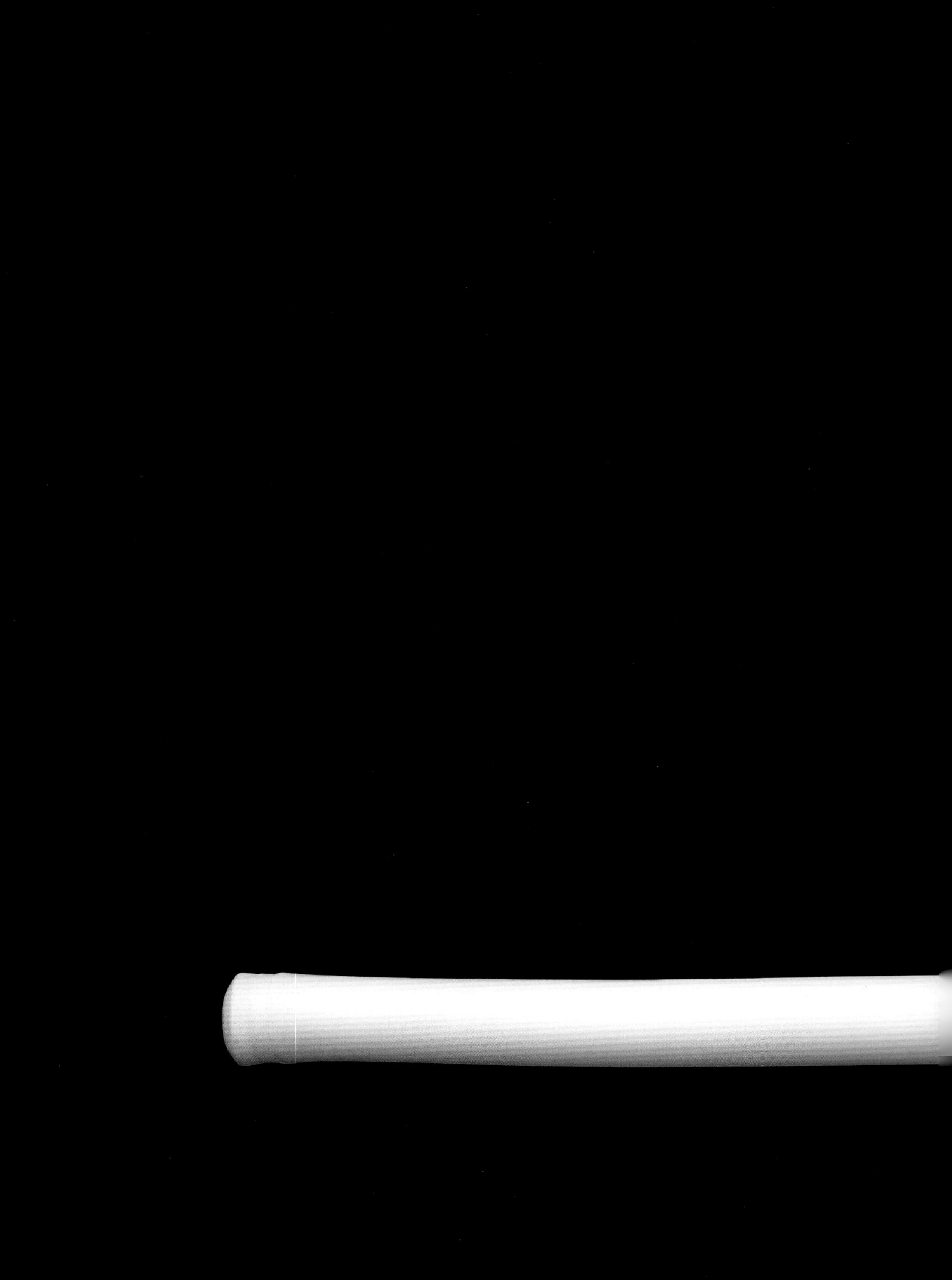

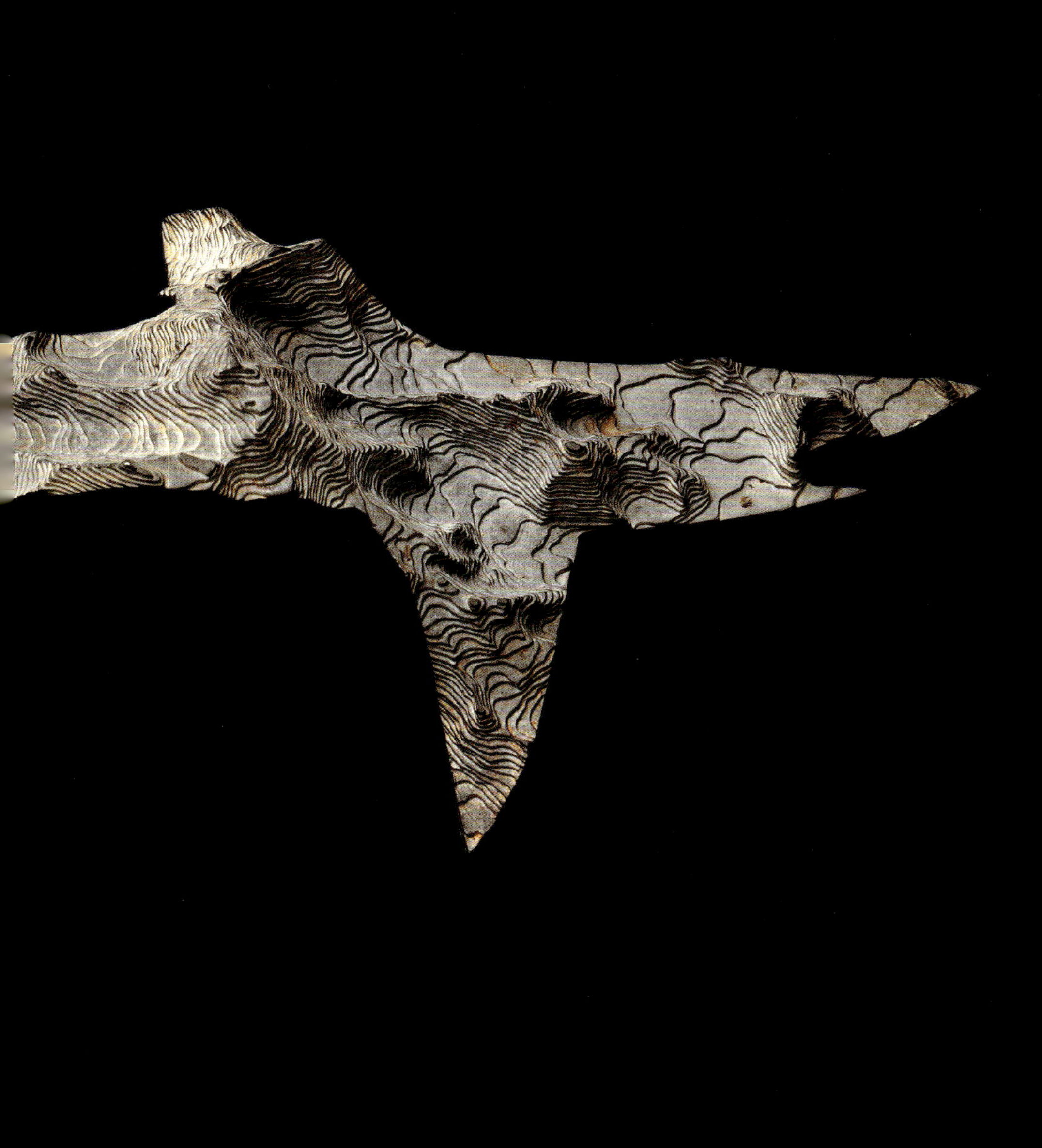

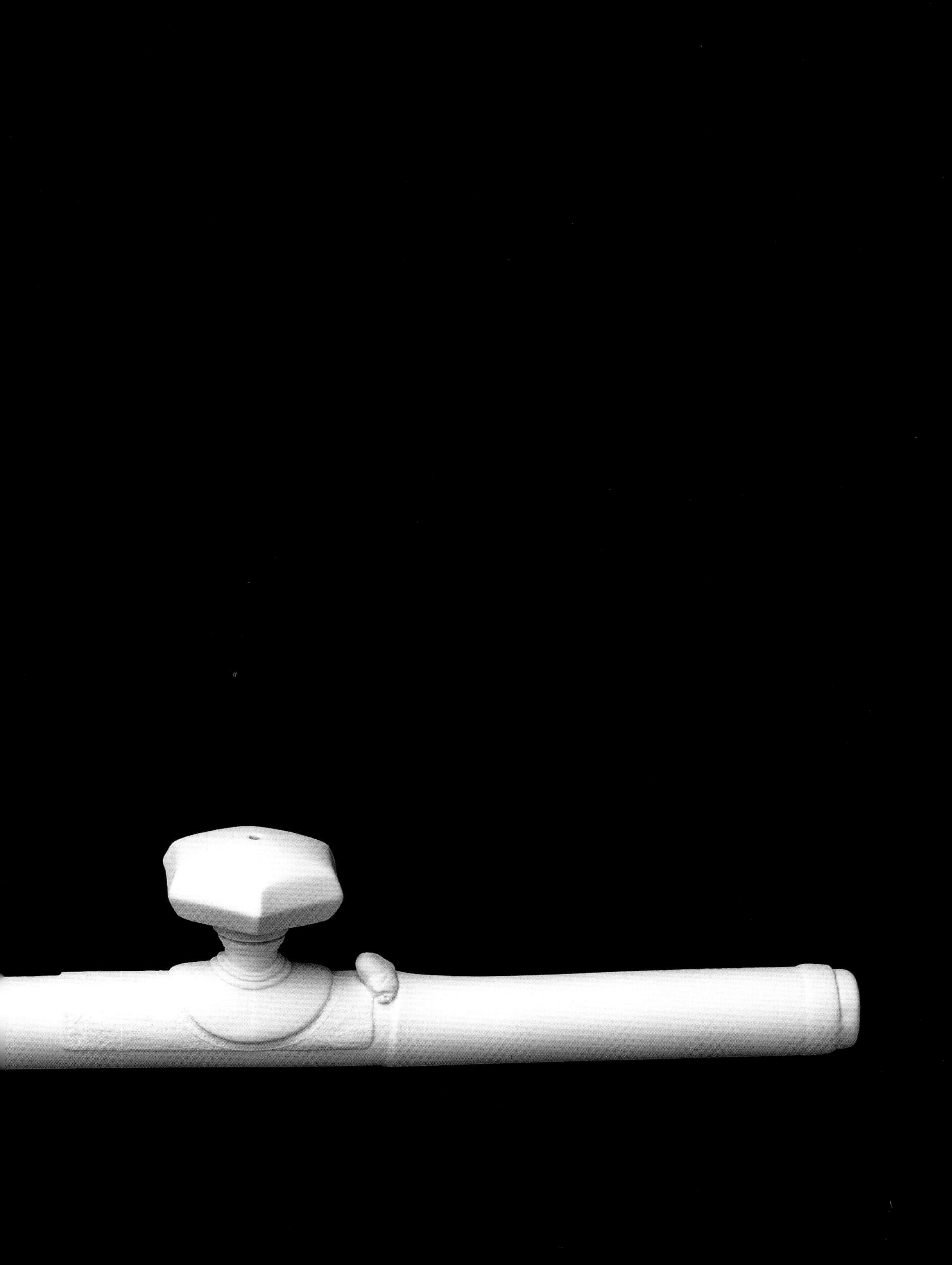

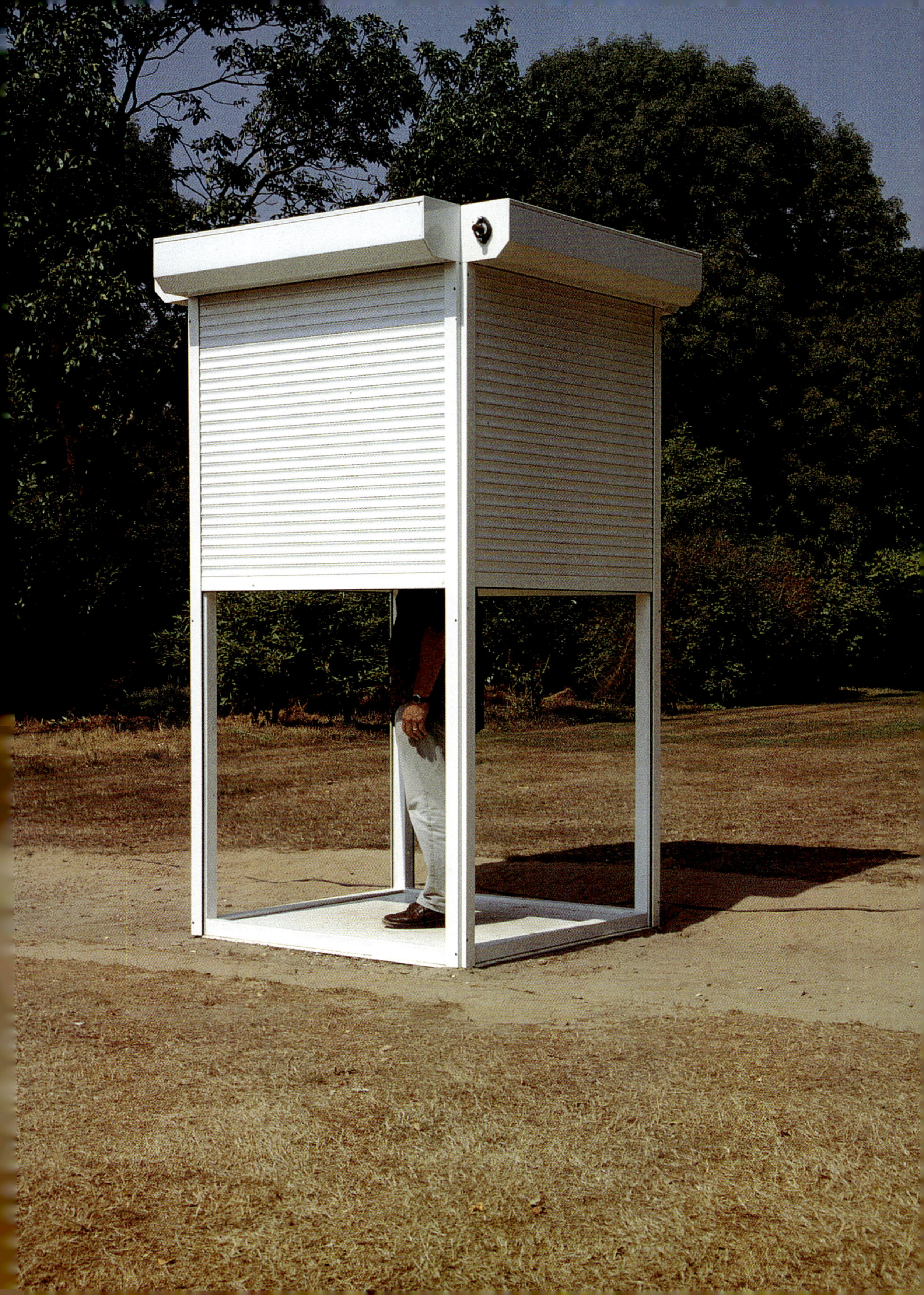

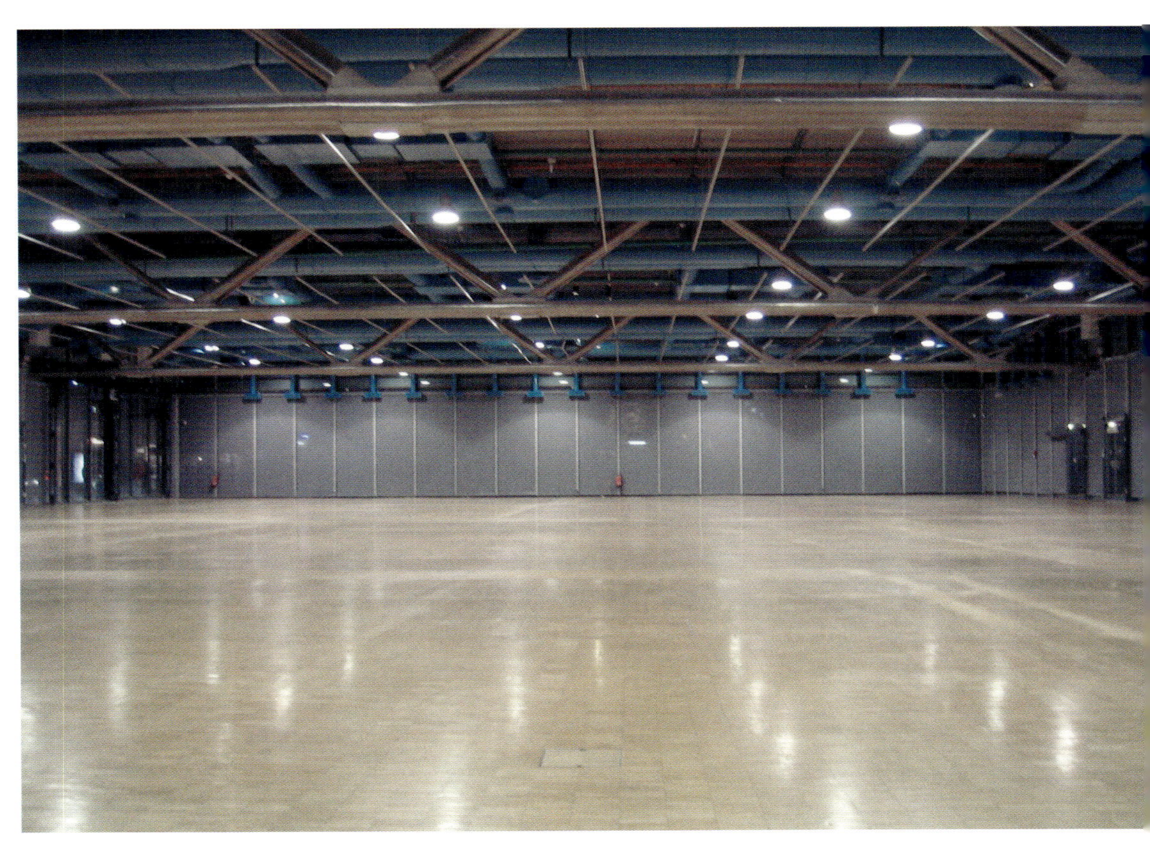

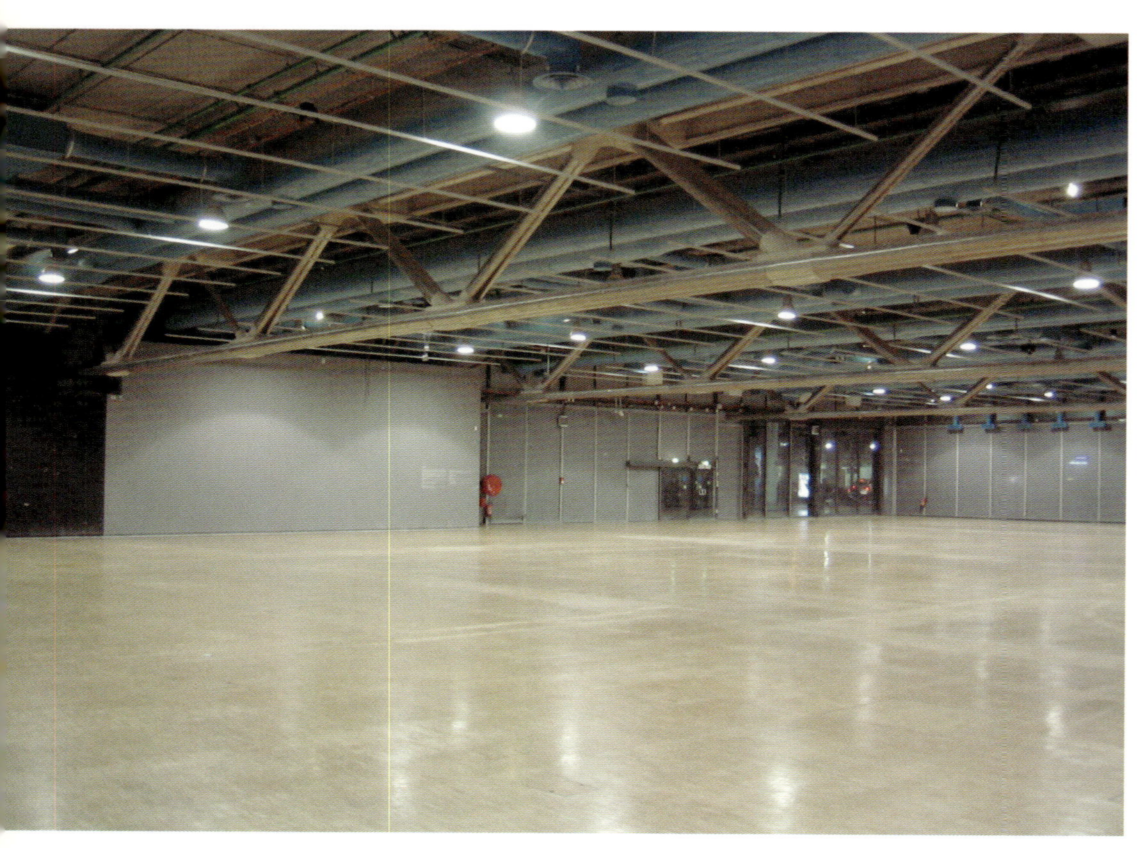

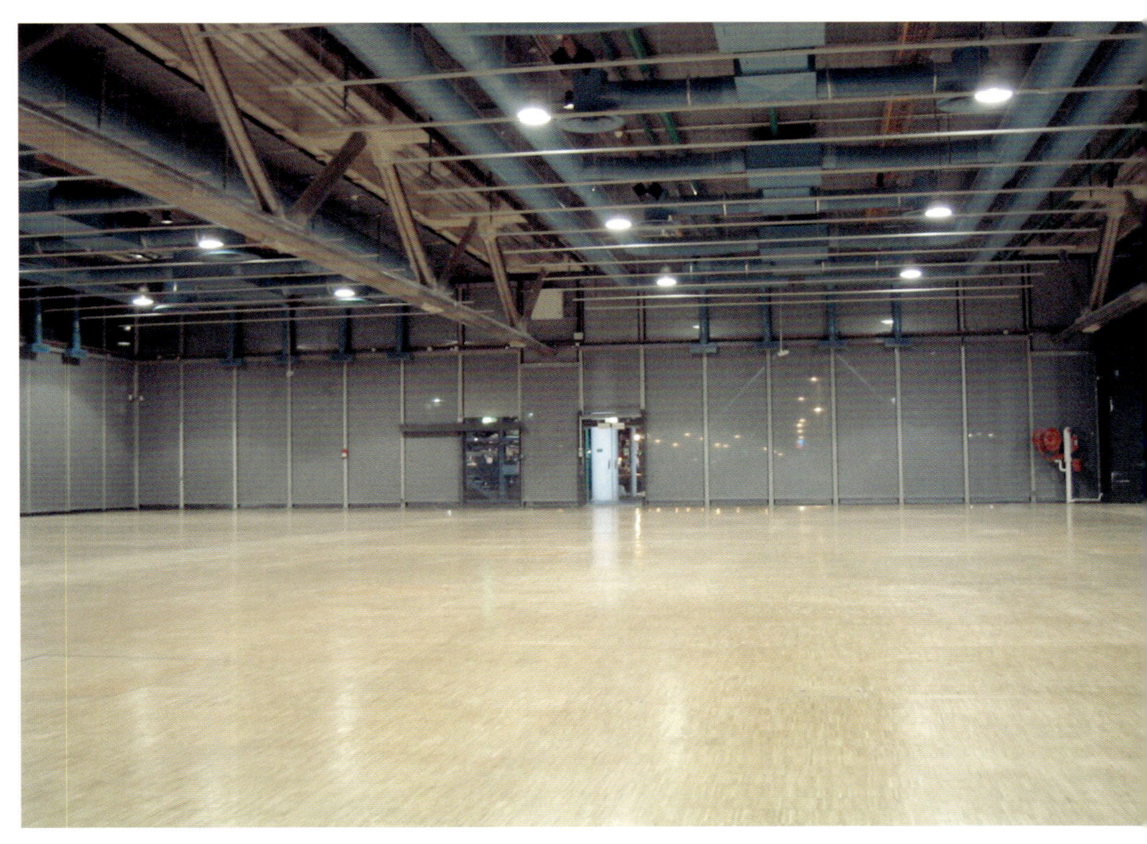

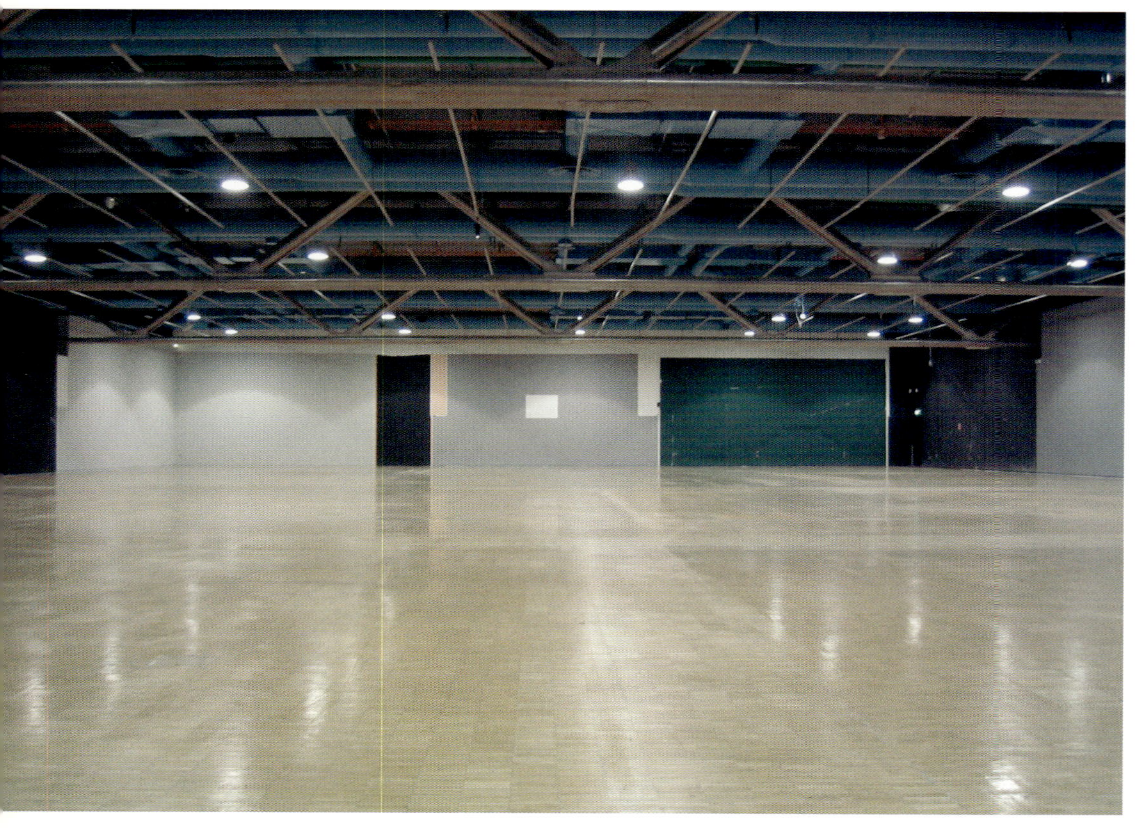

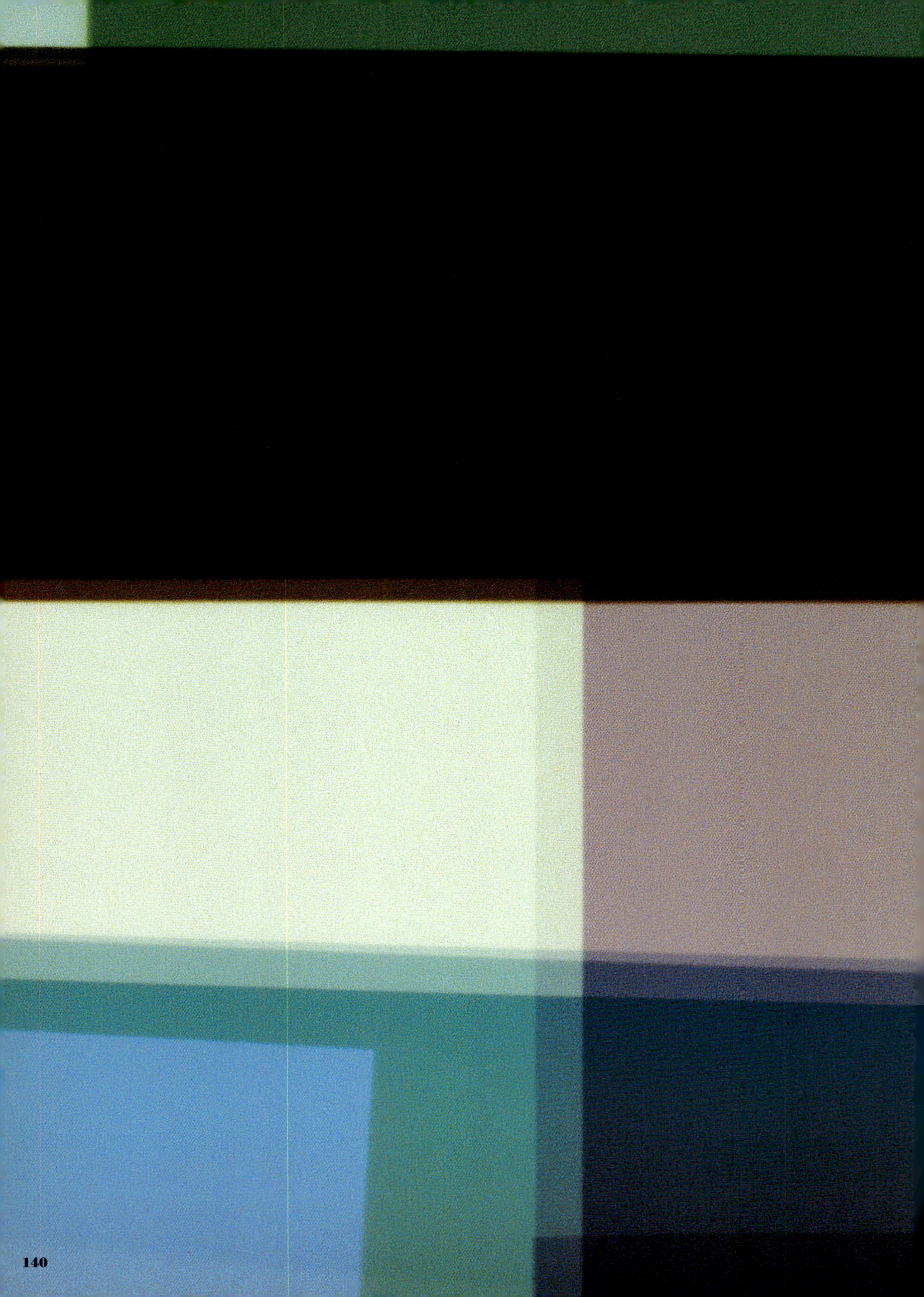

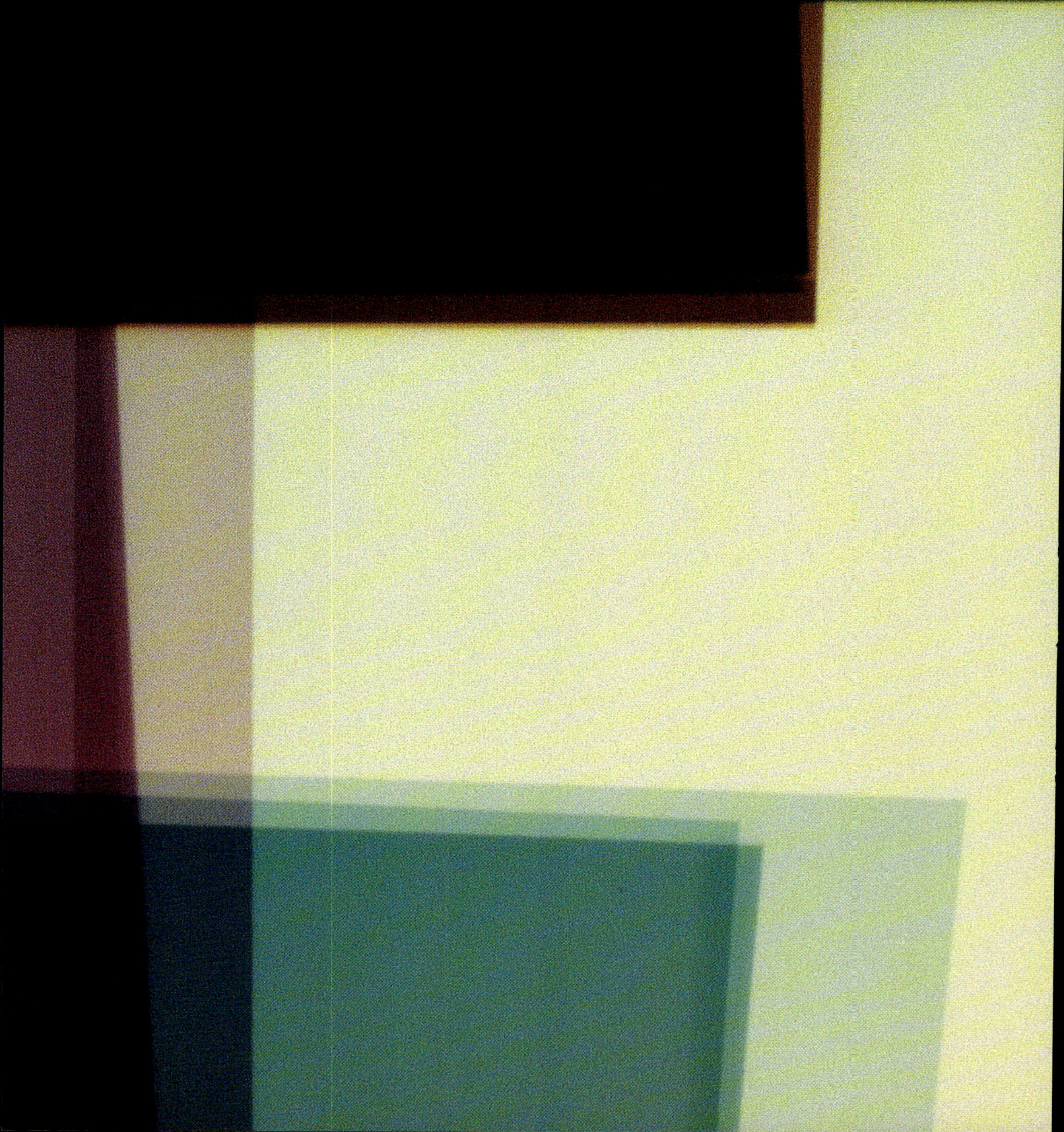

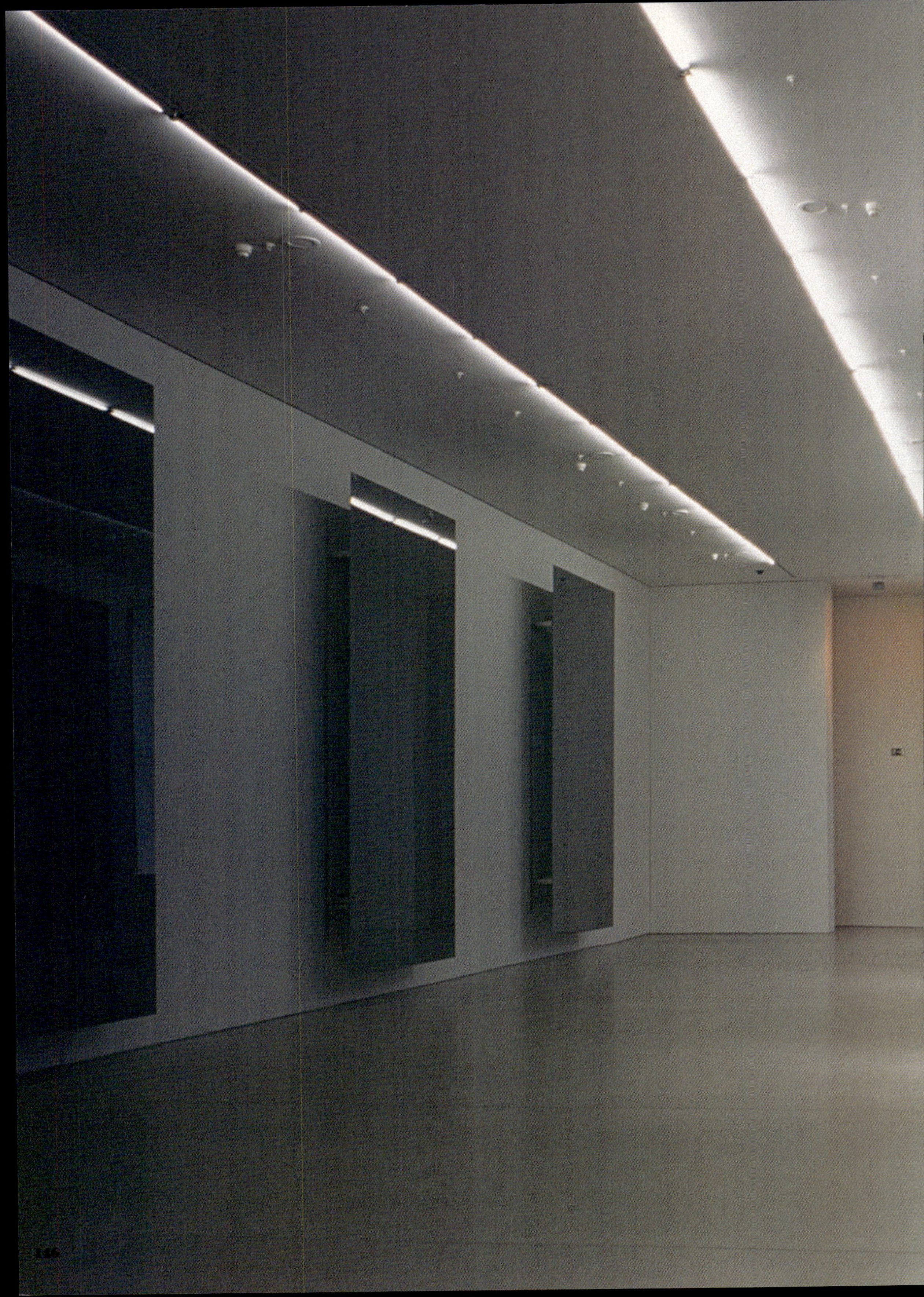

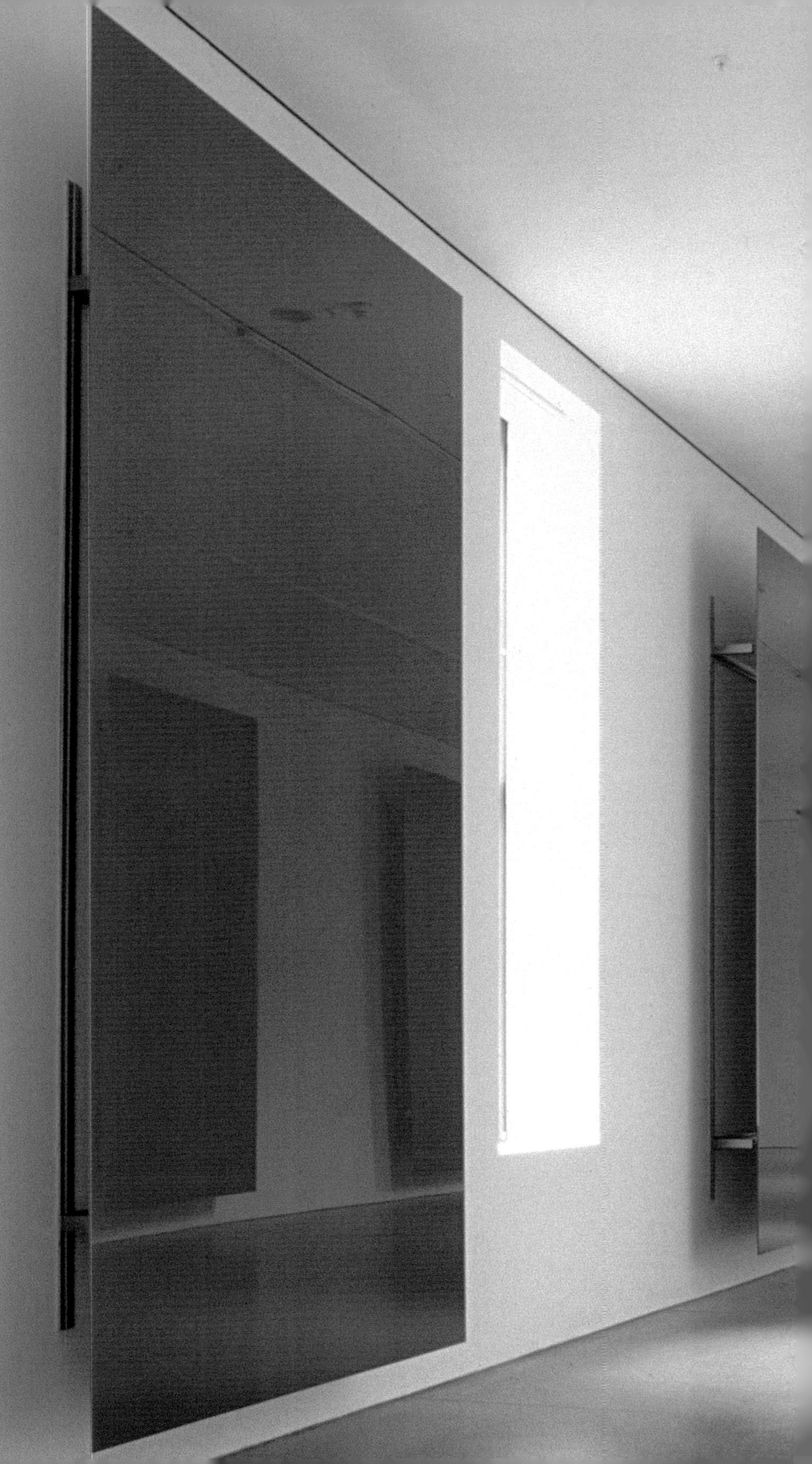

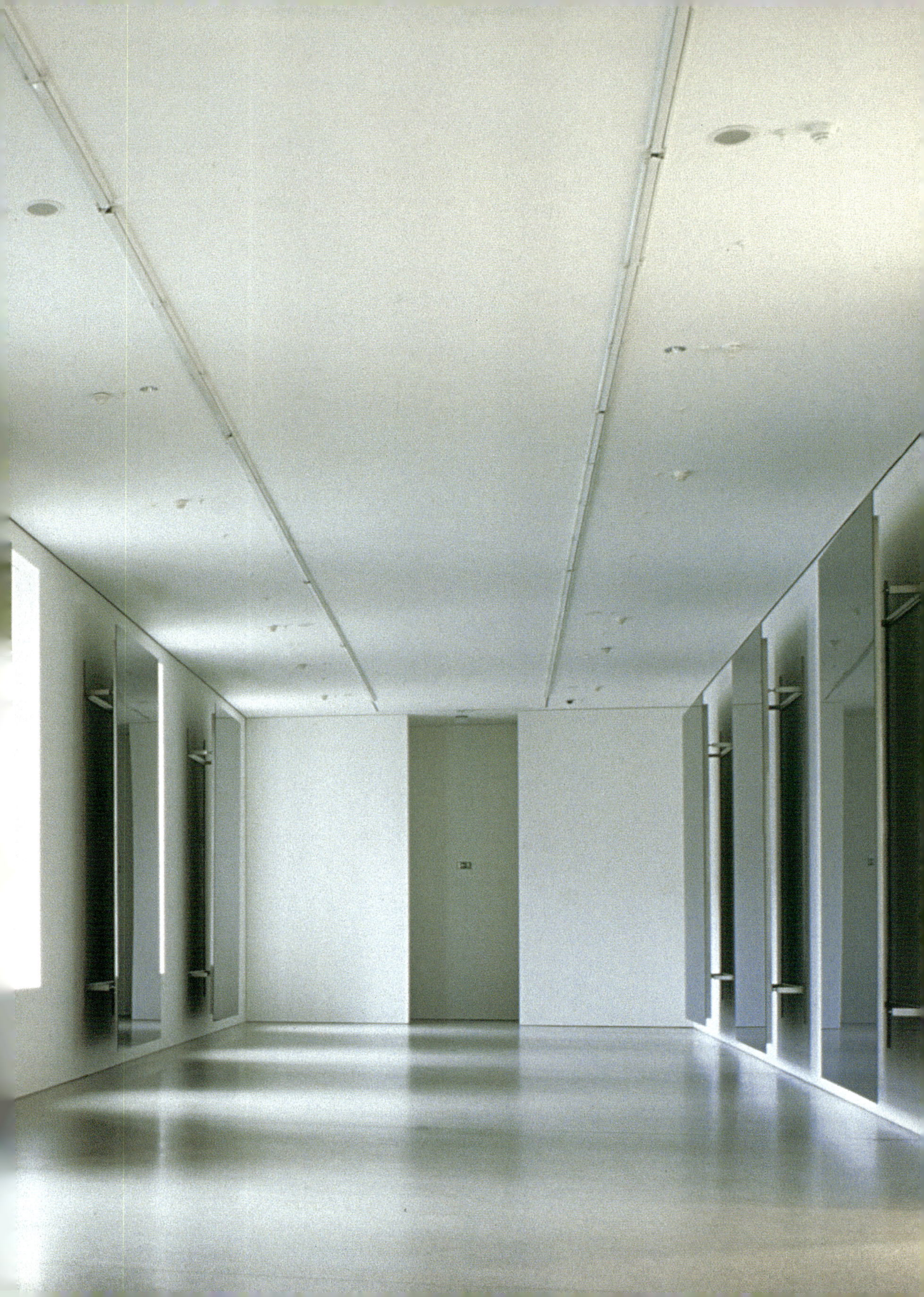

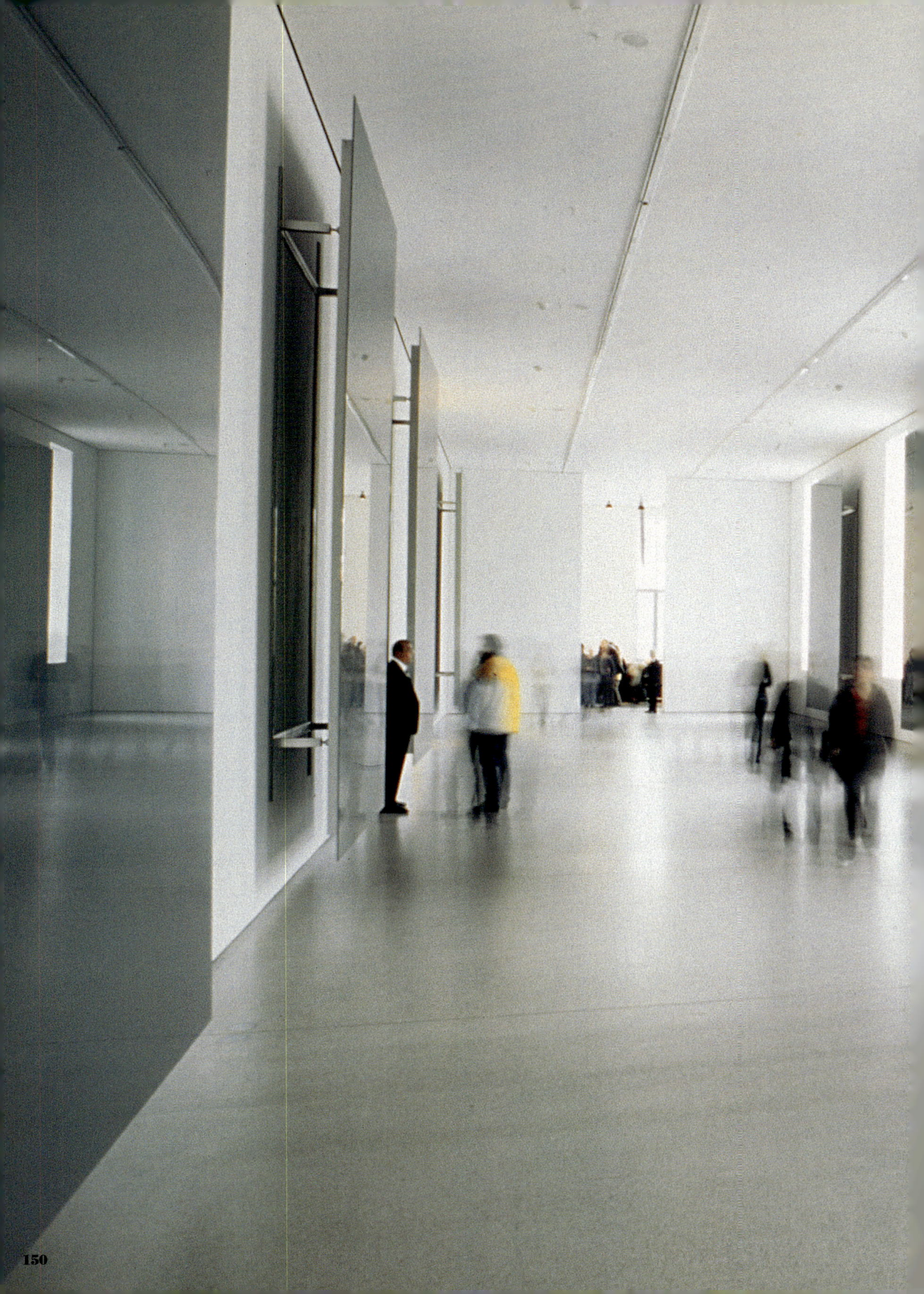

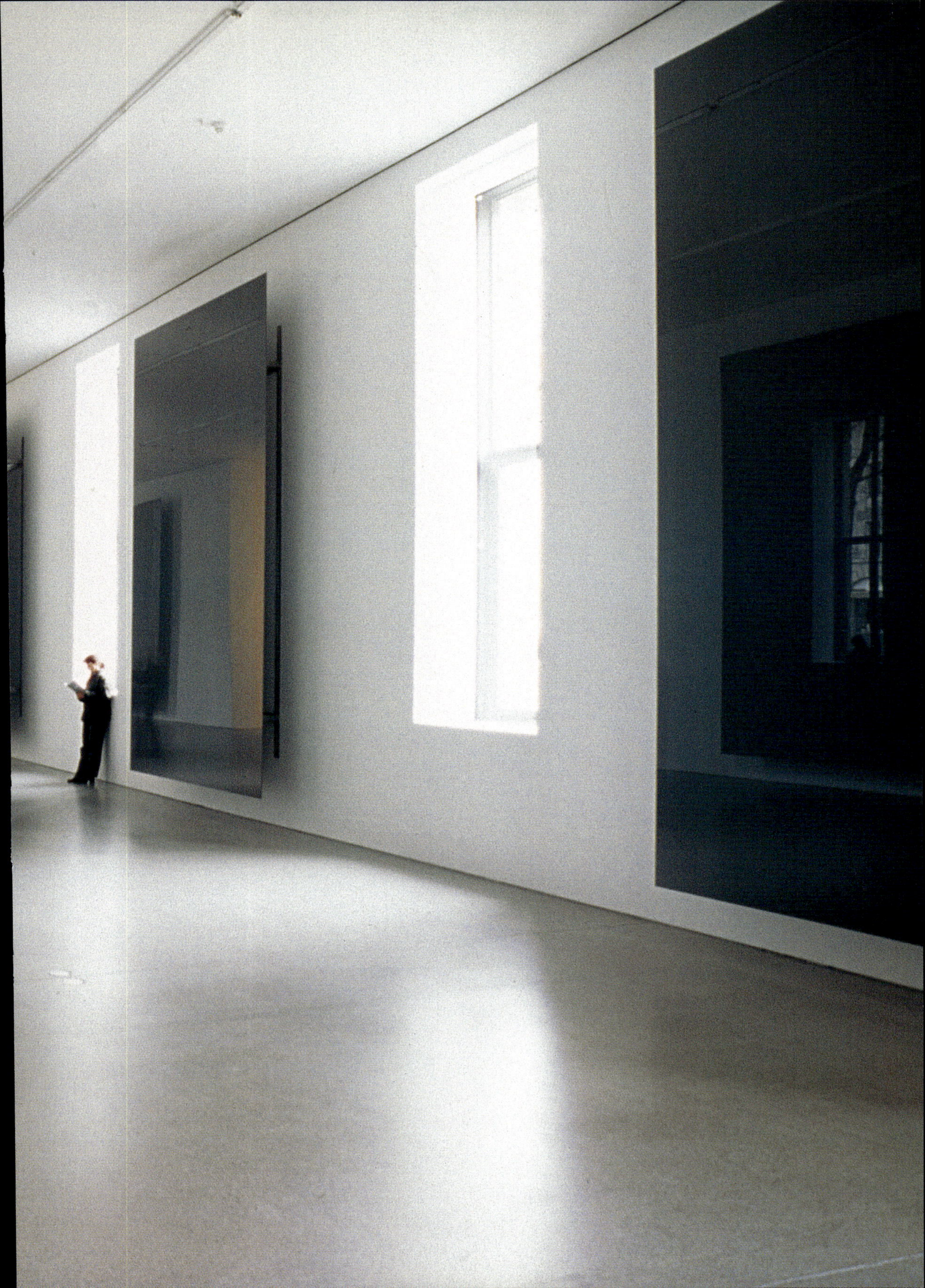

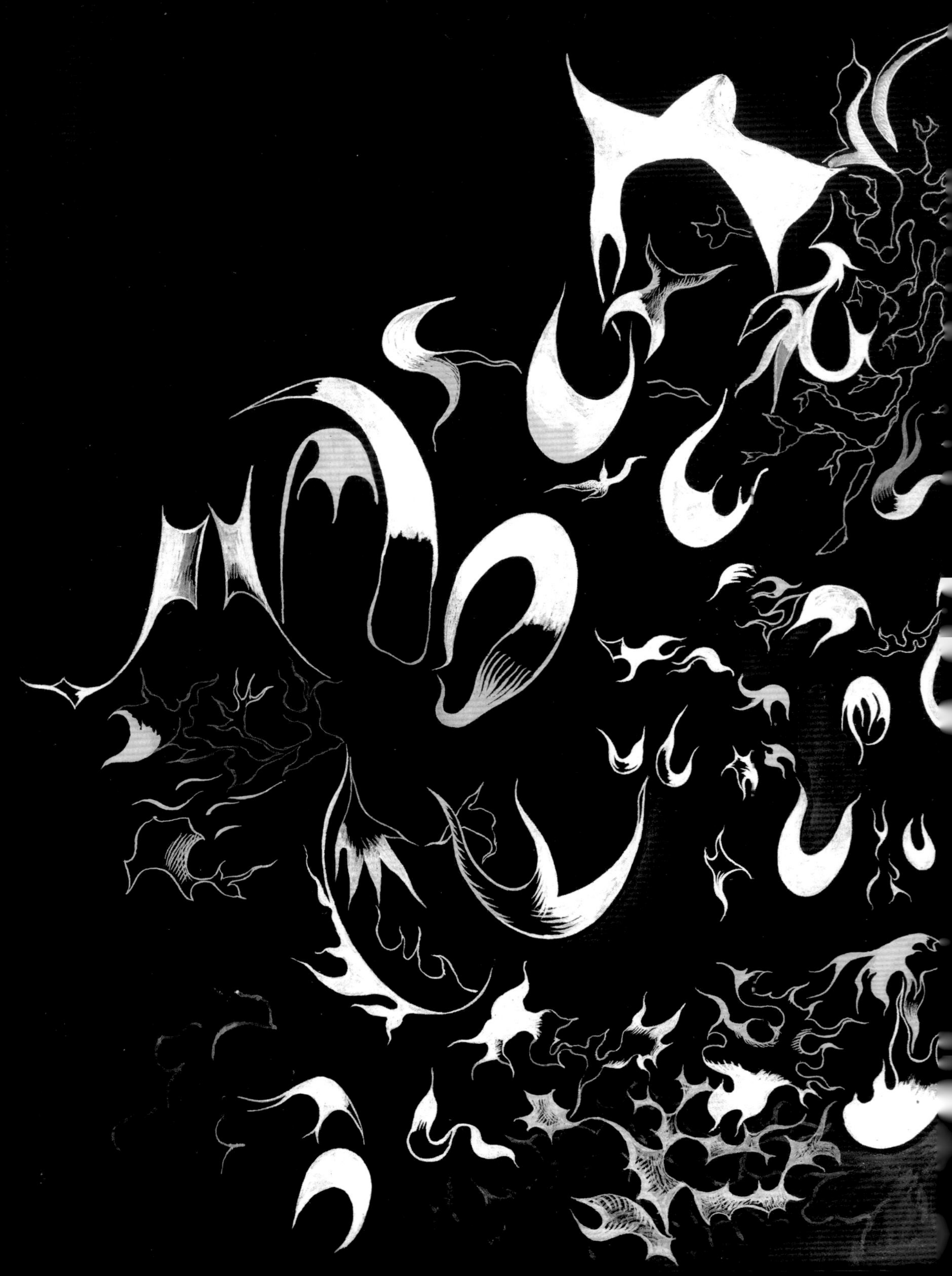

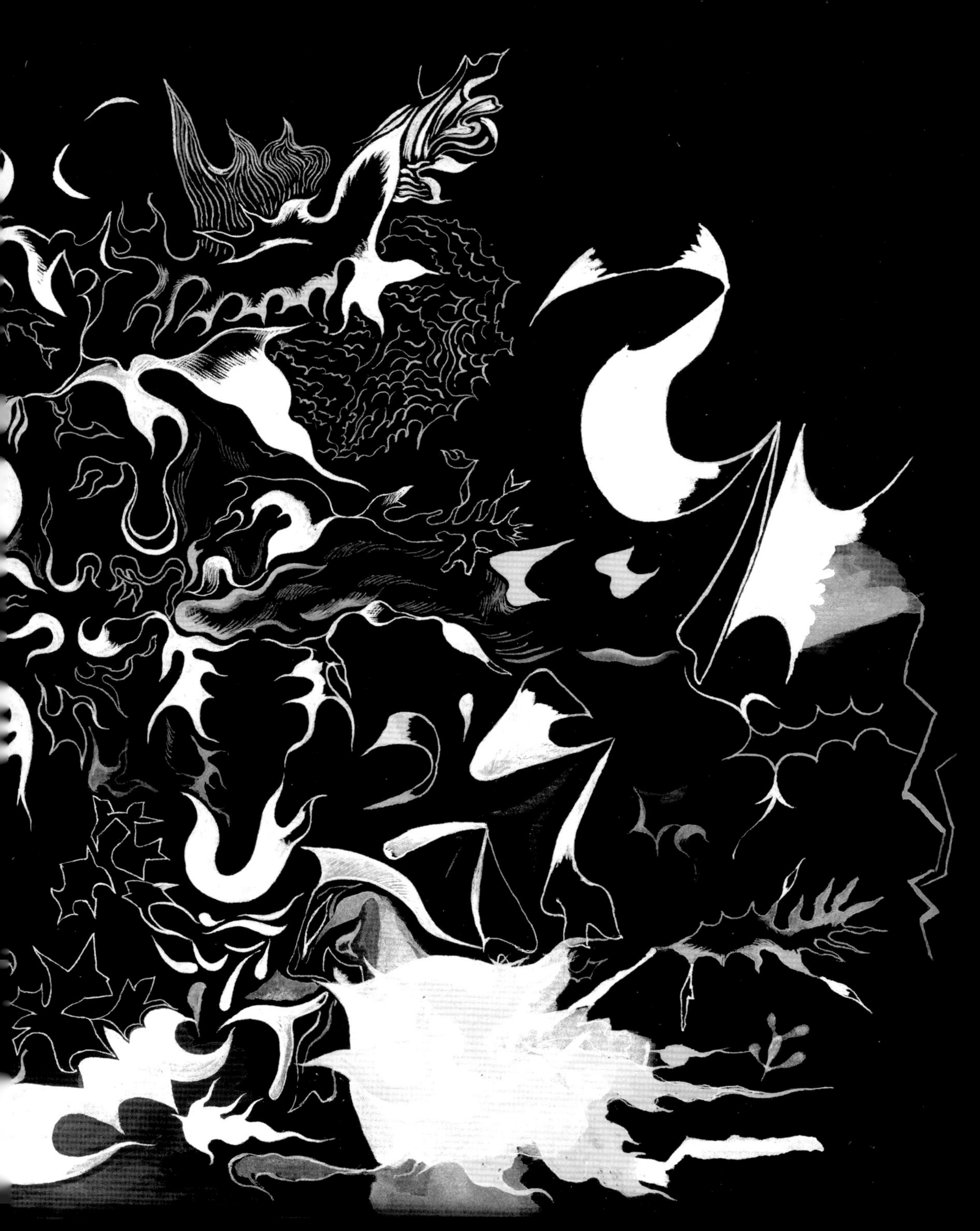

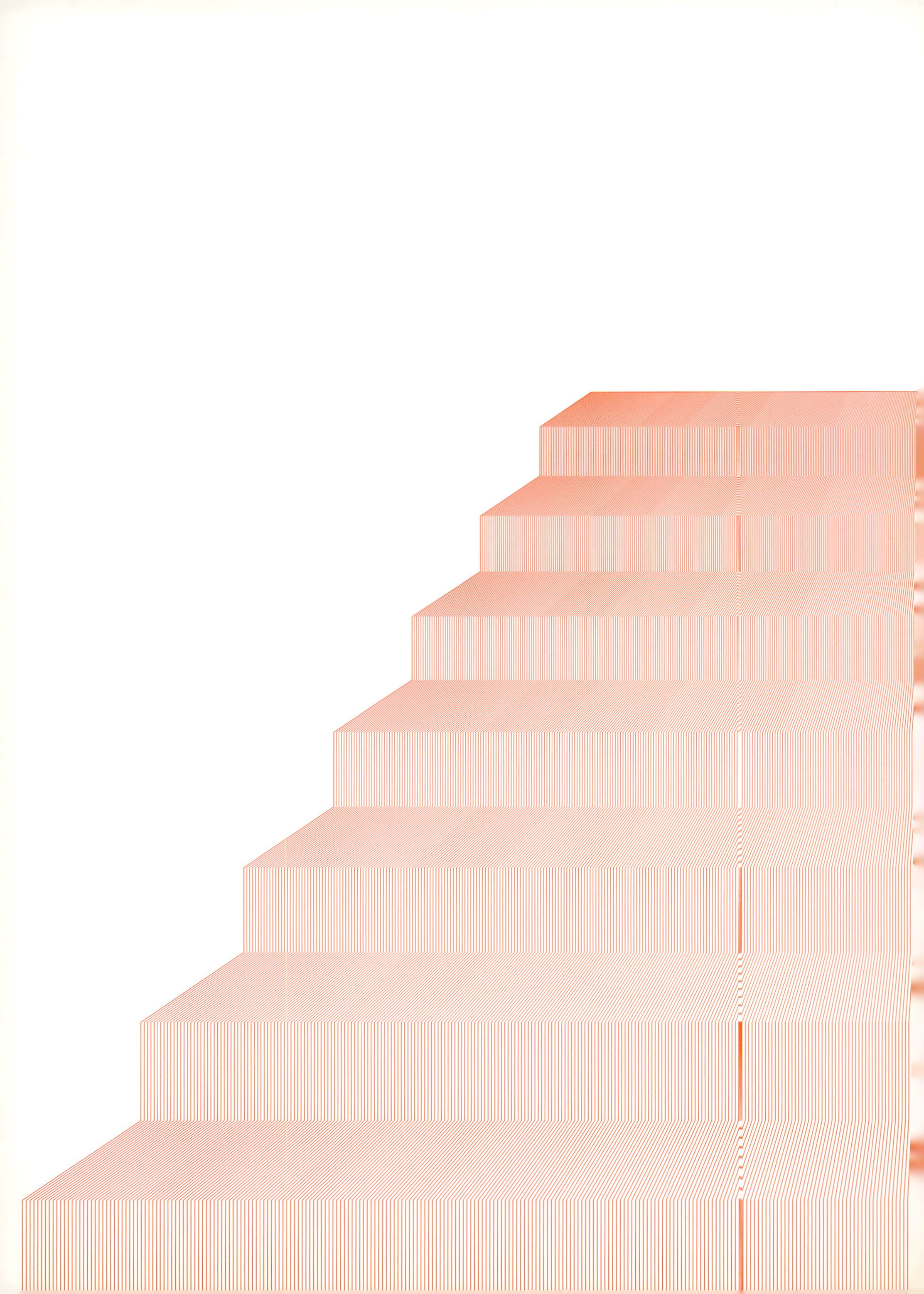

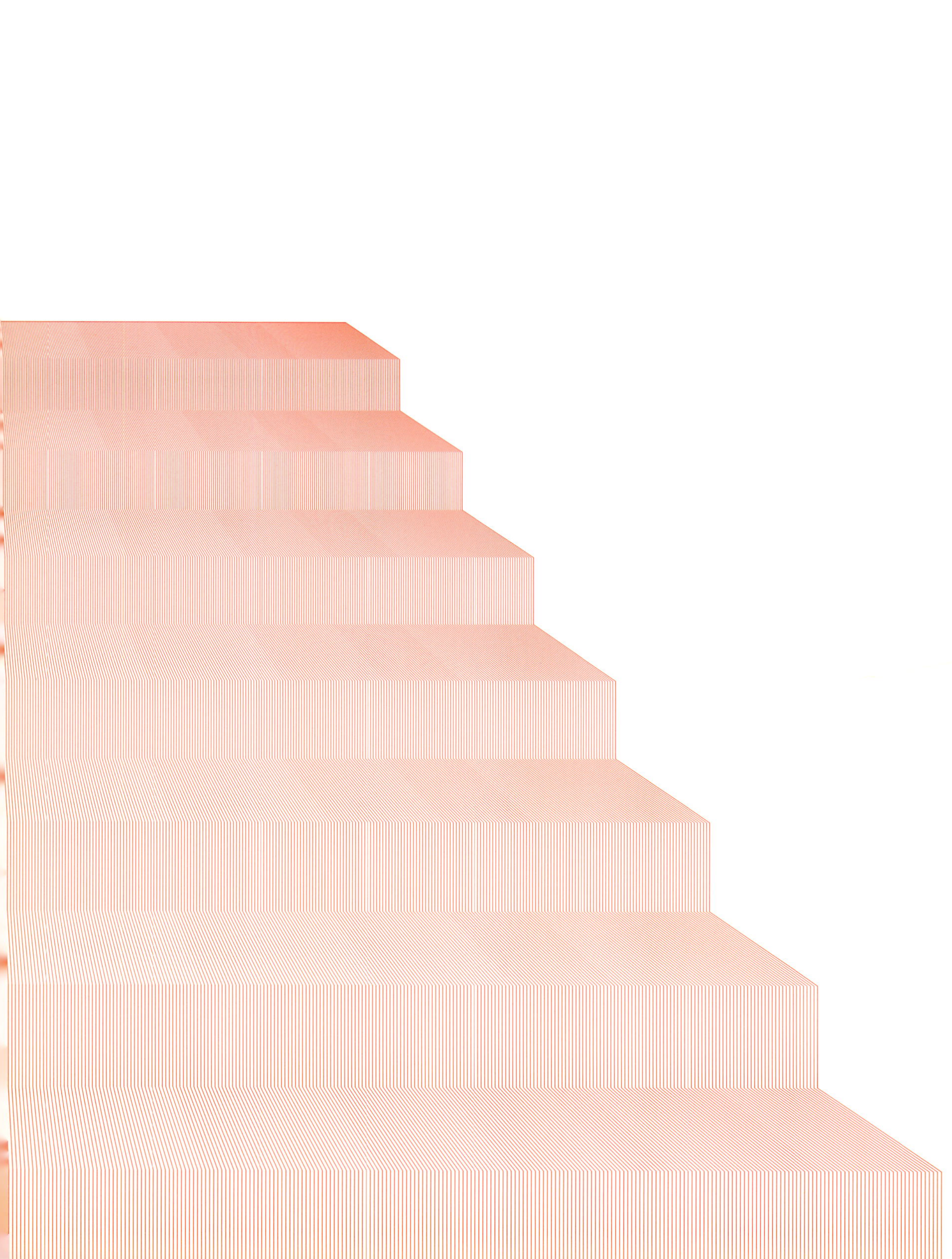

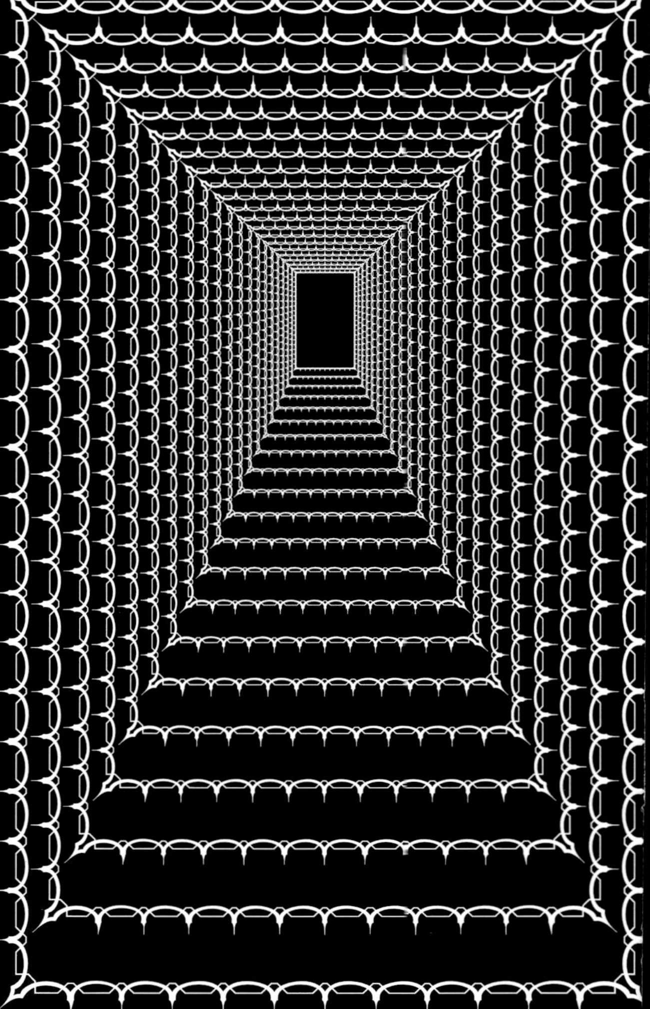

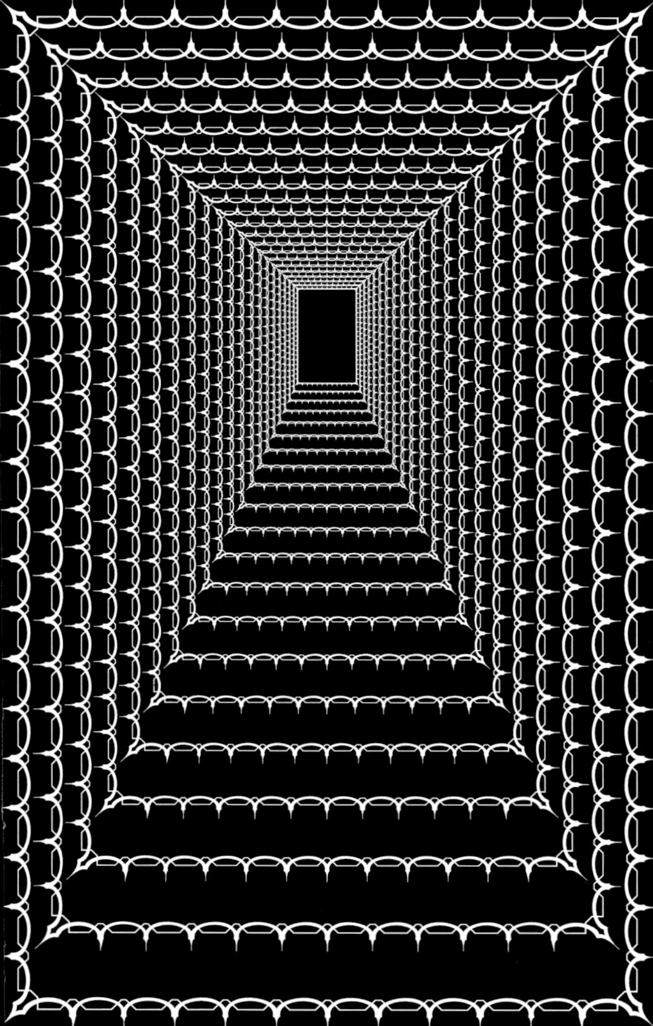

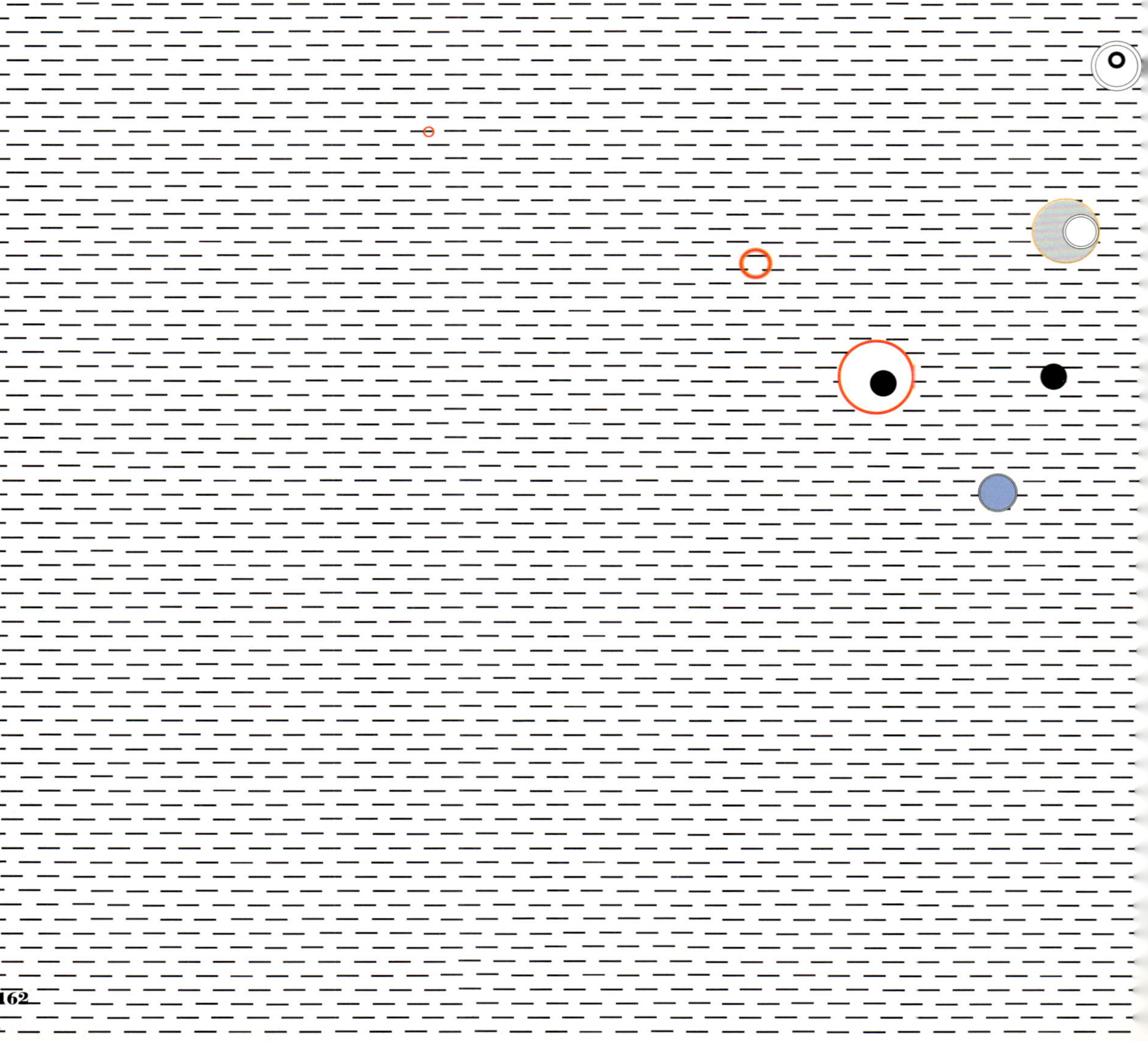

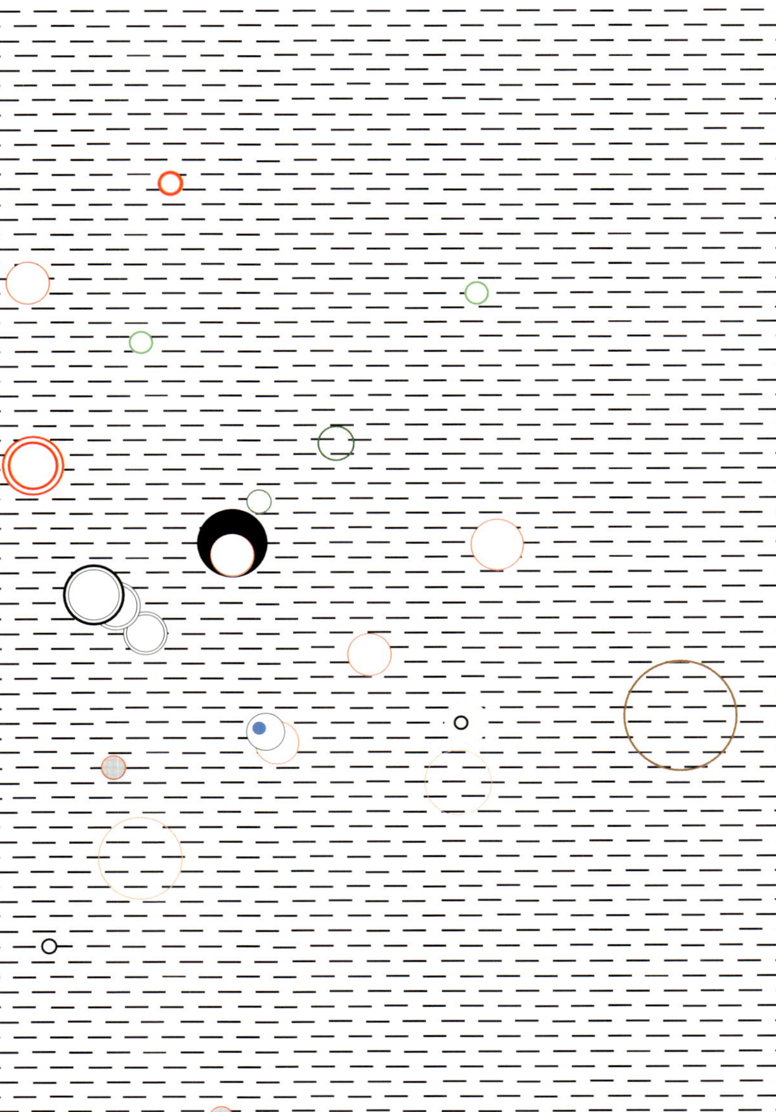

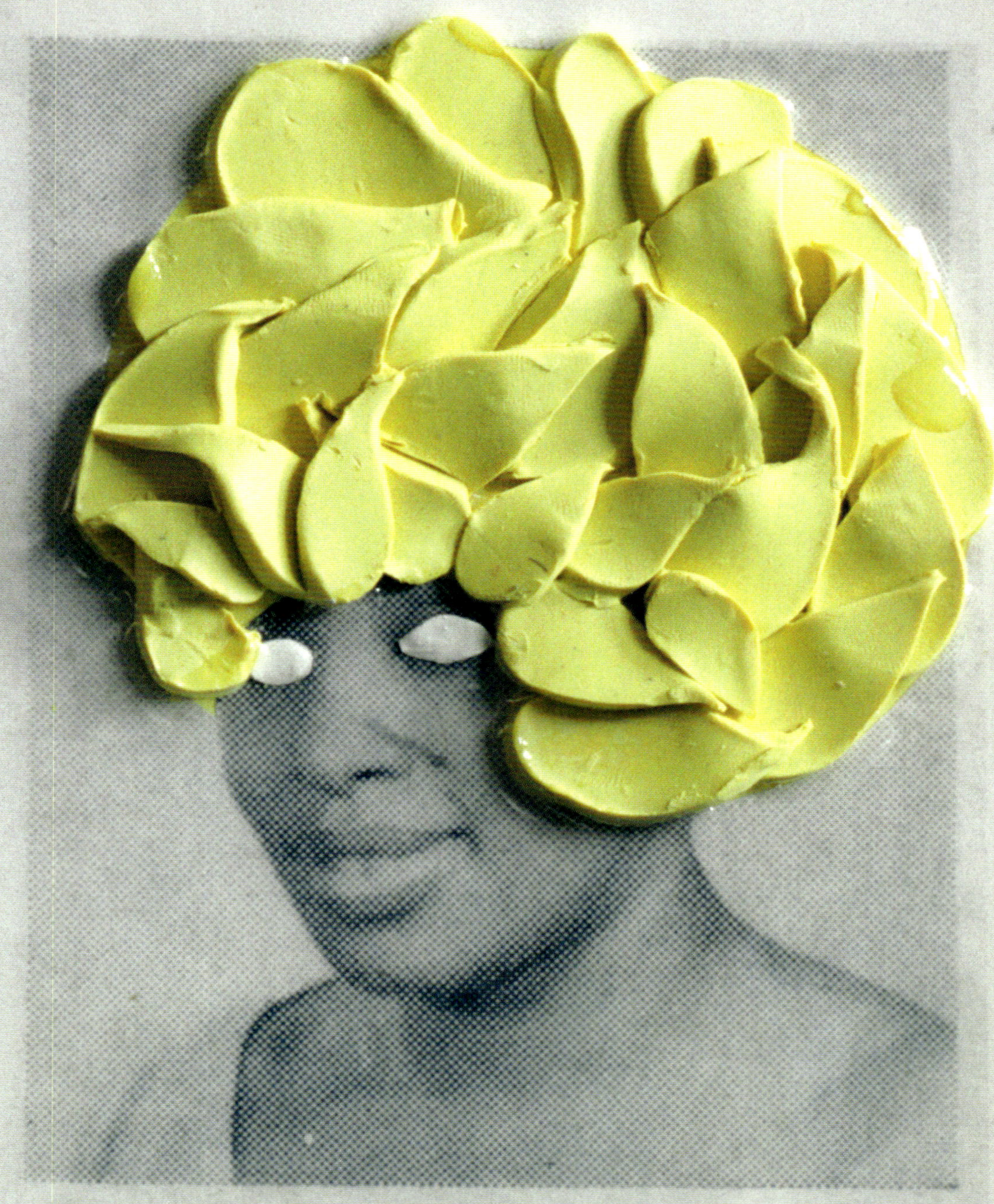

7
PIXETTE
Discreet $36.95

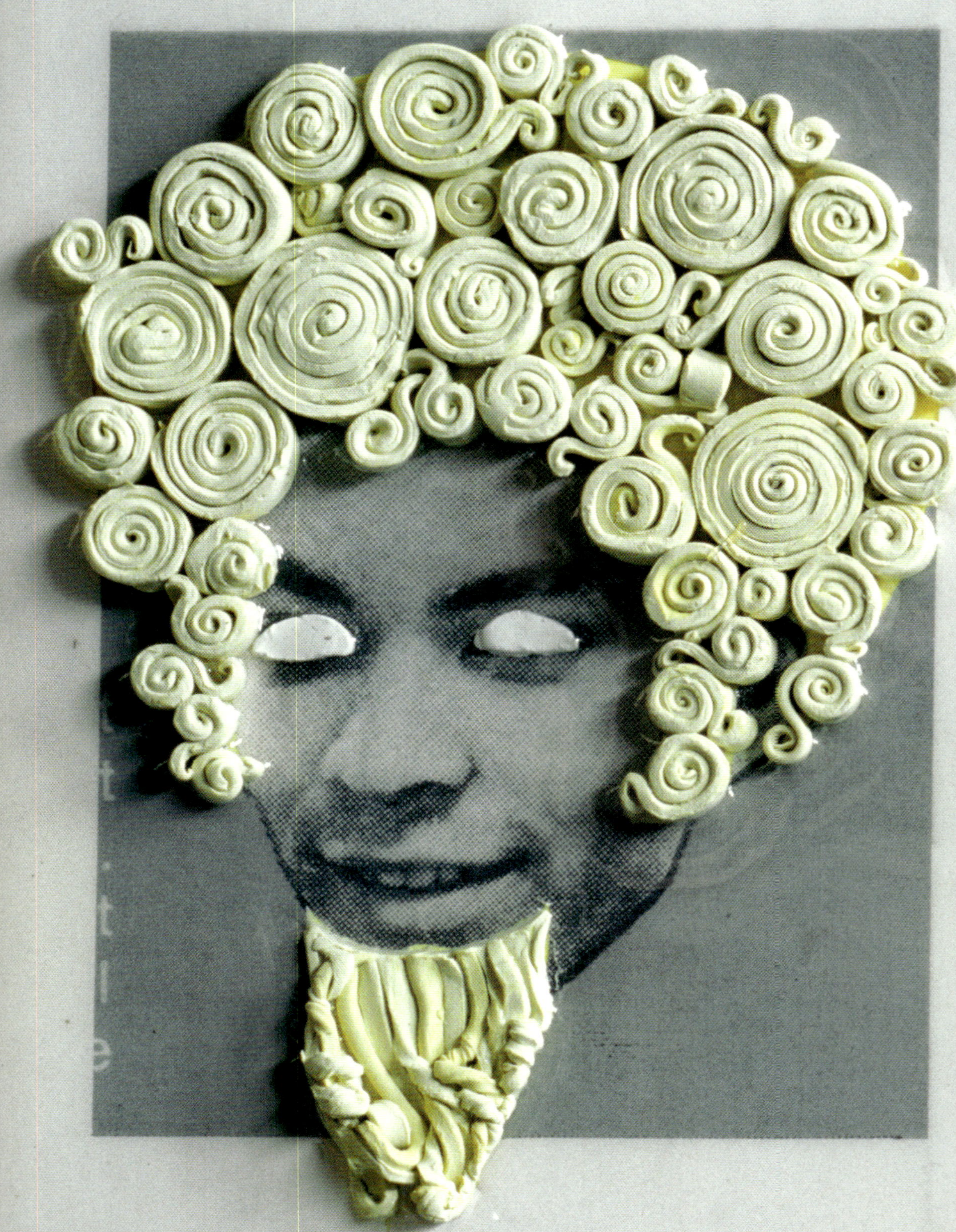

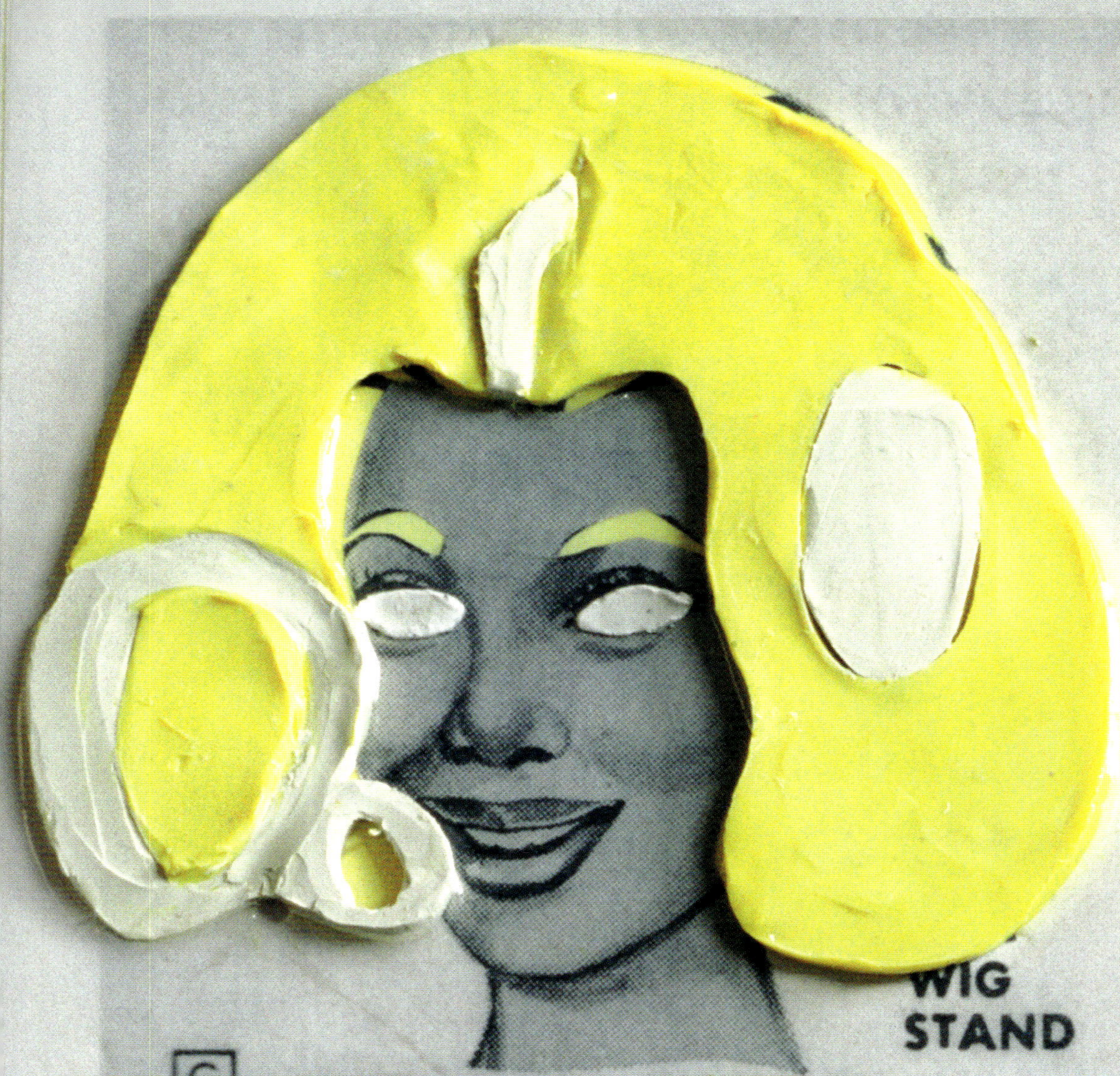

WIG
STAND
G #9036 LADY BIRD
First Lady of fashion in Frederick's
newest hair style. Lustrous synthetic
wig can be combed and restyled.
Black, Brown
or Blonde.
$8.99

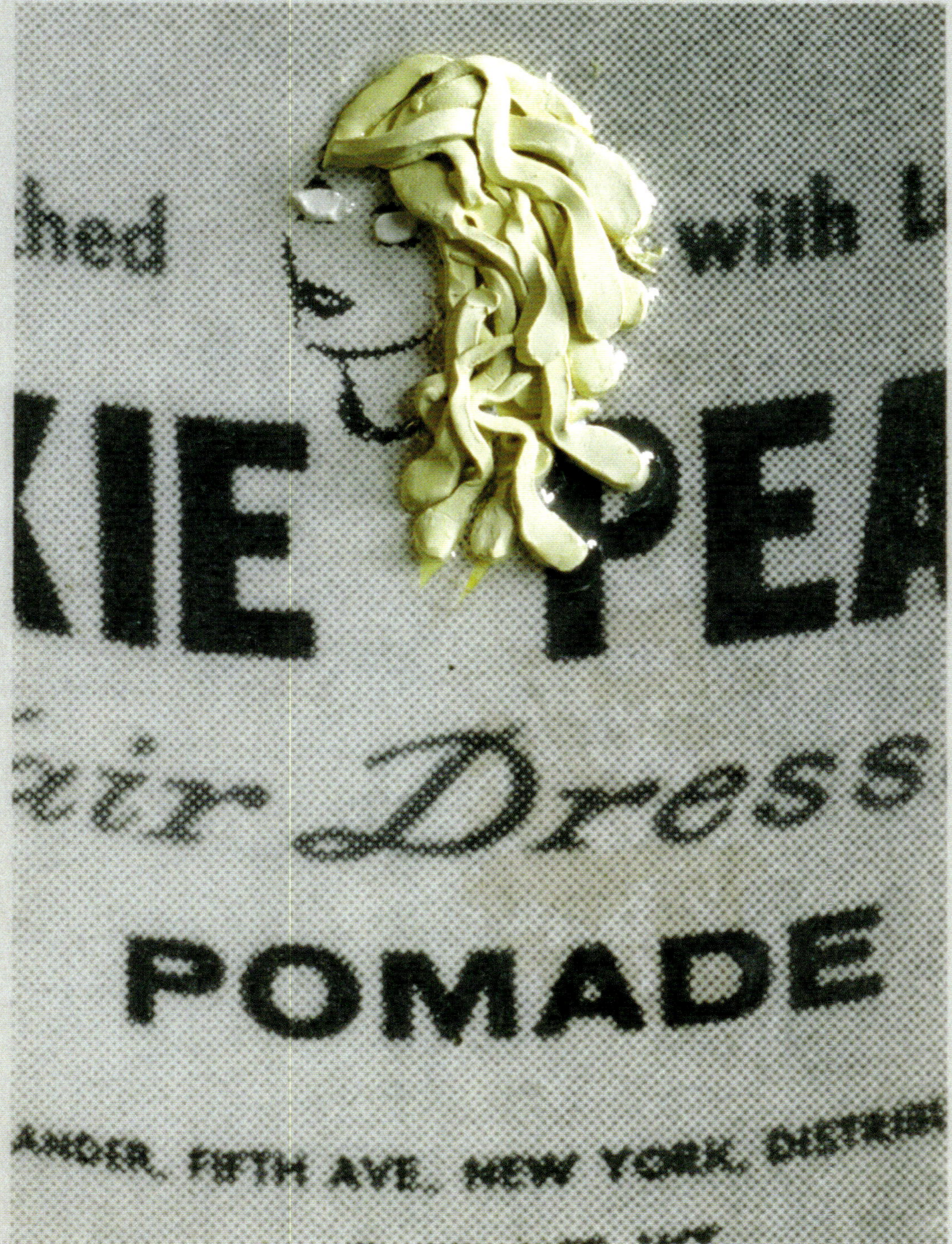

hed
with
KIE PEA
ir Dress
POMADE
ANDER, FIFTH AVE. NEW YORK, DISTRIB

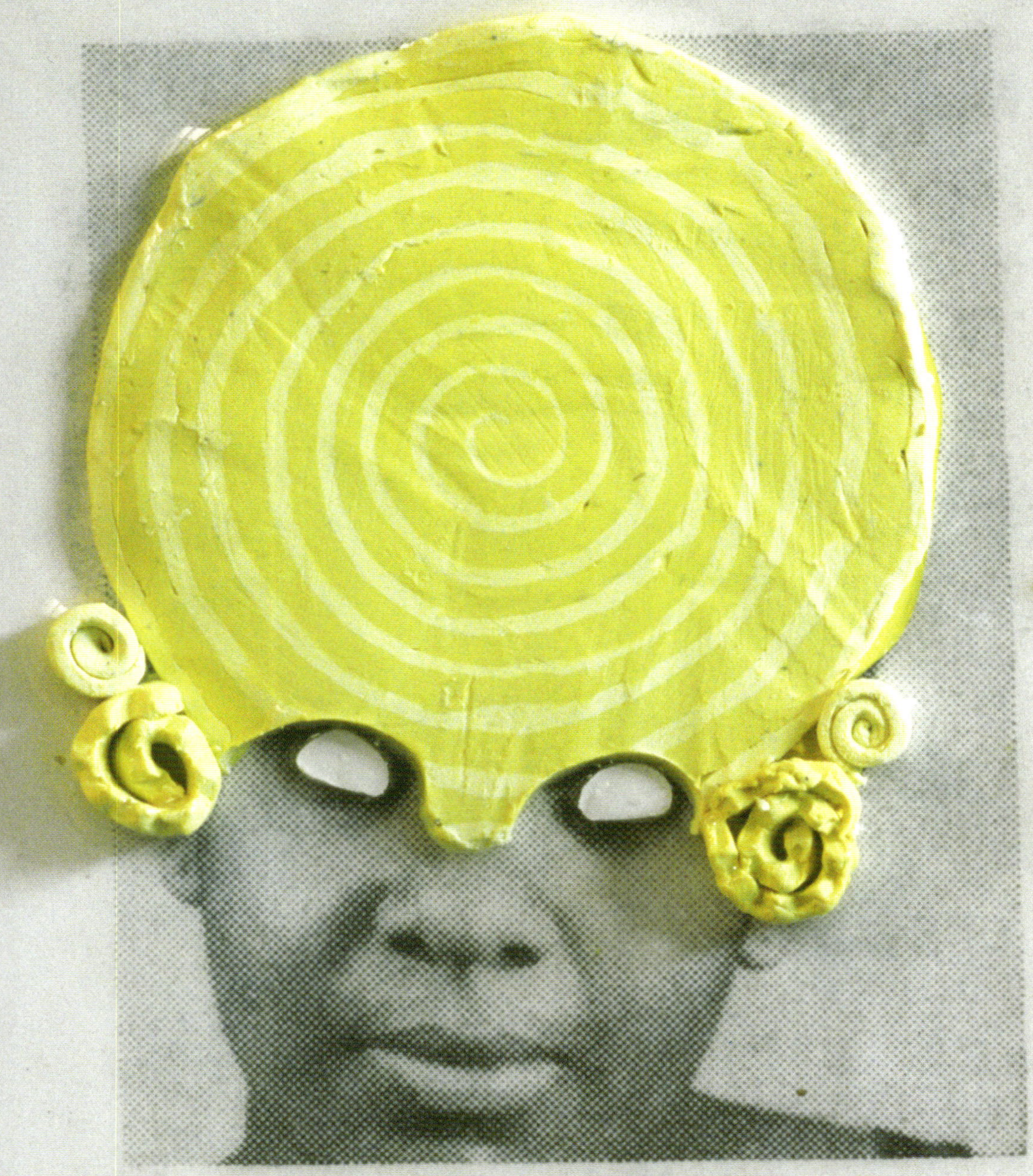

11 **WIGLETTE**
Sassy $10.95

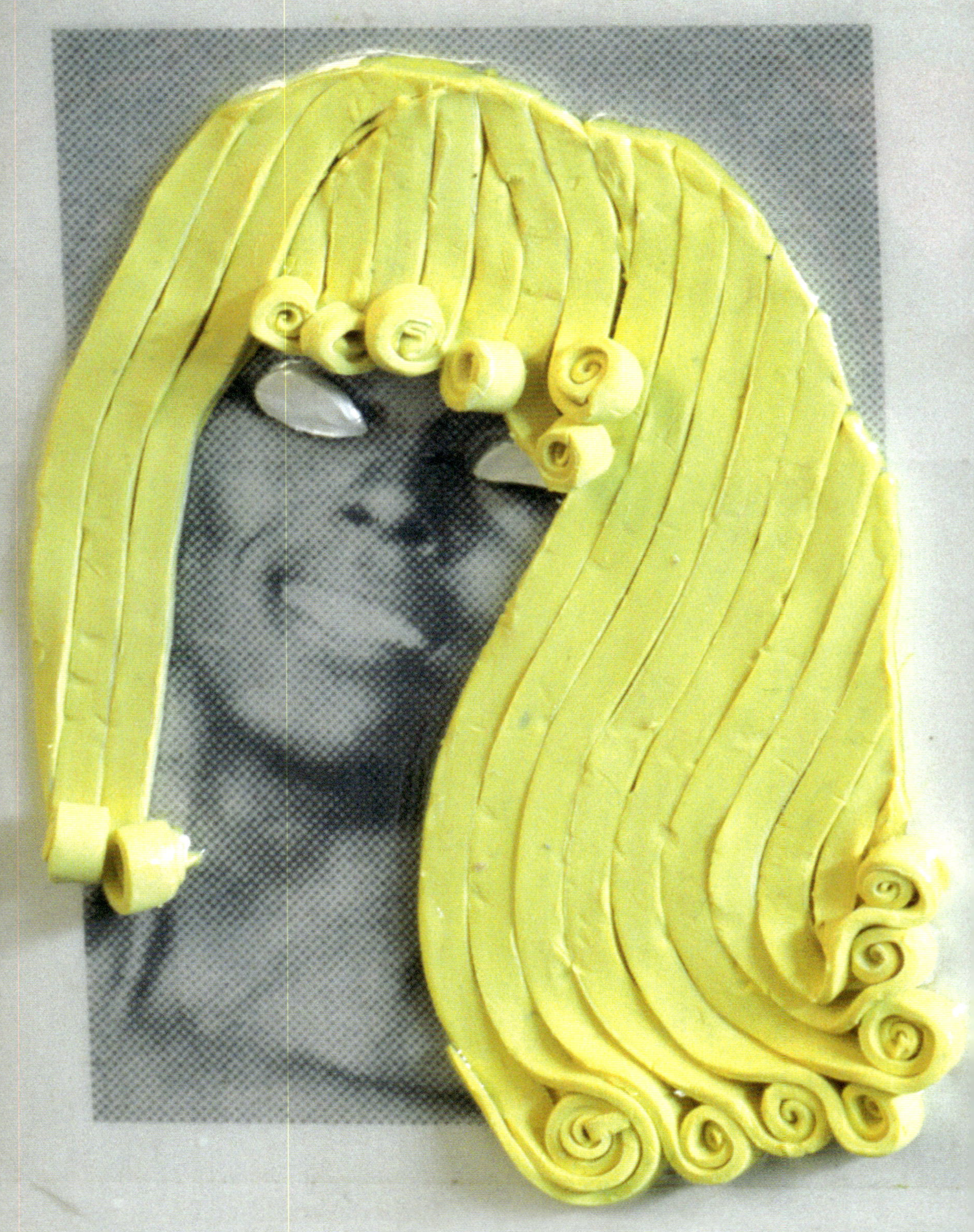

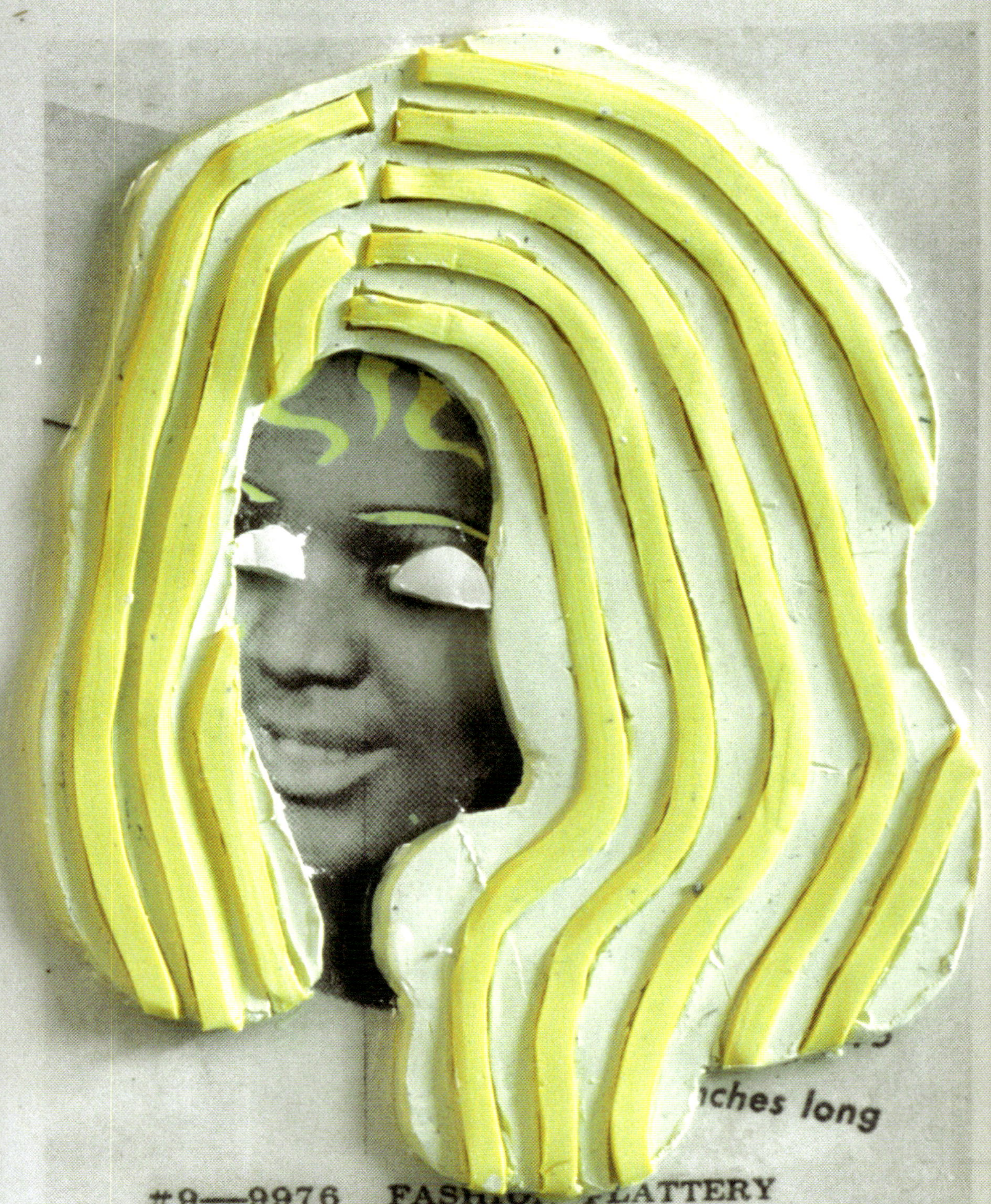
ches long
#9—9976   FASHION FLATTERY
Exquisite 100%, human hair machine
made wig gives you the fine details of

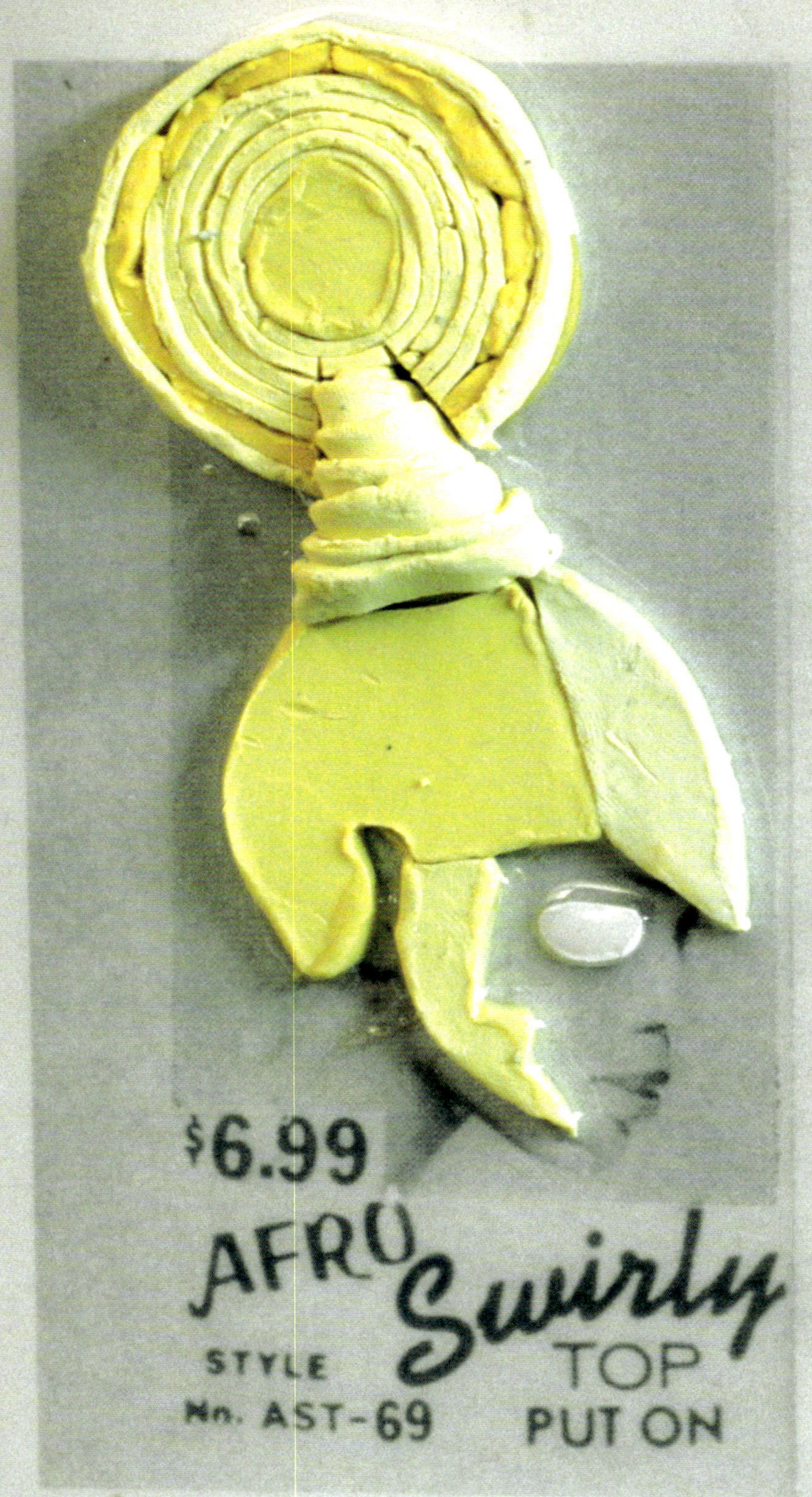

$6.99
AFRO Swirly
STYLE TOP
No. AST-69 PUT ON

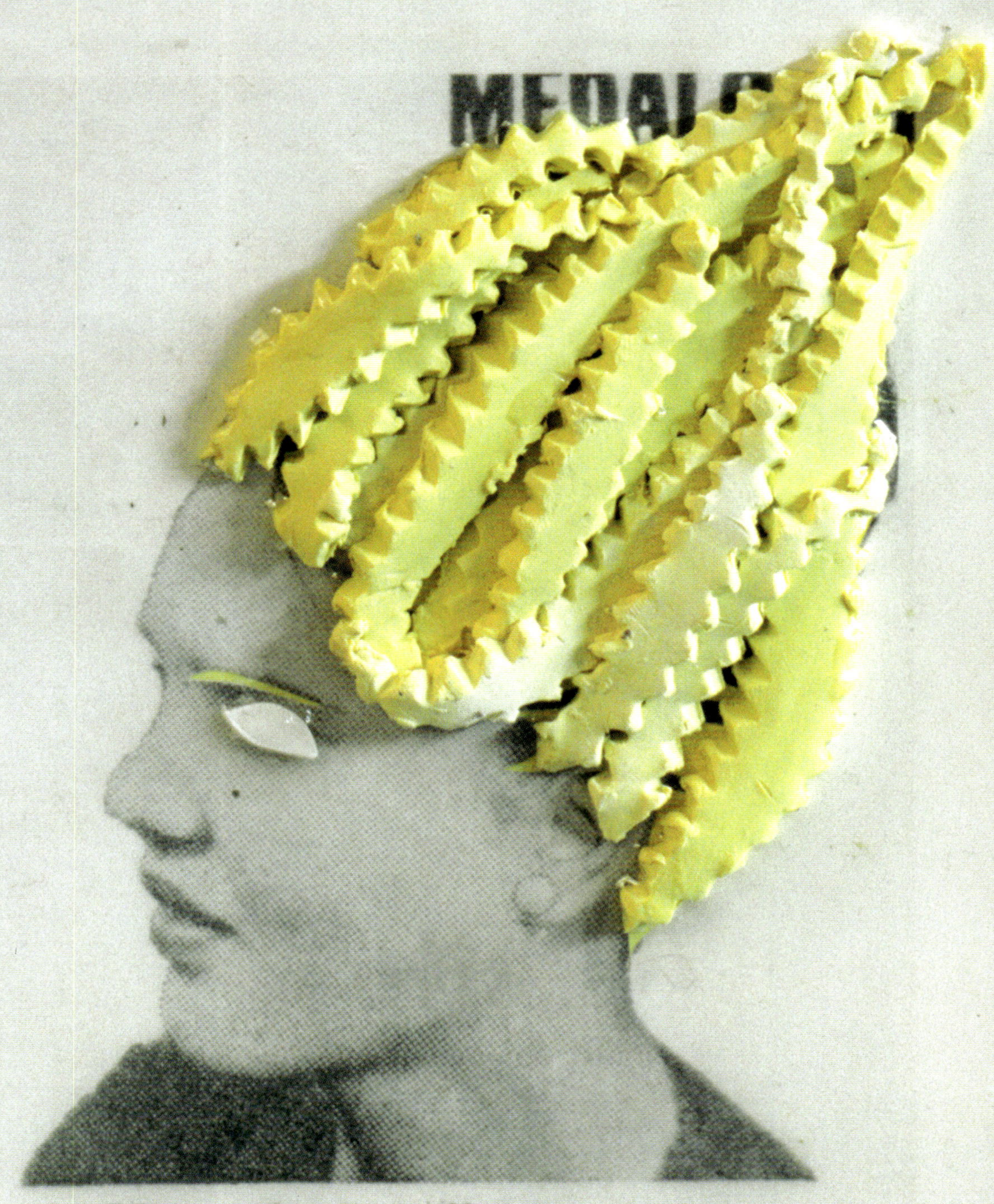

MEDAL
Hair Style #624 on your
coupon. Buy two, use them

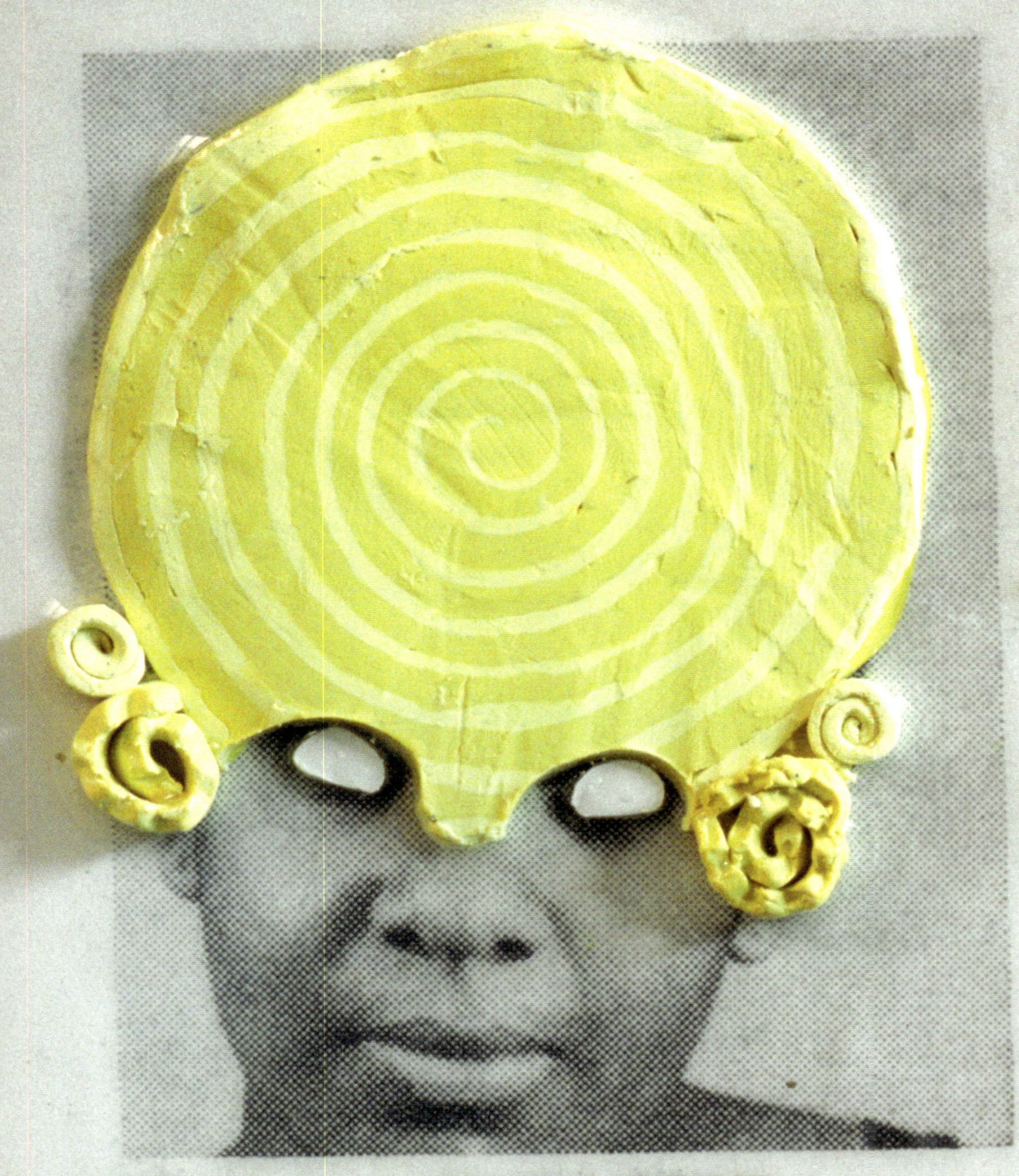

11
WIGLETTE
Sassy $10.95

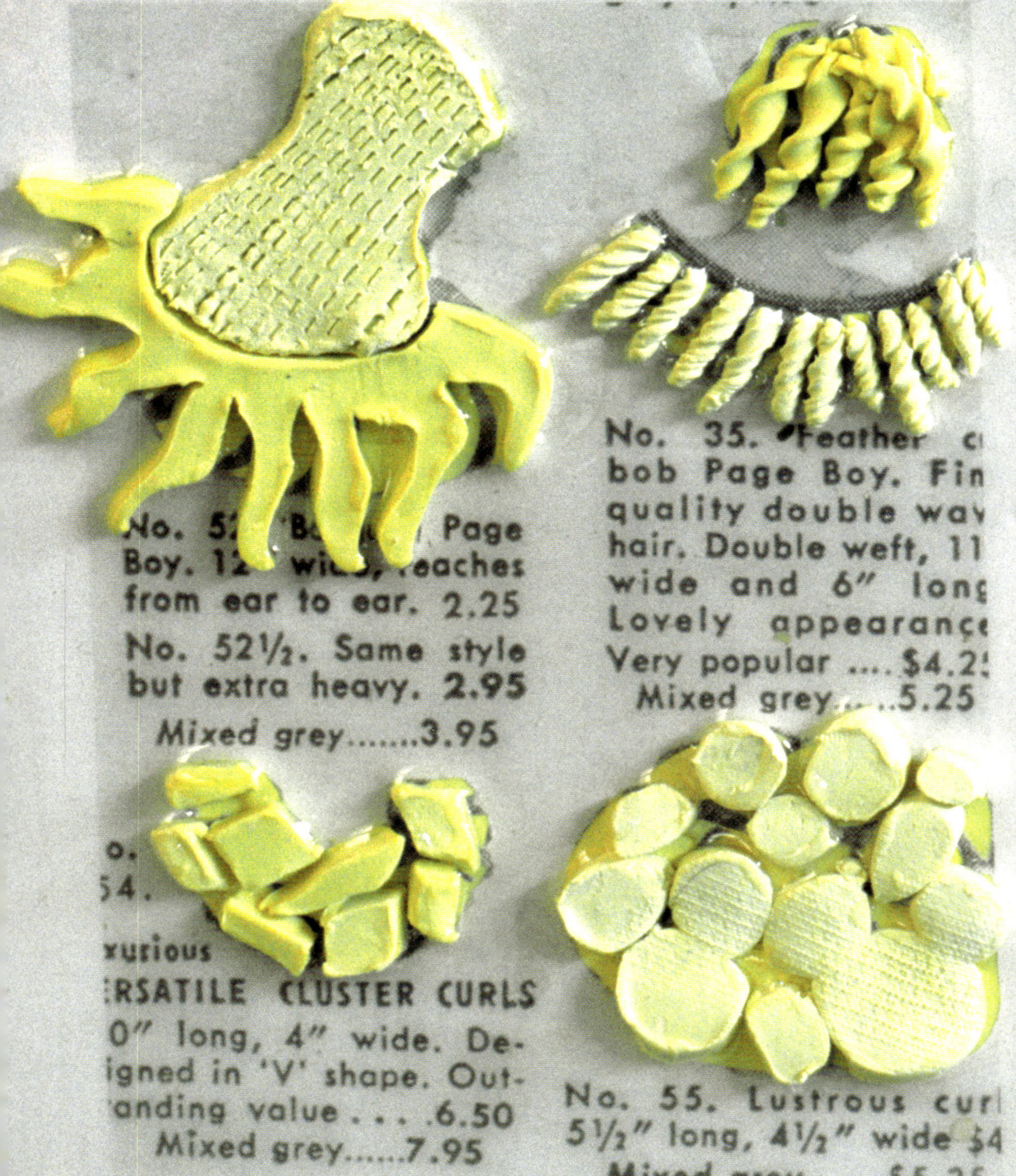

No. 52. Basic Page Boy. 12" wide, reaches from ear to ear. 2.25
No. 52½. Same style but extra heavy. 2.95
    Mixed grey.......3.95

No. 35. "Feather cut" bob Page Boy. Fine quality double wave hair. Double weft, 11" wide and 6" long. Lovely appearance. Very popular $4.25
    Mixed grey.....5.25

No. 54. Luxurious VERSATILE CLUSTER CURLS 10" long, 4" wide. Designed in 'V' shape. Outstanding value 6.50
    Mixed grey.....7.95

No. 55. Lustrous curl 5½" long, 4½" wide $4
    Mixed grey........$5.25

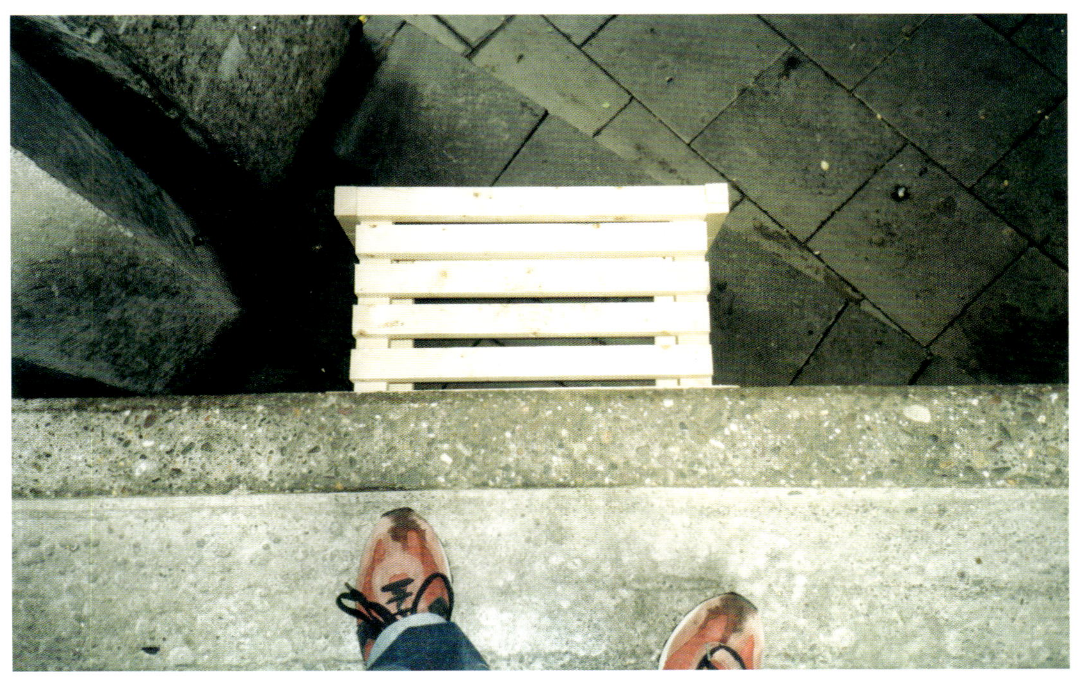

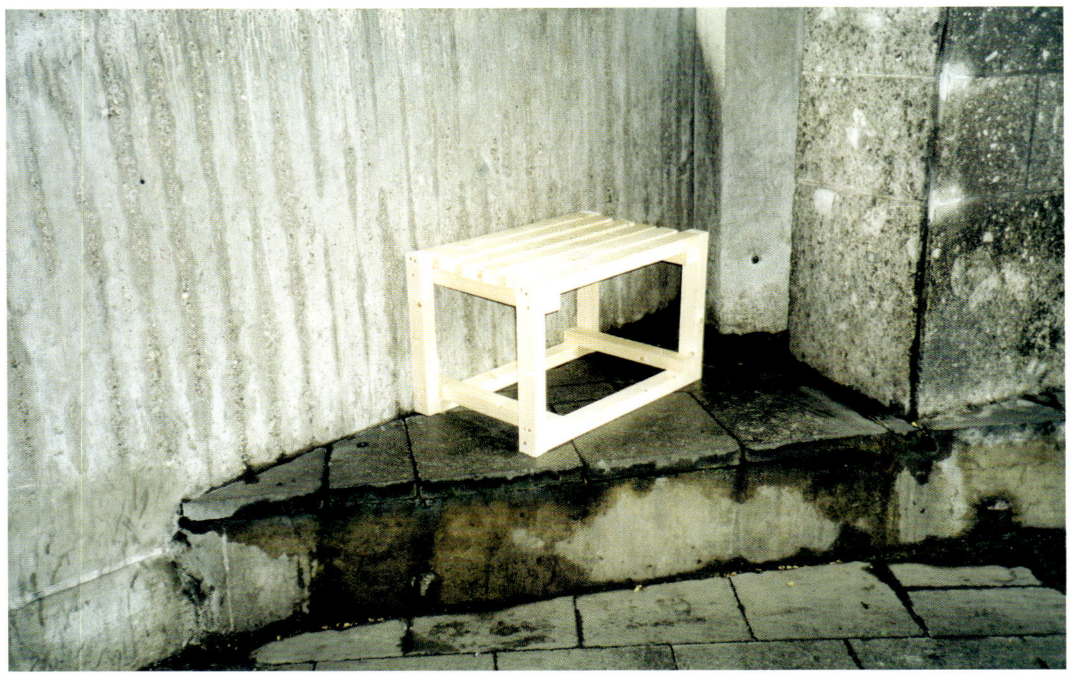

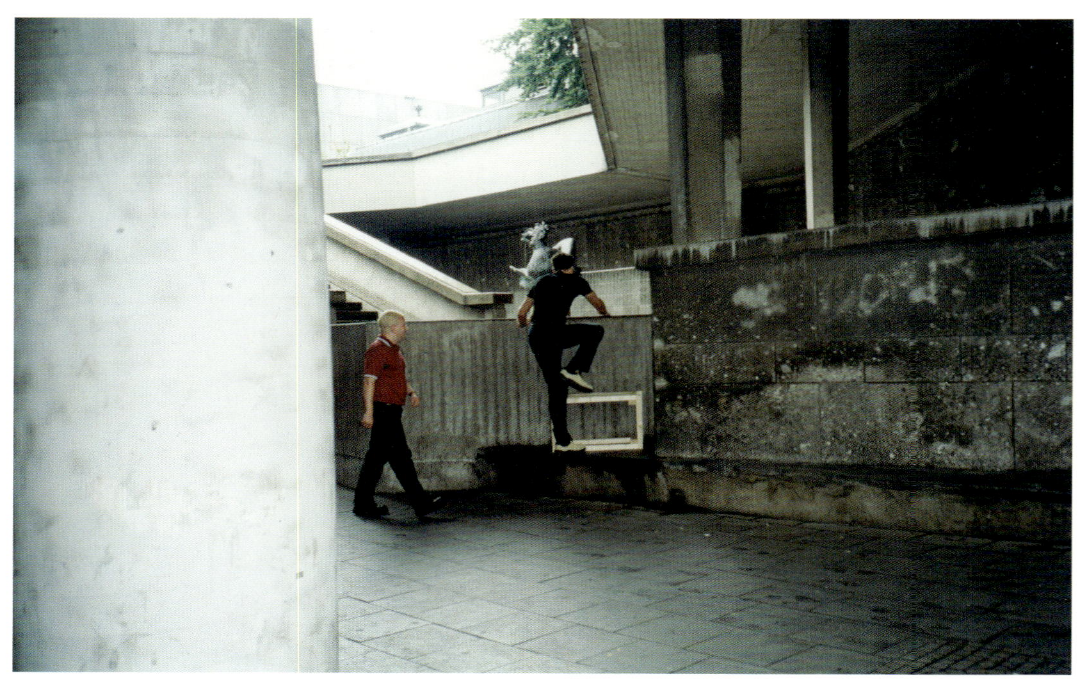

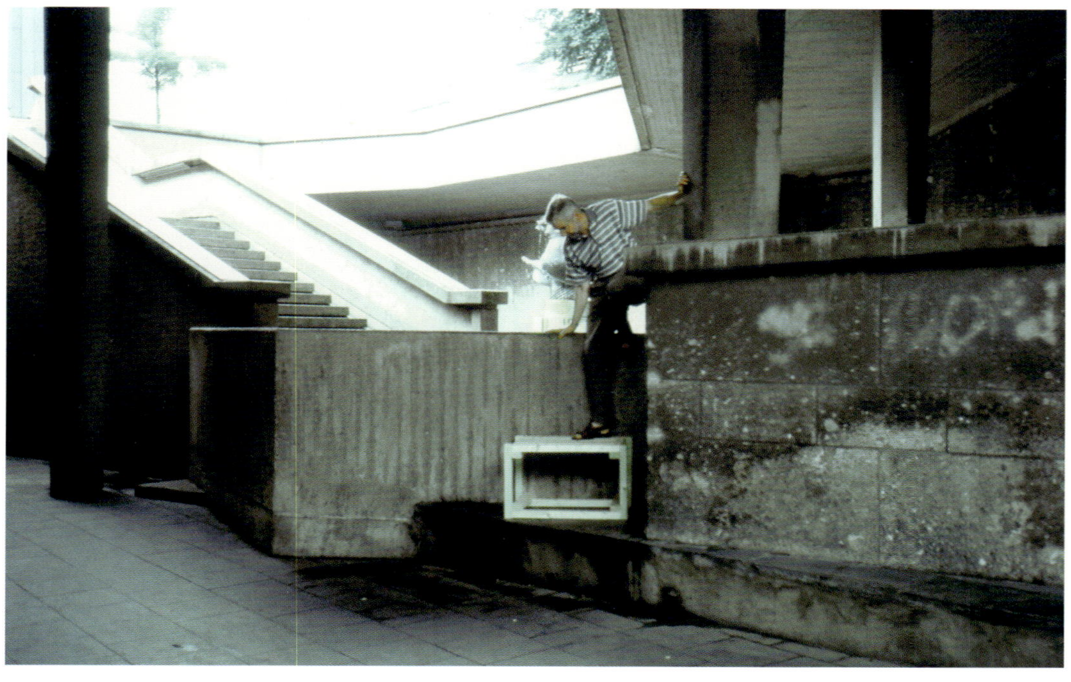

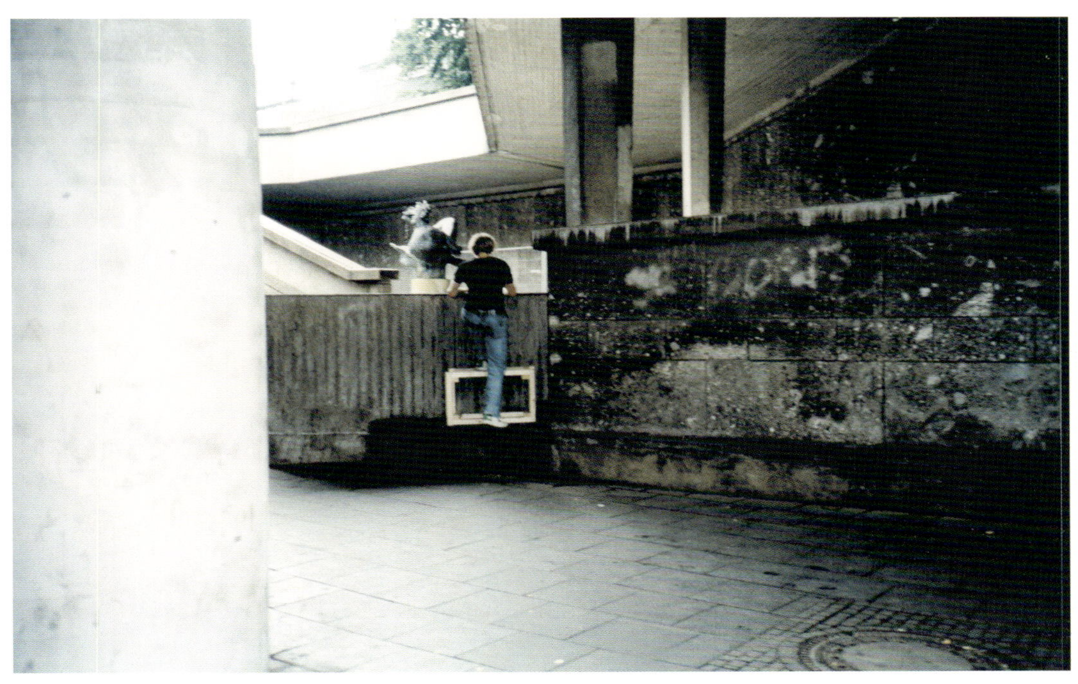

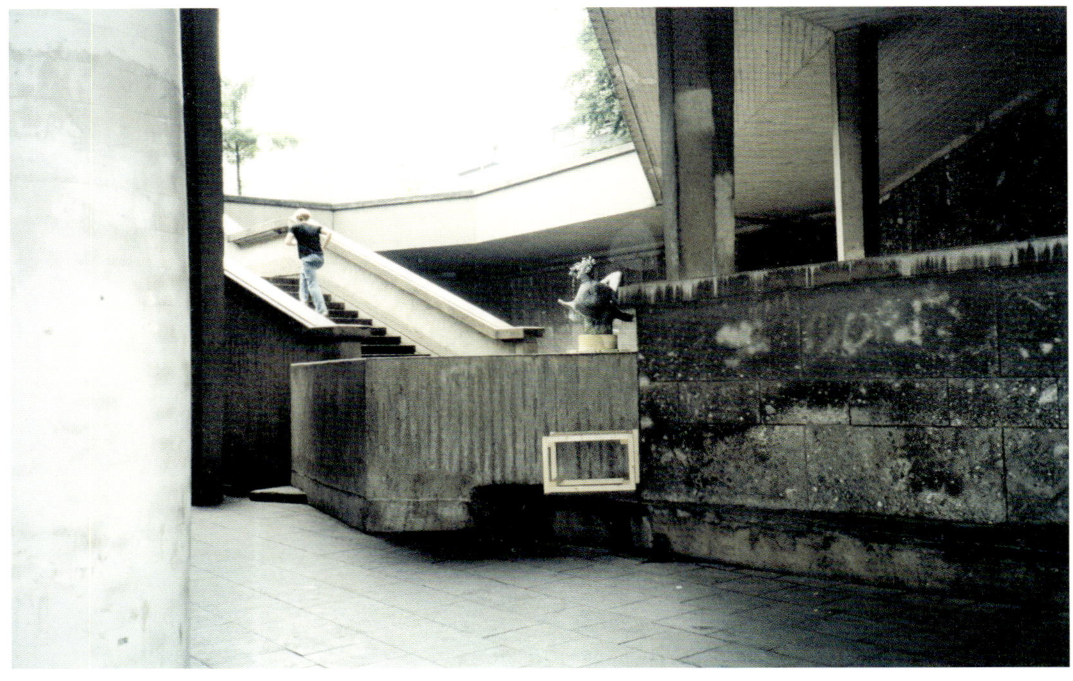

Since the beginning of time, human beings have had to negotiate the basic conditions of temperature, humidity and seasonal climate. The weather has been so fundamental to shaping our society that one can argue that every aspect of life – economical, political, technical, cultural, emotional – is linked to or derived from it. Over the centuries, defending ourselves from the weather has proved even more important than protecting ourselves from each other in the form of war and violence. If you cannot withstand the weather, you cannot survive.

To protect ourselves from the weather, we create body-friendly environments in the shape of buildings, using all sorts of energy either to heat up or cool down our immediate surroundings. Our reliance on these protective, climate-controlled, thermostat-regulated interiors has resulted in a growing awareness of energy issues over the last forty years. We are now slowly accepting, if not fully acknowledging, the fact that the post-war energy ideologies of our society have resulted in damaging that which they were supposed to protect us from: the climate. We are occupied with redefining methods of insulating our surroundings and ourselves correctly in relation to our local weather conditions and energy resources.

More than any other element in the history of spatial awareness, the weather and climate have been central to deciding the location of cities, the development of urban strategies and the forms and structures of habitation. The weather is part of the city and vice versa. Technically and logistically all cities are built for a particular weather condition, with an expected amount of rainfall, sunshine, wind etc., and any significant change to this, such as a prolonged period of unusual weather, will often result in enormous stress and an eventual collapse of the city's infrastructure. A normal chilly day in one city could be fatal in another. The weather is 'nature' in the city and is one of the central aspects in creating its look and life. Thus by observing and engaging with a city, we can sense much about the weather conditions in that particular place.

Every city mediates its own weather. As inhabitants, through our progressive experience of city space we have grown accustomed to the weather as mediated by the city. We experience the weather through the 'city-filter', as well as the other way around. The mediation of our awareness of weather in the city takes place in numerous ways, on various collective levels and in all aspects of life in the city. These range from hyper-mediated (or representational) experiences such as the television weather forecast, to more direct and tangible experiences like simply getting wet while walking down the street on a rainy day. A level between the two extremes would be sitting inside, looking out of a window onto a sunny or rainy street. The window, as the interface and boundary of one's tactile engagement with the outside, mediates one's experience of the exterior weather accordingly.

Orienting ourselves within these different mediations we are able to think about the weather. We are able to talk about it to each other and evaluate the consequences that we think it may have on us. As human beings gifted with the unique ability to reflect, we can talk about talking about the weather. One of the reasons why we have this strong preoccupation with the weather, and why we continue to mediate it through various layers of social tissue, is because the weather has such a strong relationship with time. In Latin the word for time and for weather is the same: 'tempo'. This is particularly the case in the non-equatorial regions, like northern Europe where the weather also, in its extreme diversity, its wide-ranging seasonal variations, its continuous shifts from day to day and hour to hour is an unmistakable proof of the fact that time is passing. We have through our relationship with the weather learned to use and relate to the weather as a mode of time. The weather helps us to get our senses around the abstract notion of what time is, via making time more tangible.

We can sense that the weather is changing, thus we sense that time is passing. Like this we use the weather to predict time and maybe more important, one of the largest of all collective engagements of humankind is time related. It is to foresee the future. Not in the crystal ball of the fortune teller; no, it is the vast international industry also known as weather forecasting. Via the weather forecast we look at the time ahead of us, organising our expectations. One could say that we stretch our ever-progressing 'now' to the highest possible degree of avoiding the unforeseeable.

The most common concepts of time have through modernity been compartmentalised into predictable systems, schedules and numbers, objectifying its continuous aspect. Regardless of the success in forecasting the upcoming weather, there is always the risk of the unforeseeable. As a time concept the weather has the benefit of not having lost its central aspect: duration. One can ask if maybe this element – the duration – and the non-predictable aspects that inevitably follow this idea of constant movement or flow might be one of the basic reasons for the obsessive preoccupation with the weather. Even though this will supposedly improve soon, we, through our local weather forecast, can still only look a day or two, or maybe a week ahead, stretching our 'now' into the near future. By predicting what the weather might bring tomorrow and using the analysis from yesterday, our society and its fundamental desire to control everything has extended our sense of 'now' long enough to become a massive common space constantly negotiating and in various ways mediating the weather. Because it has such a strong relationship to time, one could argue that the level of mediation of the weather is revealed, where it may have a lower degree of representation and thus a higher degree of 'reality'. In other words the weather can be communicated or experienced as an abstraction but, due to the durational and unpredictable element of the weather, to a greater extent it allows us to understand the level of abstraction.

Since this idea of how situations and things can be mediated or represented has become a crucial part of how I work in my artistic practice, I would like to elaborate briefly on what I mean by 'mediation'. Basically, by this term, I mean a degree of representation in the experience of a situation. The level or degree of representation is in a constant state of flux, varying in accordance with the different factors mediating this situation.

Let me offer a couple of examples. If you watch two people having a discussion, you experience a level of representation, though it is at the low end of the scale, defined by the particular language, behaviour and cultural codes to which this event is subject. If you watch a film of the discussion, you are experiencing the higher end of the representational scale. Significantly, the film can be replayed over and over again, and the discussion thus takes place out of its own time. In between the two extremes there are endless different levels of representation. If, for instance, one of the two people talking knows that they are being filmed and acts differently as a result, this person, by imagining what the discussion looks like from the perspective of the camera, has altered your reception of the situation. In other words, for you (and for the person in question) the situation has become slightly more mediated.

Another example would be studying a map before going out into the city. This has an impact on how we will experience and orient ourselves in the city when walking through it later. The map mediates the city, and the knowledge and expectations we have of the city before going into it mediate the map.

Seeing a movie about the same city mediates it in yet another way, while an advertisement featuring the city will affect your experience in a slightly different manner, and so on. When walking through the city, it continuously mediates itself, for example by resembling a place you have visited before, by threatening or welcoming you, by being architecturally restored in a certain historical style, or having surrendered to junk architecture. And you yourself can have a large impact on the

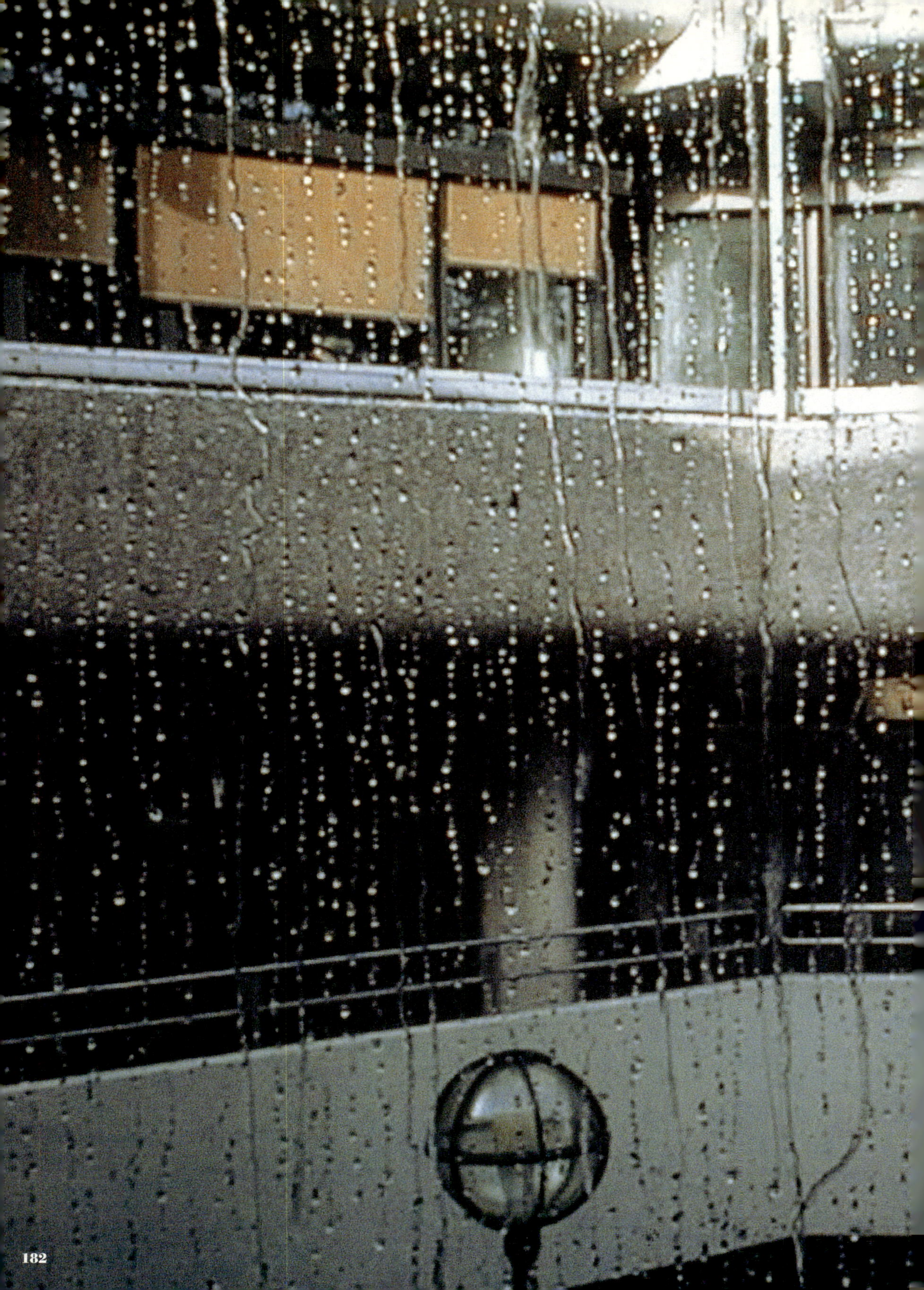

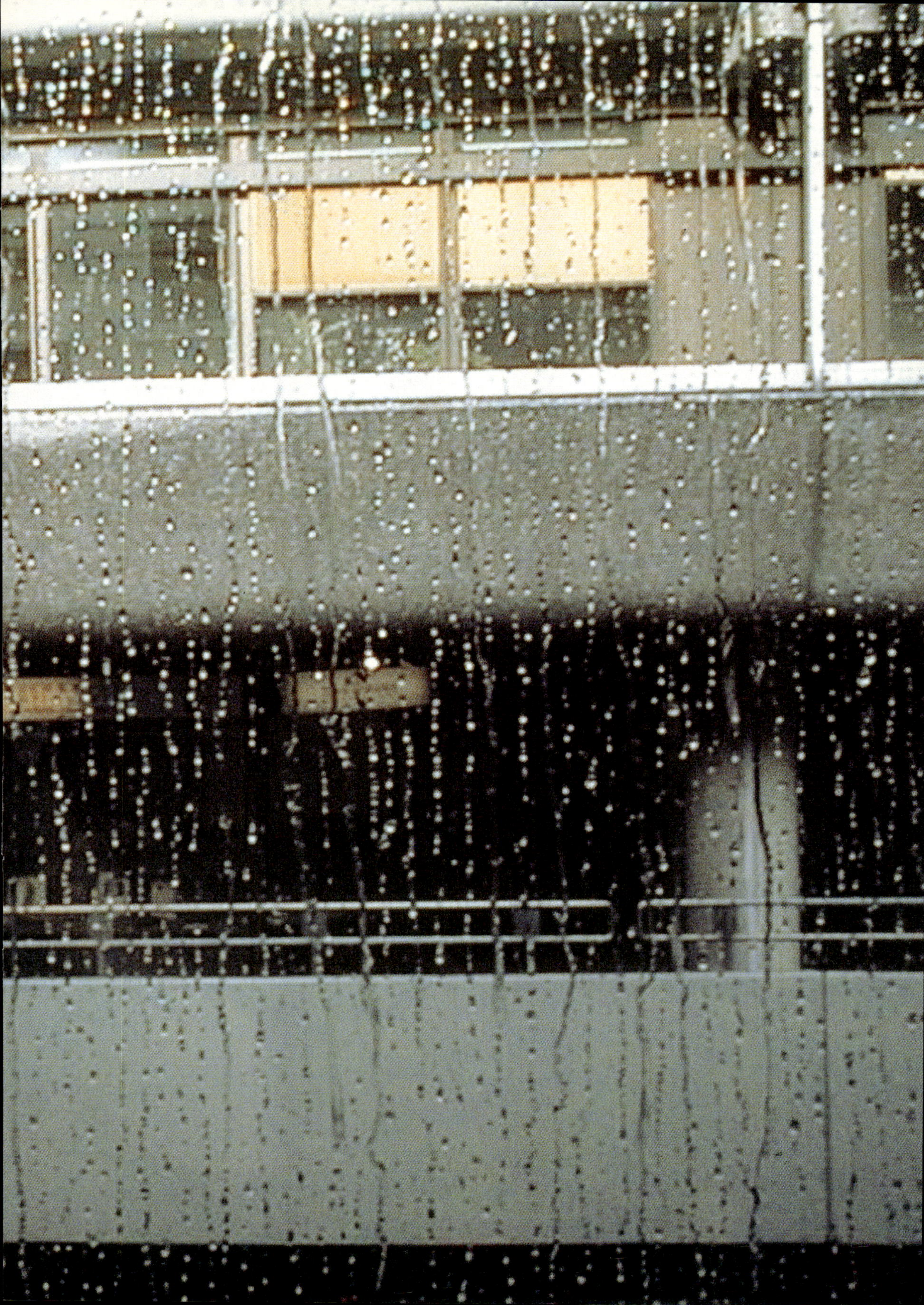

mediation. You can walk down a street wearing a personal stereo, substituting the urban sounds with an alternative soundtrack, maybe even a piece of music once used in a film featuring that exact same street. You can wear tinted sunglasses, thus altering the colour range of what you see, or soft or hard shoes, giving a different impression of the surface on which you are walking. Even your perfume will mediate your olfactory experience. We mediate our surroundings as much as they mediate us.

I have nothing against mediation *per se*. Mediation can be fundamental to our ability to take a step back and make an evaluative and critical judgement of a situation. We use the mediation or representation of our surroundings to govern them, to advocate the social, moral and ethical ideologies in which we believe. However, we are aware that the mediation can be, and to some extent always is, inflicted upon us through our surroundings. If mediated via a third party with intentions that might deviate from our own, our surroundings can obscure our means of social, moral and ethical responsibility. This happens when we, in our ongoing negotiation with space, are led to believe that something is less mediated than it is; in other words, when there is a discrepancy between the levels of mediation experienced by our consciousness and our physical body. Consequential to this, if following the ideas about the weather mentioned earlier, one could argue that what happens is a displacement of our consciousness, a displacement in time, or rather *out of* time.

The problem with mediation – in other words, this more representational experience of oneself and one's surroundings – comes when one does not recognise that the situation in which one is involved has been mediated according to the intentions of the party mediating it. One might mistakenly take a situation for granted as a 'natural' state of things, being unaware of the constructions lying behind this situation. The challenge of orienting ourselves in a mediated realm is therefore to see through and know when, to what extent and by whom a situation has been mediated; in other words, to be aware of a situation's relationship with time.

The (often cultural) elements in society who have taken it as their responsibility to participate in society by somehow reflecting it, have largely understood that reconstruction of a past time, like an earlier model of seeing, is by definition not possible. It has become agreed upon that regardless which 'time' that the cultural institution sets out to display, it can only be seen from the point of view of our own time. But one has to understand that also this 'new idea' is also a model. A construction. It is important to understand that we cannot, like any other modern venture, just replace the old model with a new solution of how to present for instance art in a museum. The challenge lies in understanding the premises of the (singular) engagement in a situation in an institution. In understanding the mediated layers and their manipulative power to the extent that we can make them 'transparent', for example, enabling a museum visitor to understand that the institutional ideology and given display is itself a construction and not a higher state of 'truth'.

When we can 'see through' the mediation of a situation, when it is transparent, we may experience a degree of heightened self-awareness due to the self-evaluative potential that lies within a situation like this. We can never not have mediation, since our memory and expectations alone give us the first of many mediated layers. There is always some inescapable level of representation, except perhaps for the moment we are born and the moment we die. Apart from these two basic events in life, 'reality' as we know it is relative.

By allowing for transparency and thus the mentioned time in the mediated experience, one becomes more responsible for a given situation through awareness that it is part of a larger system of causalities, and not an autonomous element. It's a construction.

In a society, the use of mediation as a way of allowing evaluation, critique and reflection has been the central nerve of cultural practice in general and artistic practise and presentation in particular.

As long as we have had art history, we have had the discussion about whether art should be referred to as a representational system (reflecting society like a mirror) or whether it is an integrated part of society itself. Considering art as one of many cultural trajectories in a society, these questions are little different from asking if the weather is separable from the city. Of course the art institution is an integral part of the life of a city. Cultural institutions are among the many 'immune systems' of a society's self reflection. When a 'virus' such as the commodification of our senses attacks us, and the developing identity of the city's life are challenged, the immune system is (or should be) active in restoring a plausible dialogue involving some sense of resistance. It is important to note here that I doubt whether art has any power to change things directly; I consider the field of artistic practice to be more like a giant laboratory, where research on multiple fields is constantly being conducted. And it is of particular interest to me that artistic practice – not unlike other scientific fields – has made an effort, as a part of its content, constantly to negotiate its relationship with society, to the extent that its method is now becoming integrated into its form, and its form is no longer fixed according to an ideal paradigm. Thus what gives art its unique influence on society is its obsessive desire to define and redefine its position (or lack of it) in relation to that society, and this provides a magnificent resource with which to challenge one's own relationship (or lack of it) with society.

When working on projects in different art institutions, however, I have sometimes been challenged by the general problem that the museum continues to define itself according to the modernist standpoint, assuming that it is possible to stand 'next to' or 'outside' of society and somehow reflect it from there. This standpoint is like assuming that the weather can be separated from the city, experience from interpretation, form from content, or time from space. It means that the institution is not acknowledging its responsibility with regards to society in general and the value of a singular experience in particular. When the *ideology* of a display or exhibition is not acknowledged as a part of the exhibition itself, the socialising potential of that exhibition is sacrificed on behalf of formal values. To avoid this situation, any chosen ideological strategy, any marketing choice, any architectural detail, must not only be considered as a condition and part of the project, but must also somehow be revealed to visitors and thus allow for some transparency in the mediation. I believe that in order to achieve a challenging engagement with art that avoids the manipulation of the viewer, every part of the construction behind the presentation of art must be made a transparent part of that presentation. Thus art can finally achieve both its social function and make visible the relationship with time with which it is engaged: to be *of* time rather than *in* time. An exhibition cannot stand outside its social context, and we have a responsibility to understand that we are a part of what we are evaluating as well as the result of it. Museums can be radical.

Olafur Eliasson

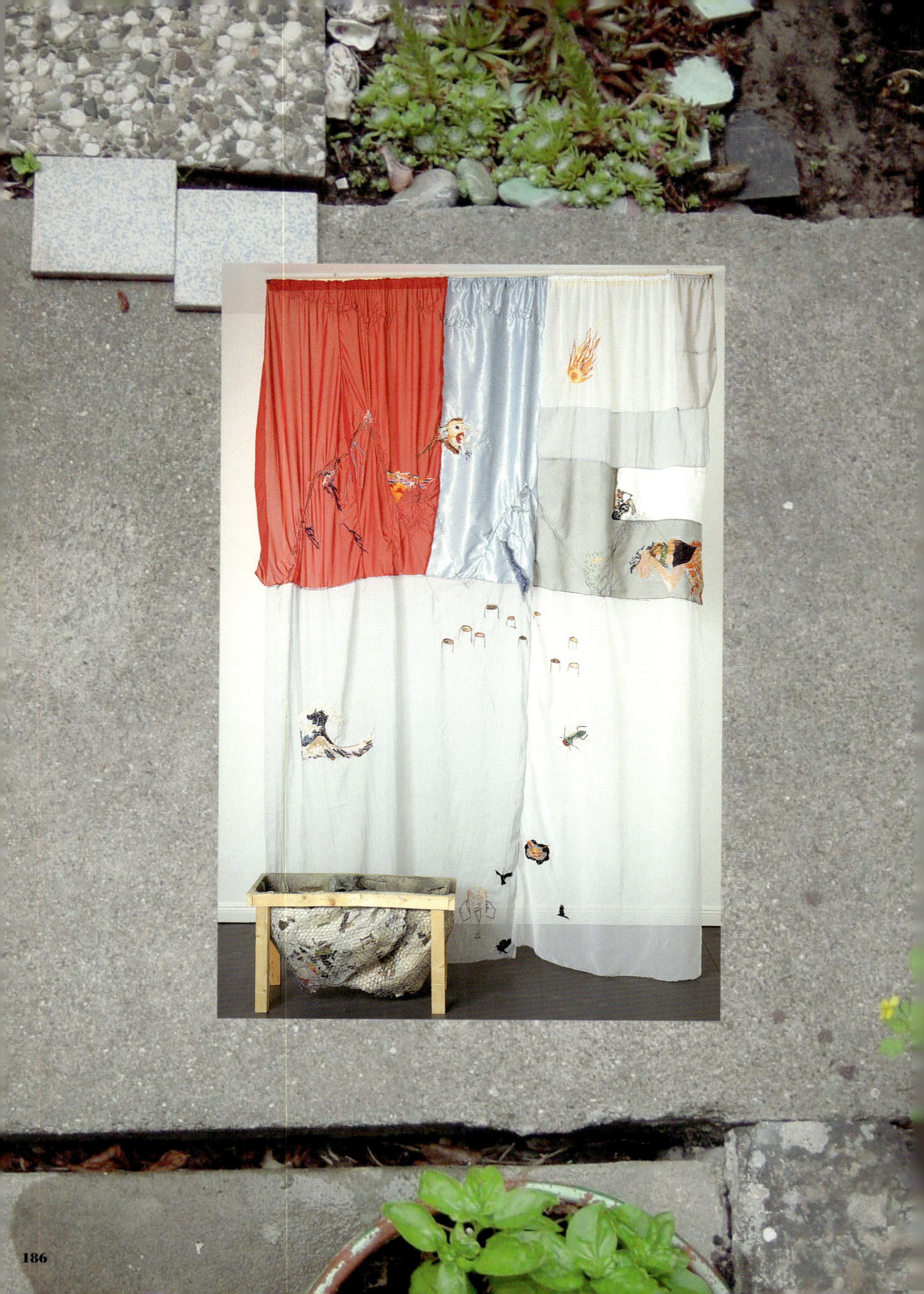

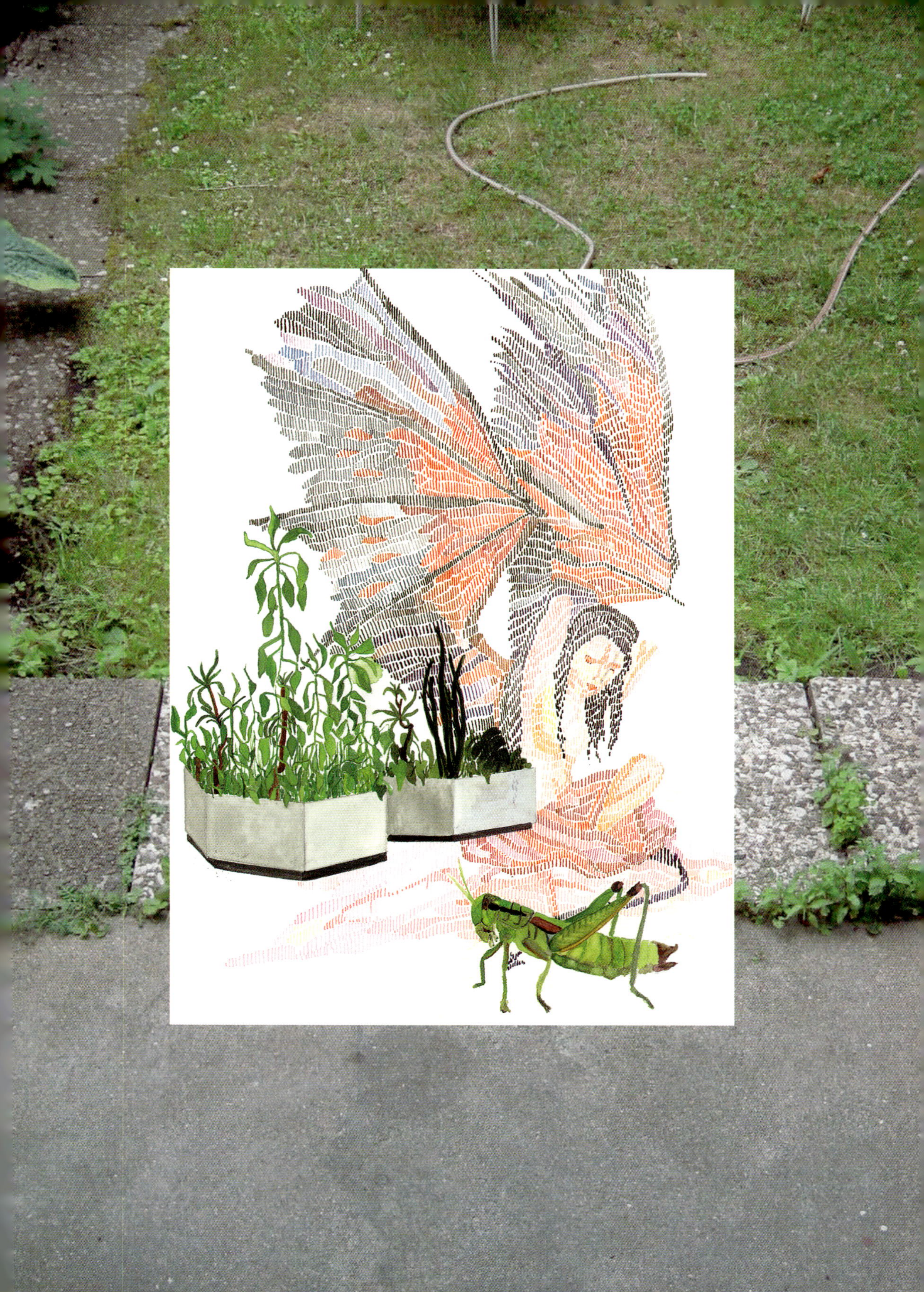

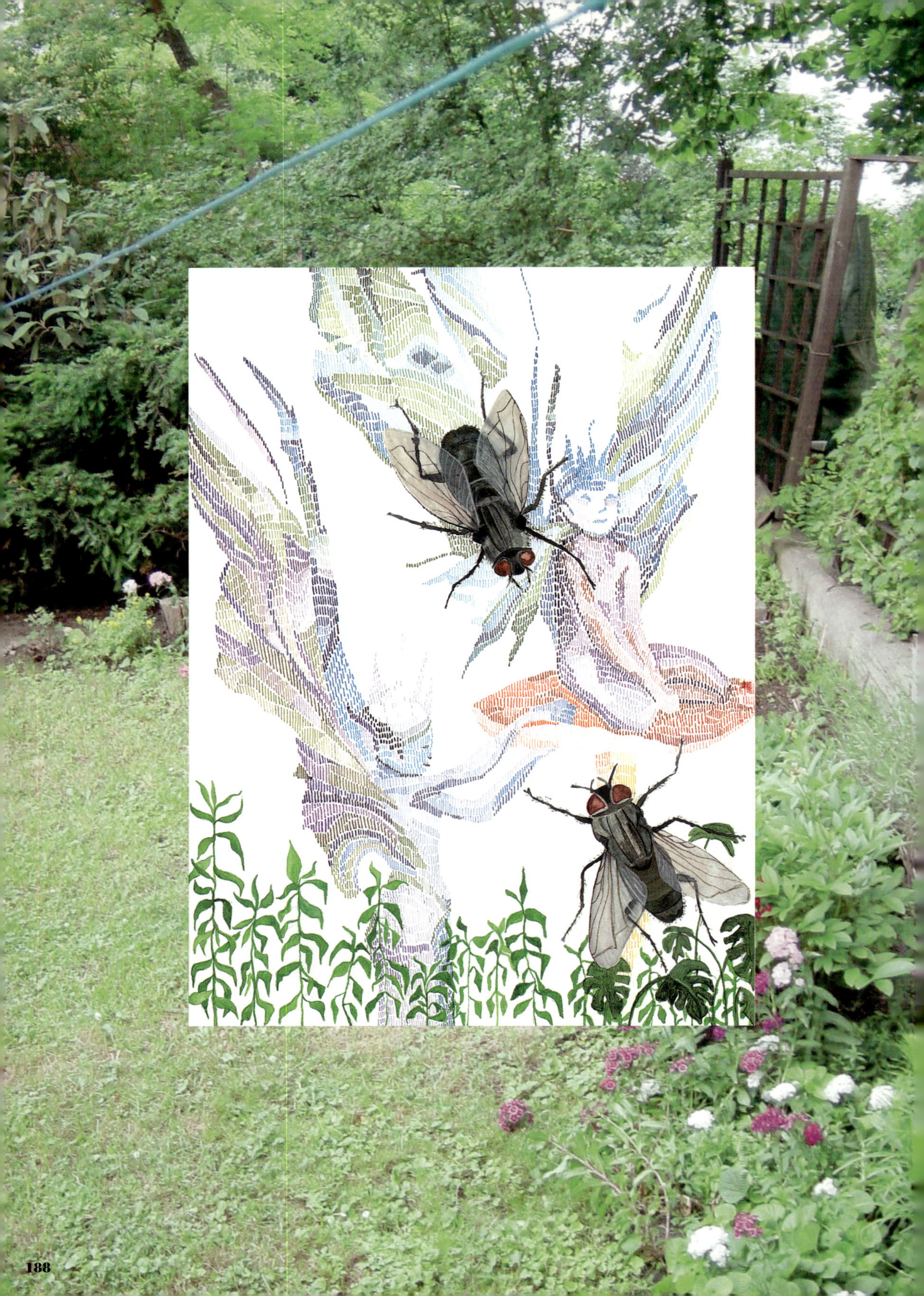

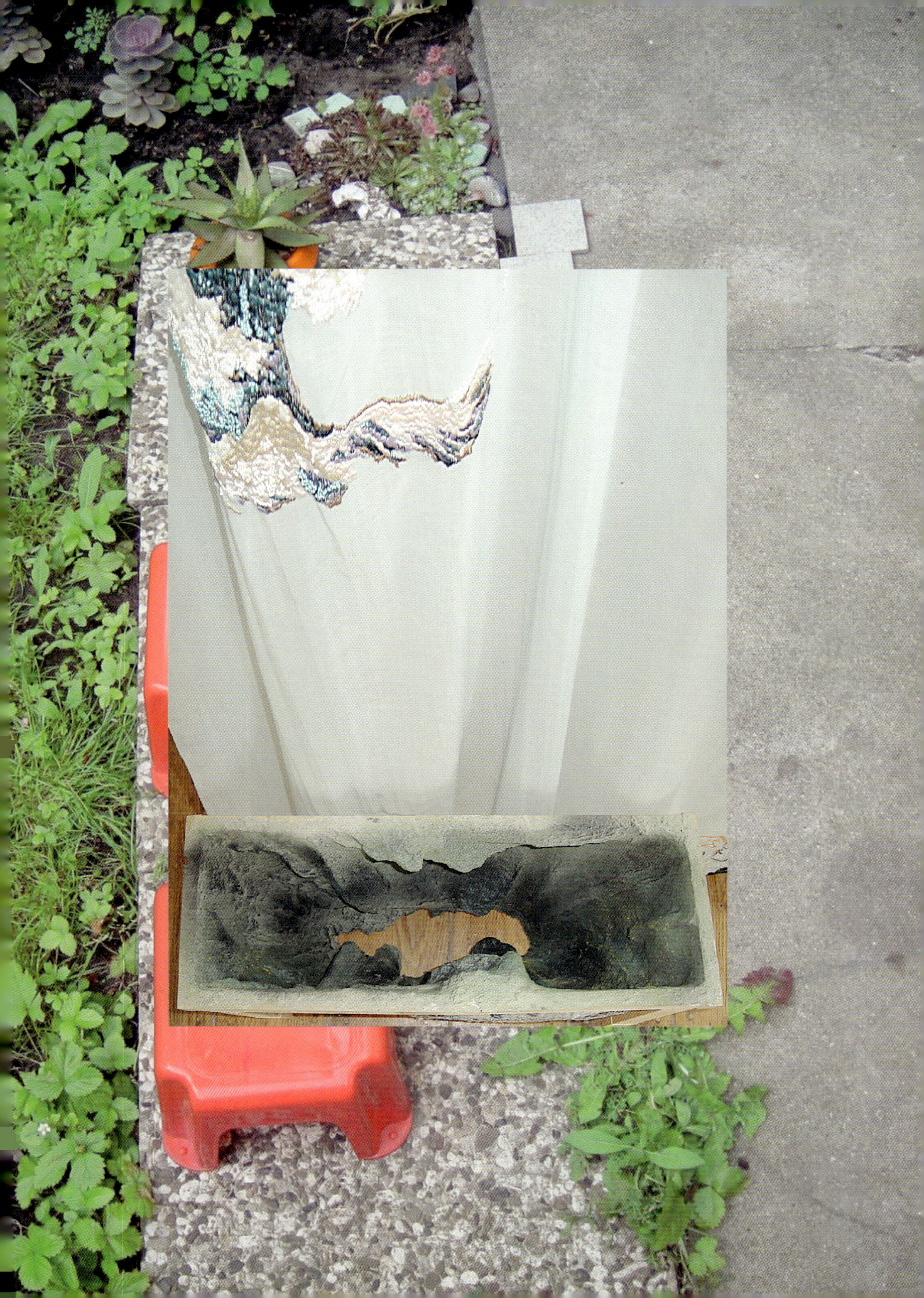

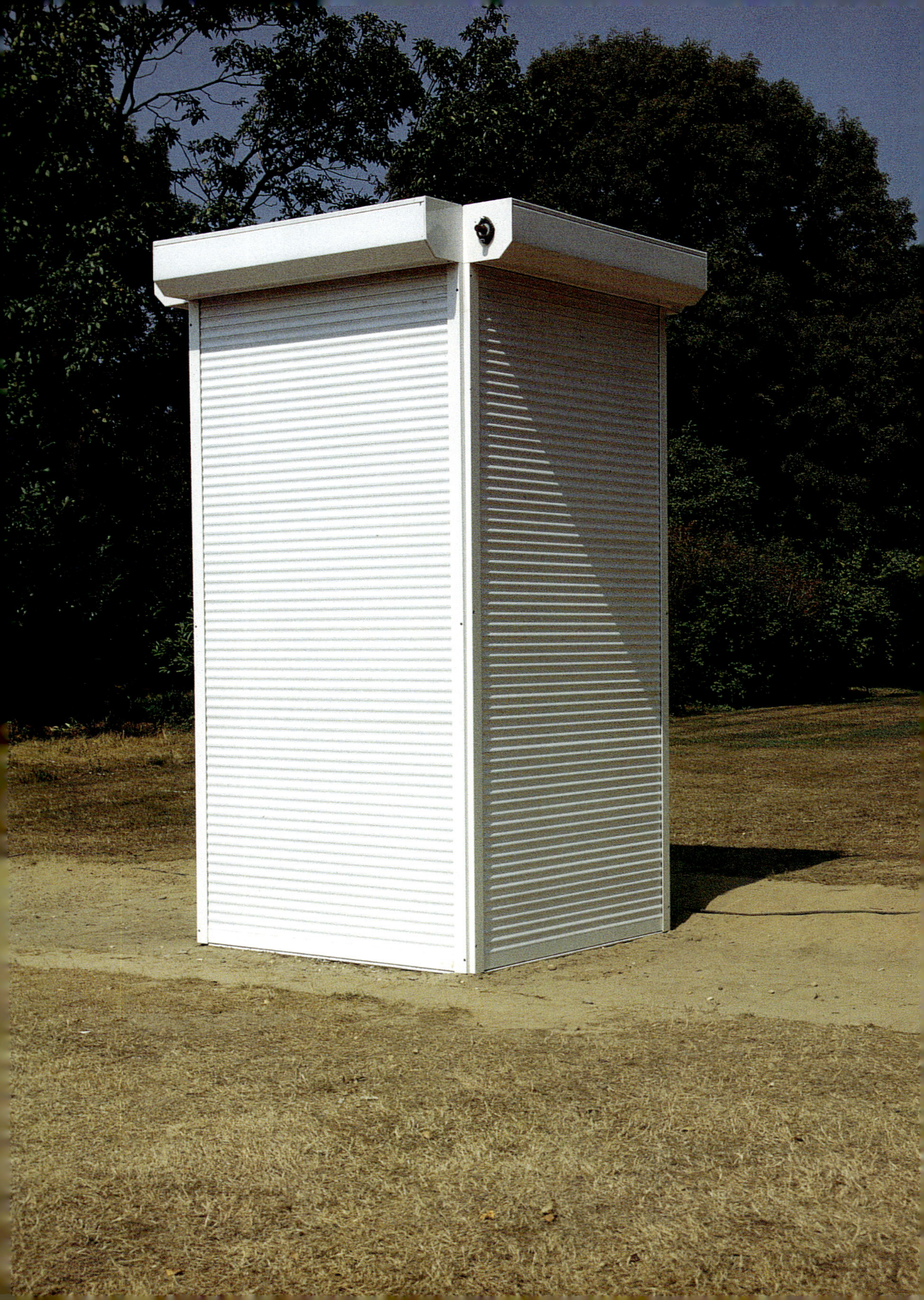

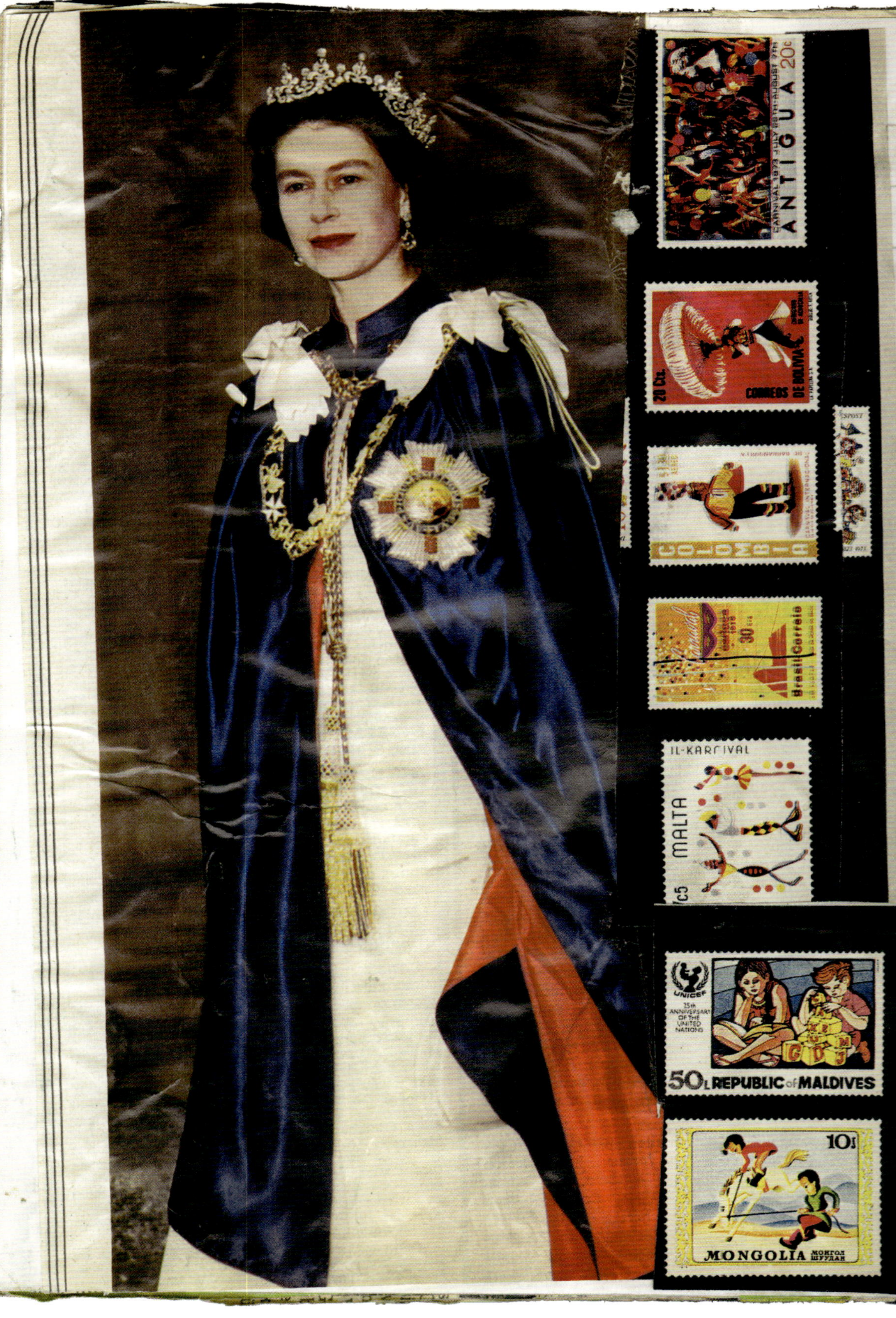
CARNIVAL 1973 JULY 28TH-AUGUST 7TH
ANTIGUA 20c
20 Ct. CORREOS DE BOLIVIA
COLOMBIA
Brasil Correio 30
IL-KARNIVAL
MALTA
5c
UNICEF
25th ANNIVERSARY OF THE UNITED NATIONS
50L REPUBLIC of MALDIVES
10
MONGOLIA

Mit Trimm-Rolli gegen Fettpölsterchen

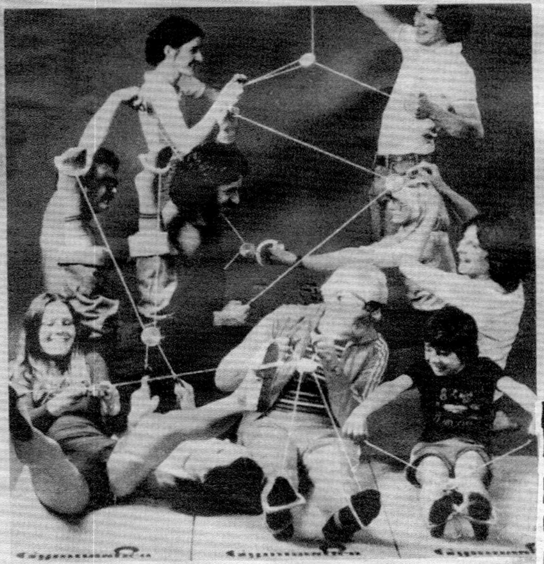

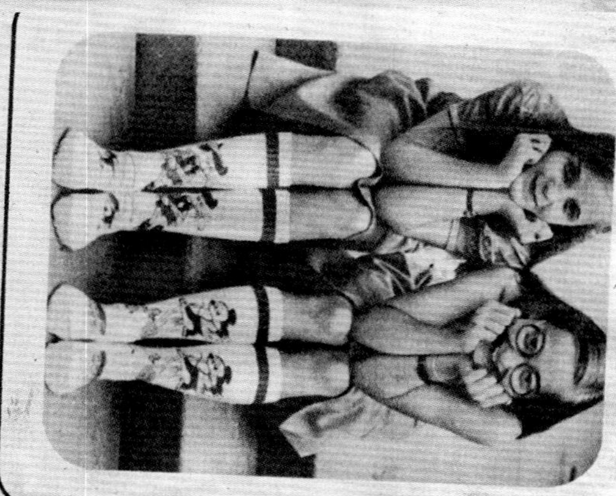

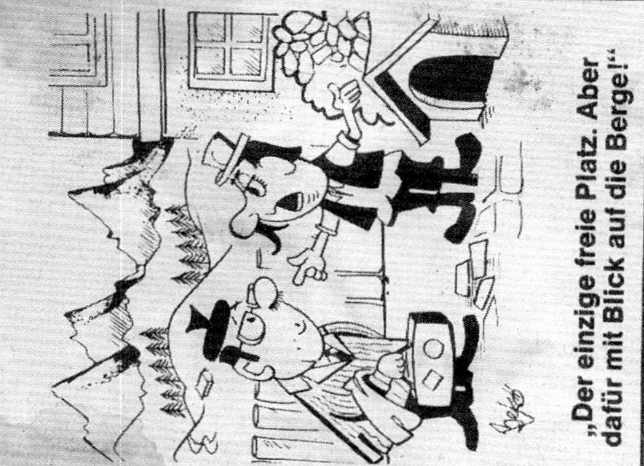

Bay City Rollers: Striktes Alkoholverbot!

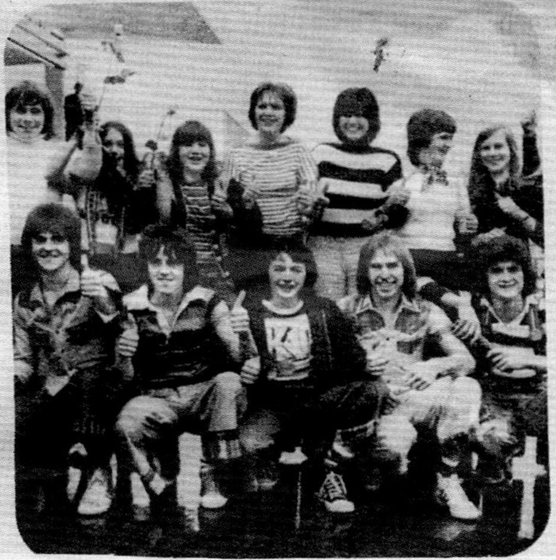

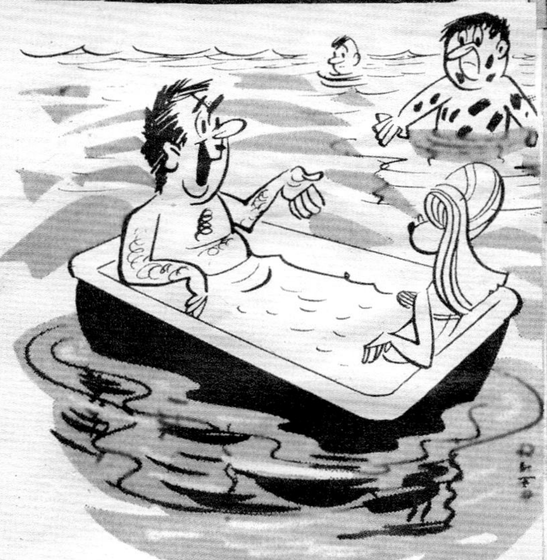

Das Gasthaus heißt „Georg und der Drachen". Eines Tages versucht ein Hausierer, dort seine Waren anzubieten, die Wirtin schlägt ihm jedoch die Tür vor der Nase zu. Zwei Sekunden später klingelt es wieder, fragt der Hausierer: „Könnte ich jetzt vielleicht einmal mit Georg sprechen, bitte?"

Dieter Melkus, Mudau

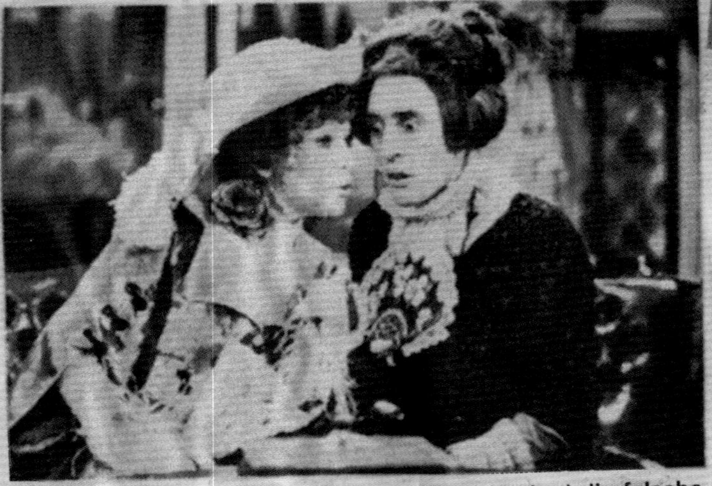
Gisela Trowe spielt die echte, Jörg Pleva (rechts) die falsche Tante von Charley. Unverwüstliche Klamotte am Donnerstag

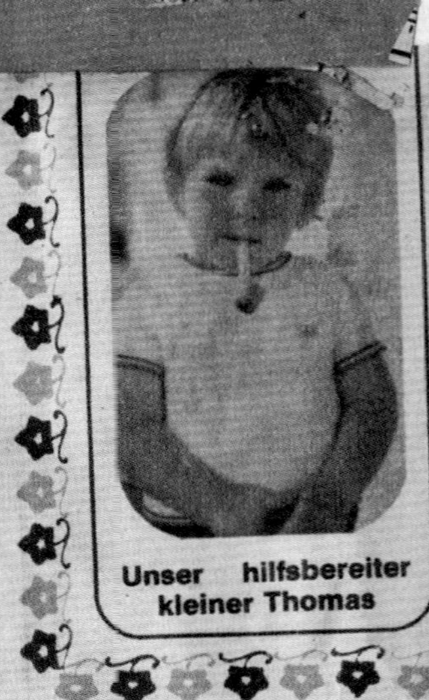
Unser hilfsbereiter kleiner Thomas

en Kronprinzessi
as Leben zur Höll

en Kummer
Schwestern
ald machen
ben schwer

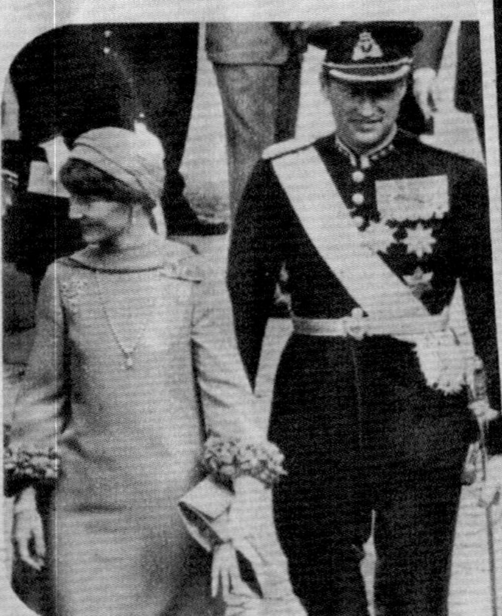

Bild rechts: Sonja übernimmt an der Seite ihres Gemahls Harald heute die Repräsentationspflichten, die früher die Prinzessinnen Astrid und Ragnhild (ganz re. ob. und unt.) ausübten

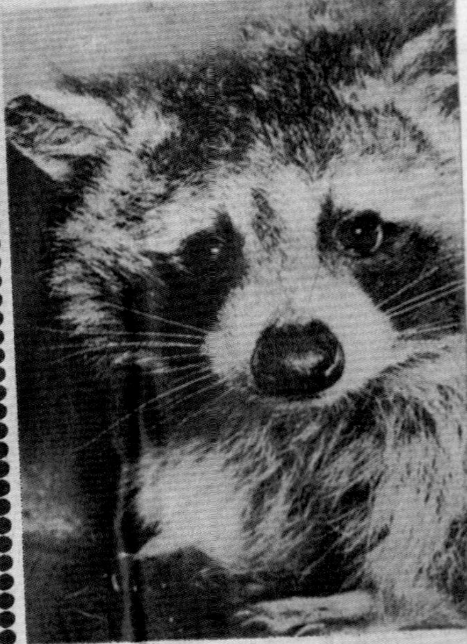
Waschbär   Foto:

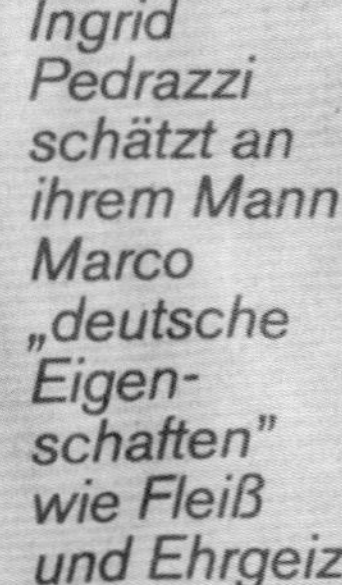

Ingrid Pedrazzi schätzt an ihrem Mann Marco „deutsche Eigenschaften" wie Fleiß und Ehrgeiz

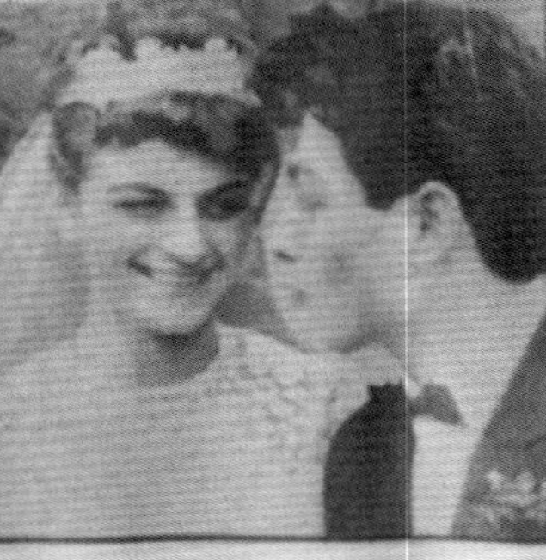

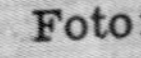

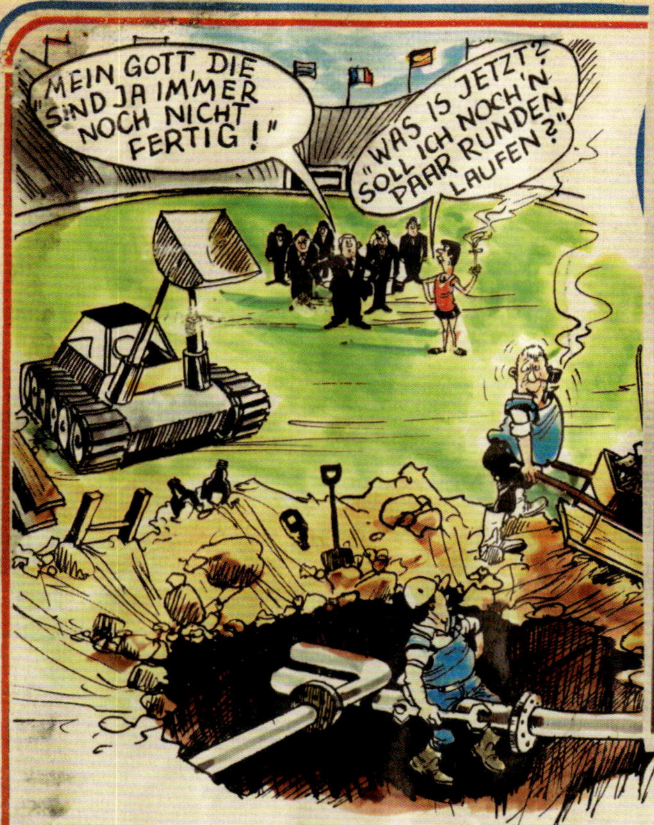

„Jetzt keine Panik, Jack! Pfuscharbeit kommt für unsere Firma nicht in Frage!"

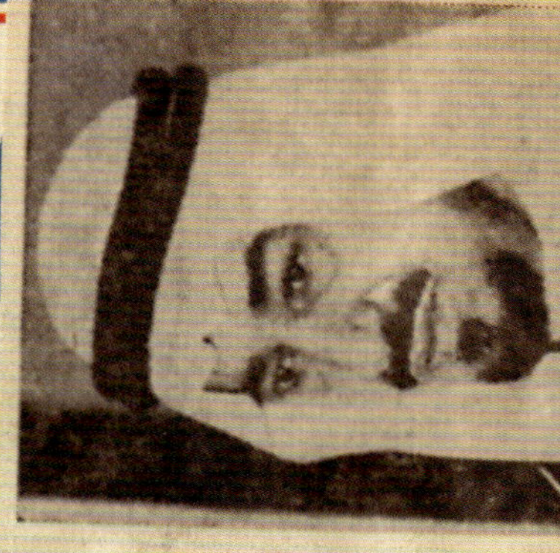

König Chalid hätte Helmut Schmidt gern als Finanzminister.

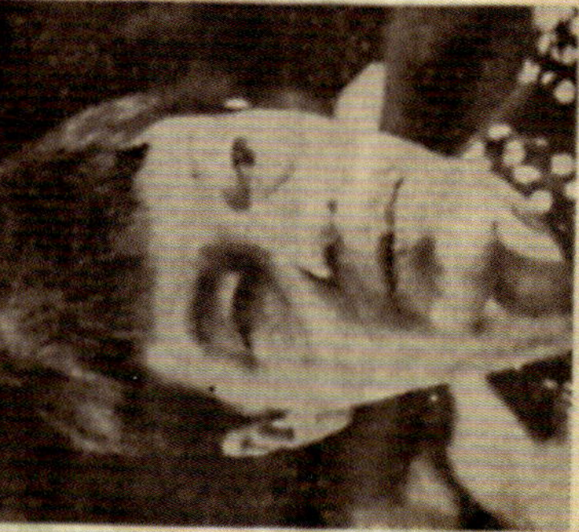

Hannelore Schmidt war als erste Europäerin Gast der Königin.

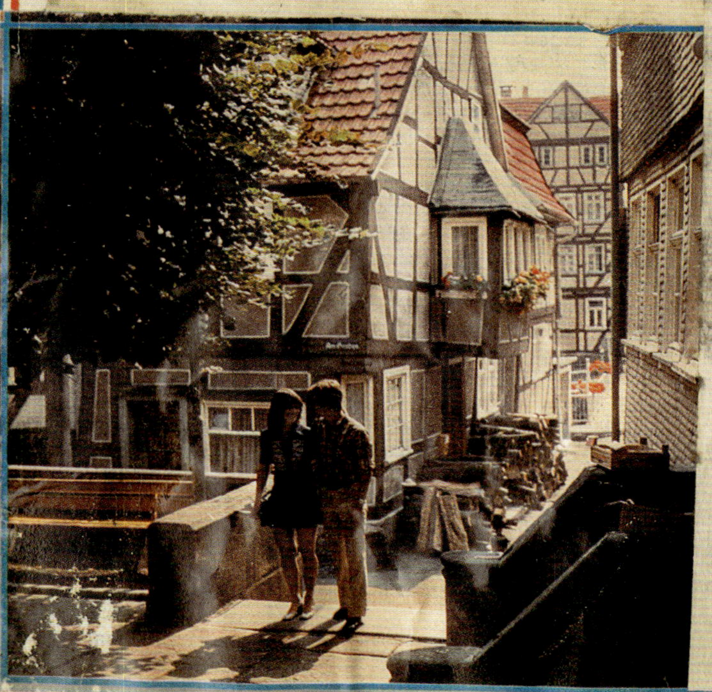

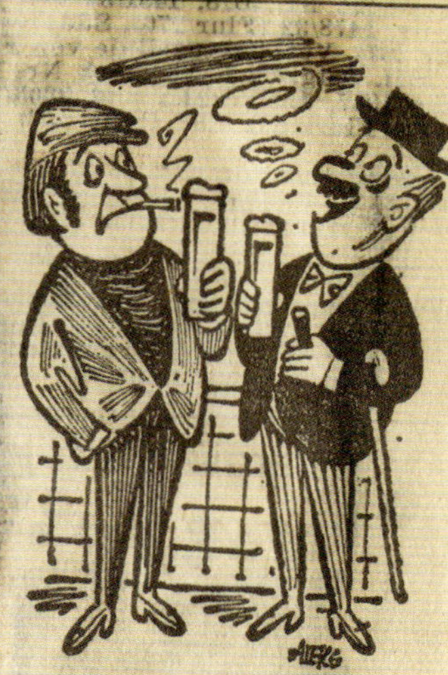

DER HERR SCHMITZ

„An der Saar hattense op eine Schlag 5 Liter Rejen op der Quadratmeter. Dat is ävver noch janix, ich han jestern he op dem halve Quadratmeter 25 Jlas Kölsch verdrück . . ."

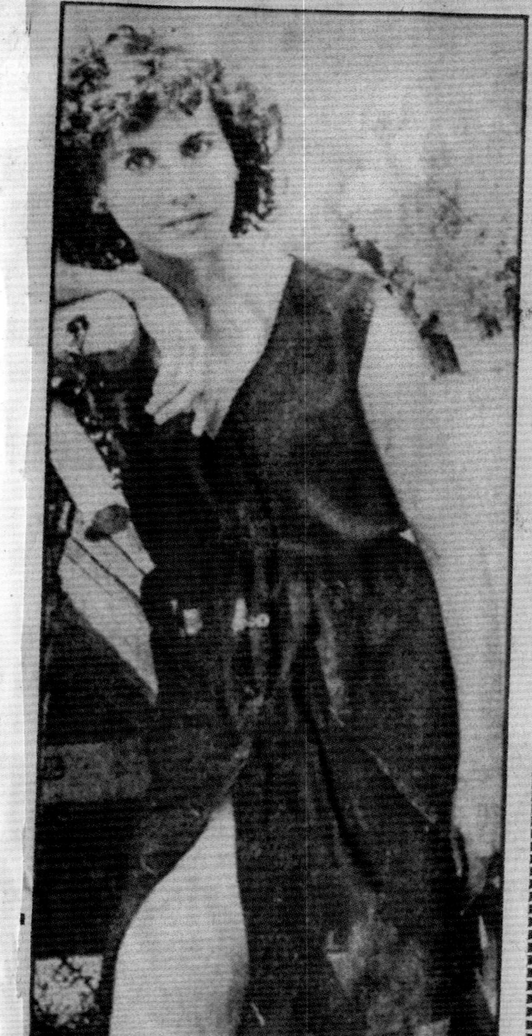

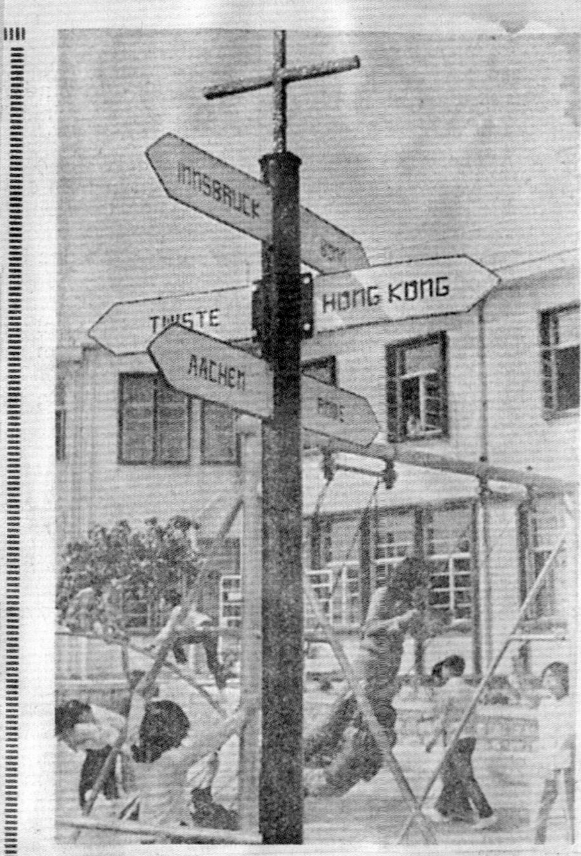

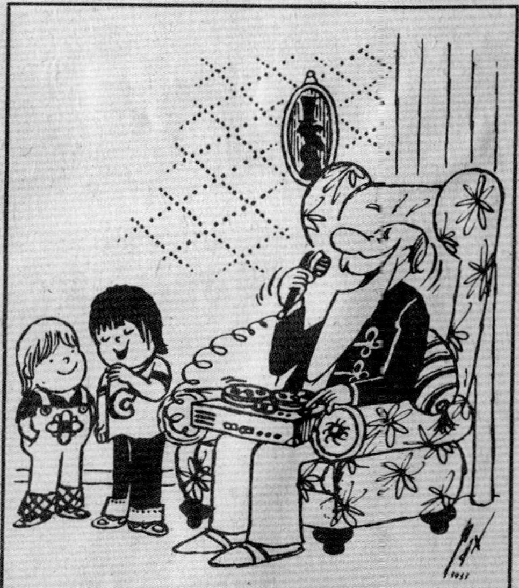

„Opa nimmt seine Lieblingswitze auf Band für den Fall, daß er sie selbst nicht mehr erzählen kann!"

Hübsche Neuentdeckung aus Italien:
Paola Pitagora

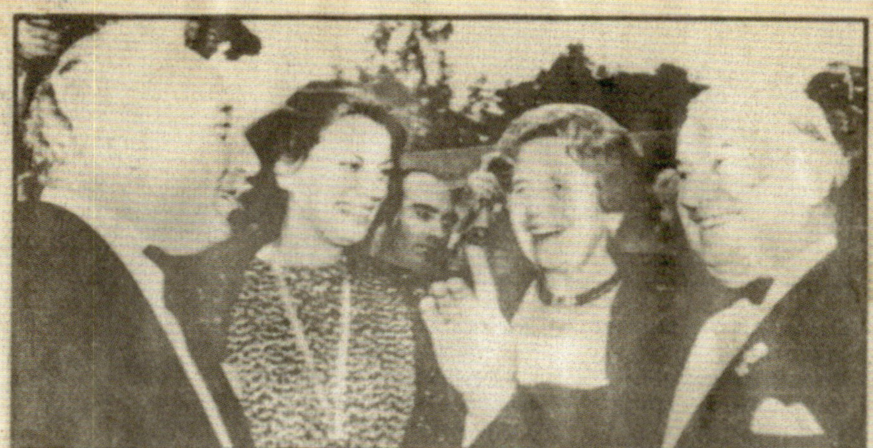

Auch diesmal wieder in Bayreuth: die Ehepaare Scheel und Goppel.

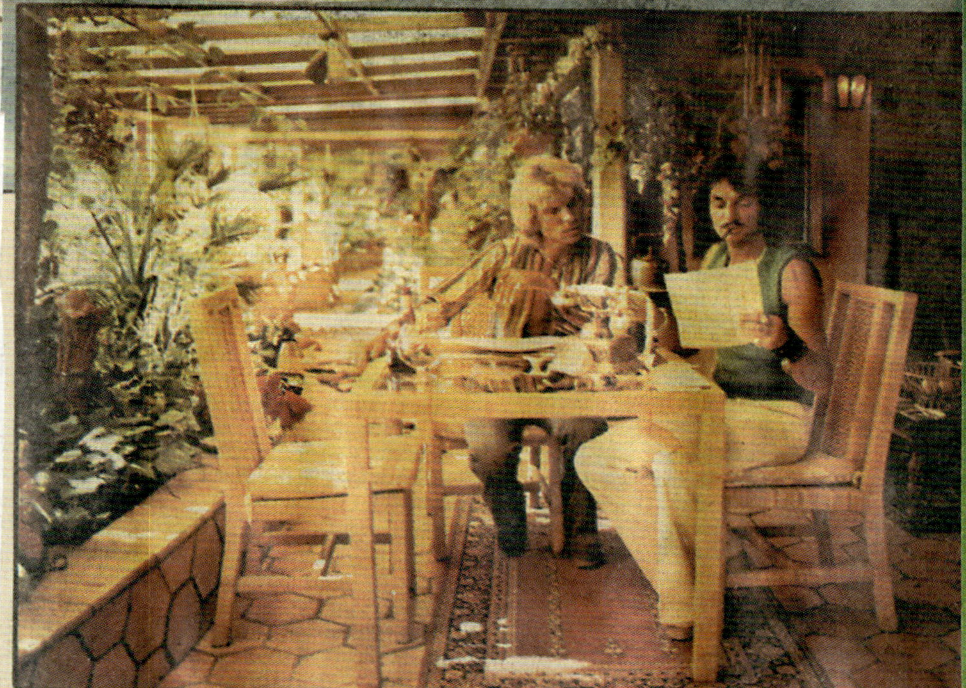

Ihr Wohnraum sieht aus wie ein Gewächshaus, ist aber sehr gemütlich. G...
veranstalten Roy und Siegfried in ihrem Bungalow magische Part...

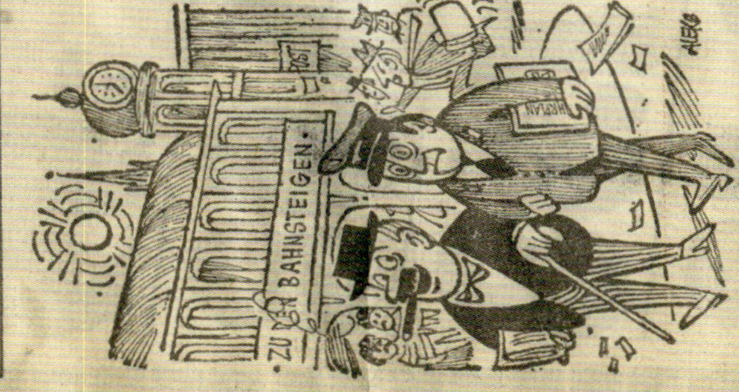

Wer nach seiner "inneren Uhr" lebt, bleibt länger gesund

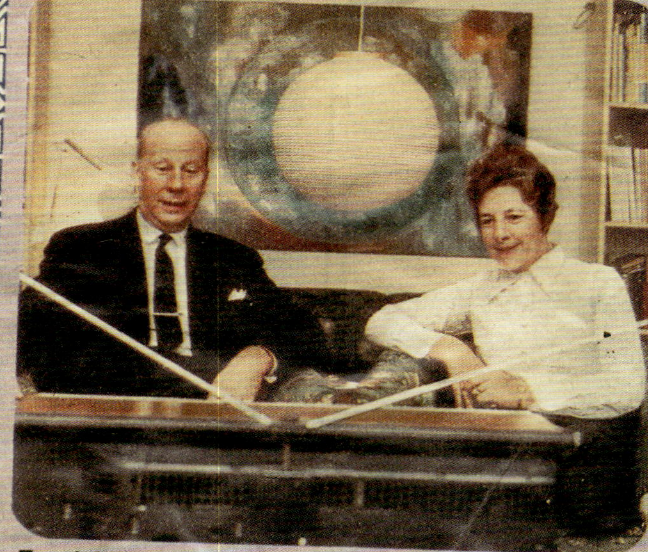

Zur richtigen Zeit entspannen – das steigert nicht nur die Lebensfreude, sondern auch die Leistungskraft

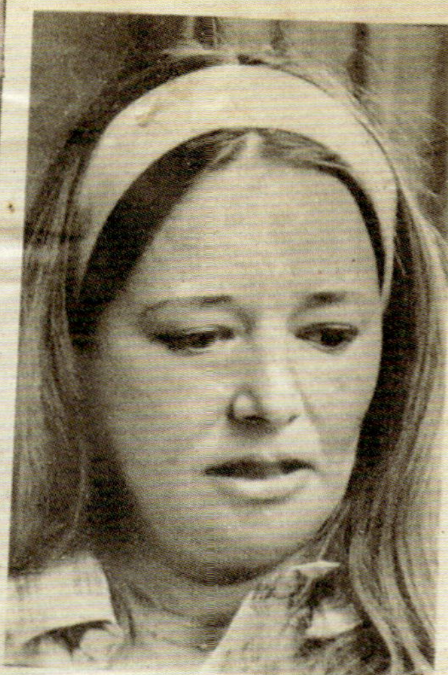

Eine Frau kann heute auch ohne Begleiter ausgehen

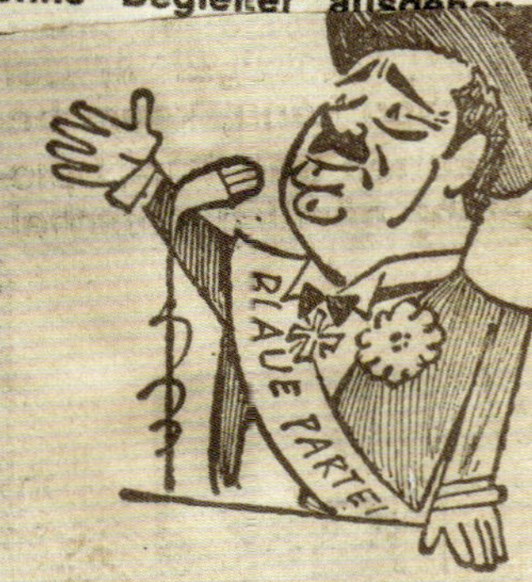

Toni Geller
„Führer der blauen Partei"

„Frauenmord" – Fritz Eckhardt als Kommissar Marek muß heute einen komplizierten Fall lösen

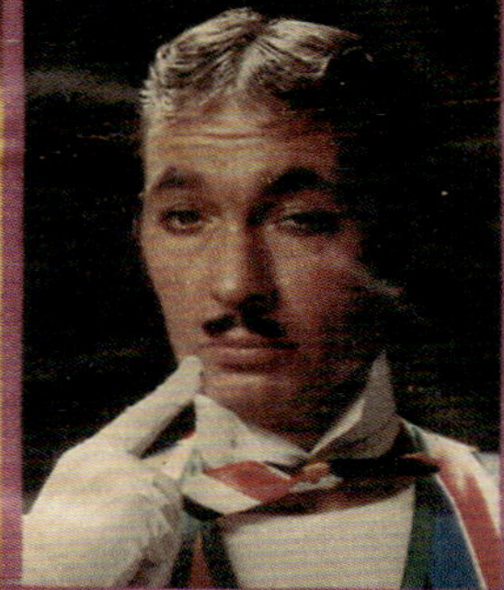

Unwiederstehlich! Mit Mittelscheitel und Klebe-Bärtchen kann jeder Mann so schön sein . . .

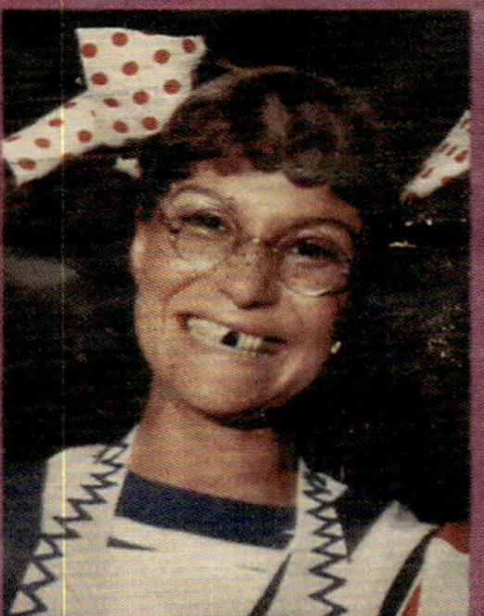

Schwarzer Zahn-lack, Sommer-sprossen, Ratten-schwänze – fertig ist die „Klim-bim"-Horror-Göre

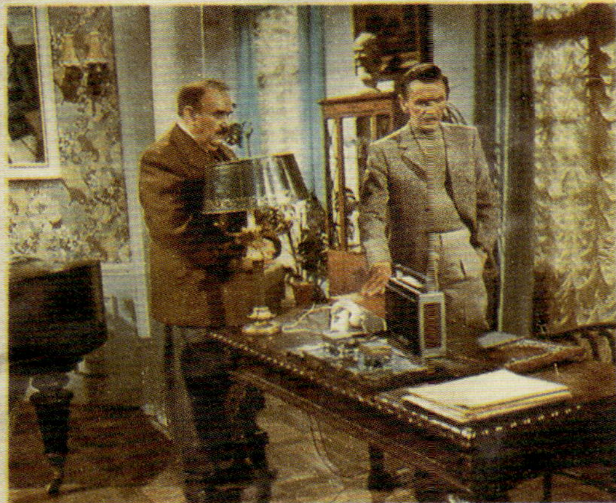

Oberinspektor Marek (Fritz Eckhardt, l.) redet mit Erwin Rahl (Leopold Rudolf), dem Mann der Toten

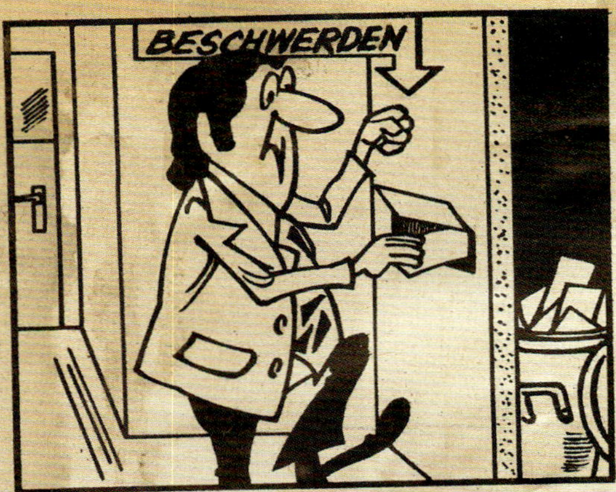

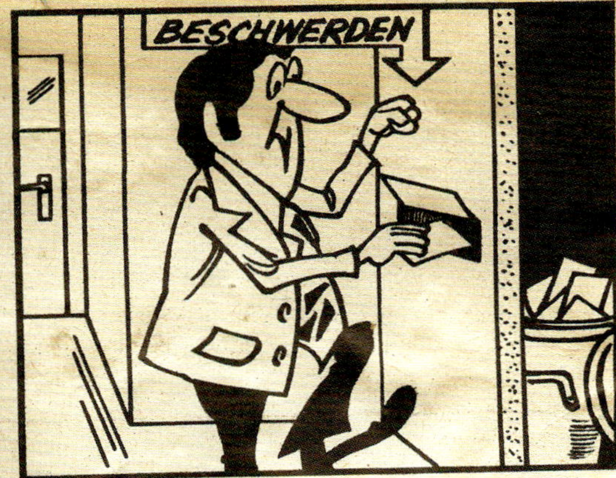

Die Lösungen der Aufgaben finden Sie diesmal auf Seite 98

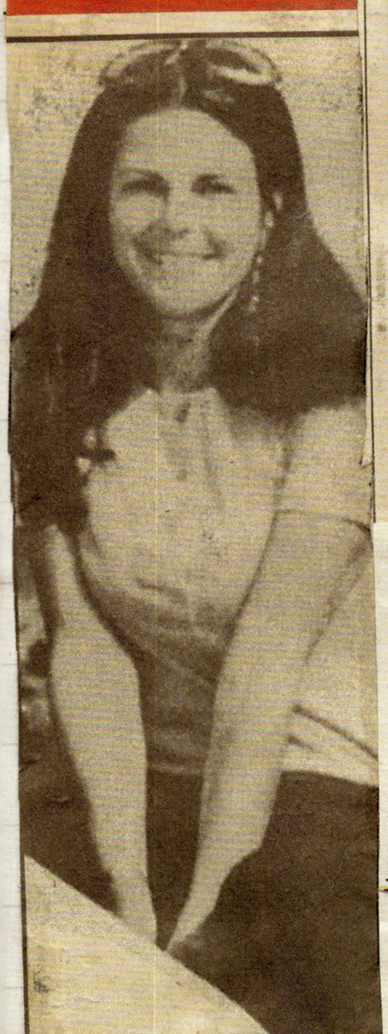

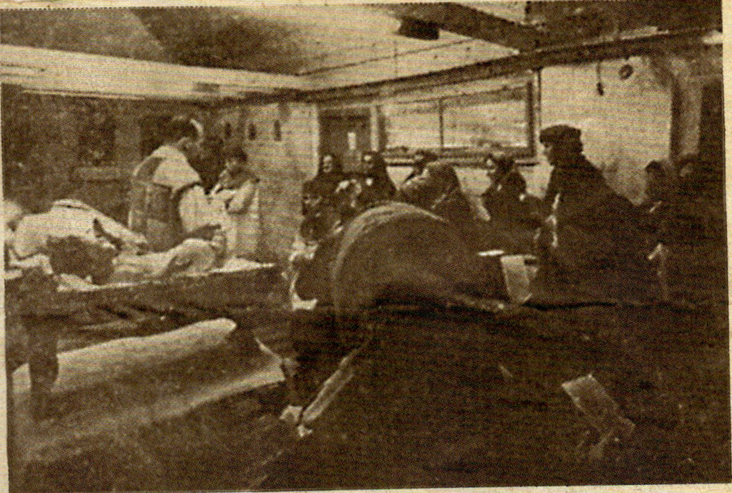

In aller Welt wird Weihnachten gefeiert: eine Gemeinde in Jugoslawien

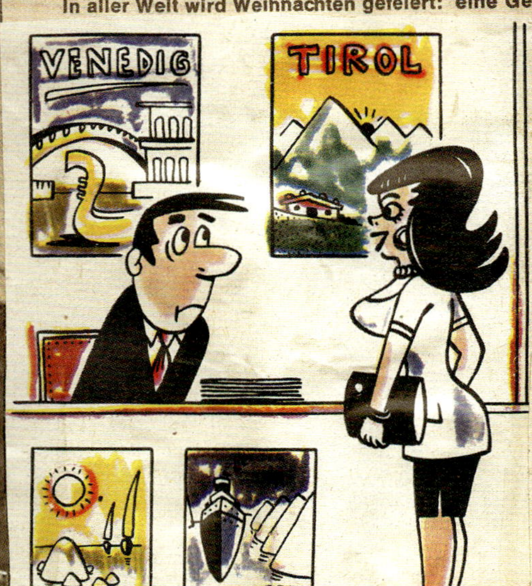

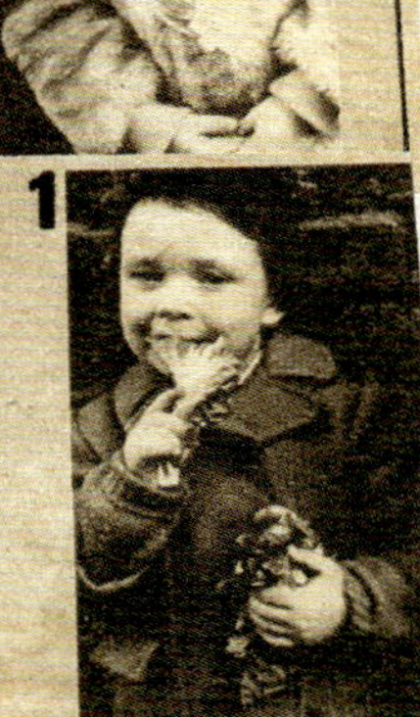

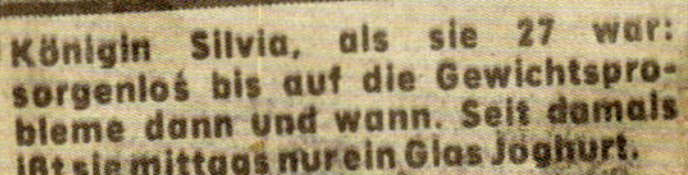

Königin Silvia, als sie 27 war:
sorgenlos bis auf die Gewichtsprobleme dann und wann. Seit damals
ißt sie mittags nur ein Glas Joghurt.

Kostbarkeiten –nd zerstört

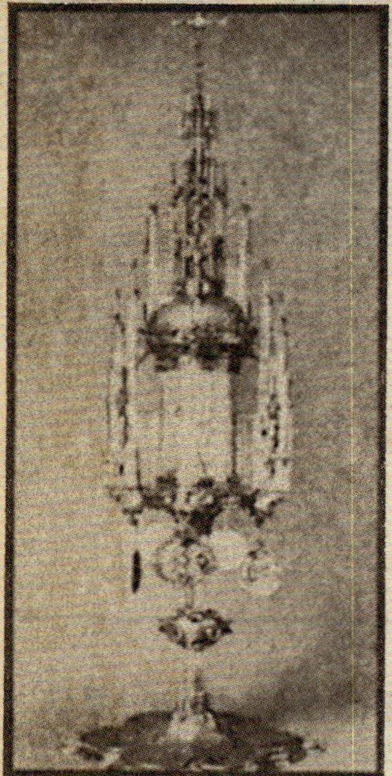

Die Silbermonstranz

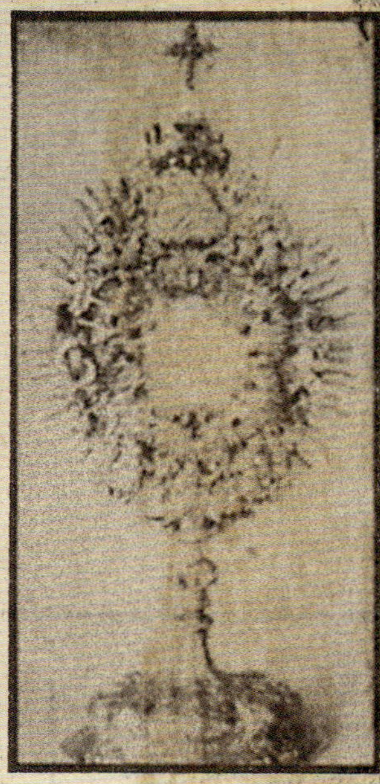

Die Strahlenmonstranz

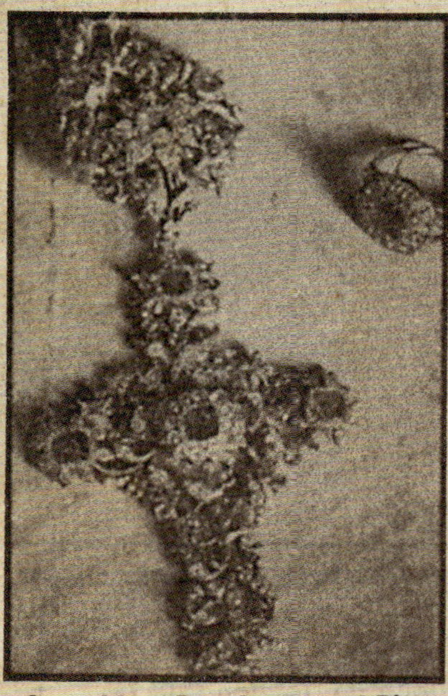

Gestohlen: Brustkreuz und Ring

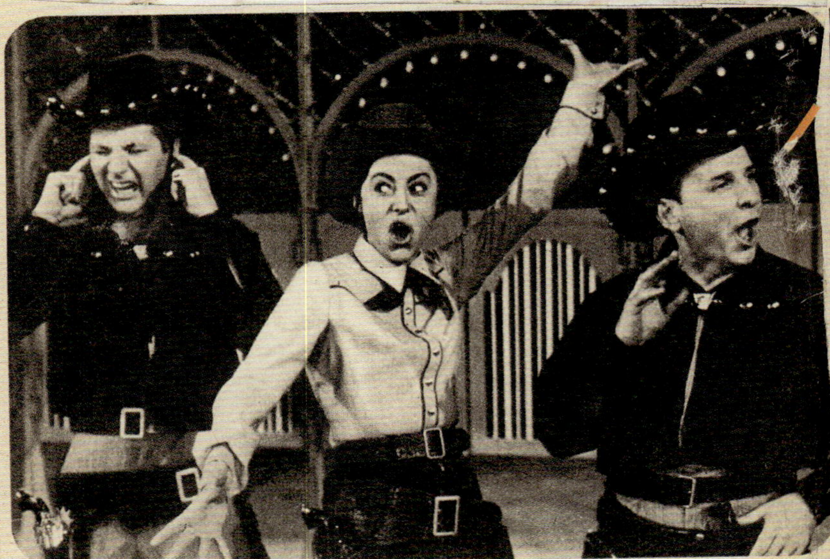

Viel Schwung, Humor und prominente Gäste in der Caterina-Valente-Show „Bonsoir, Kathrin": Georg Thomalla (rechts) und Boy Gobert

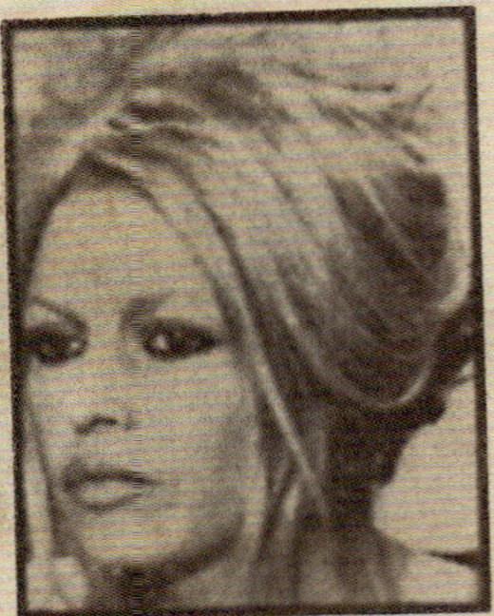

BB schickte Scheck für den Storch

exp Paris — Brigitte Bardot (Foto) wurde vom Mitleid übermannt. Das Unglück eines Storches veranlaßte sie, dem Vorsitzenden des Tierschutzvereines von Chambery einen Scheck zu schicken.

Millionen-Räuber krach

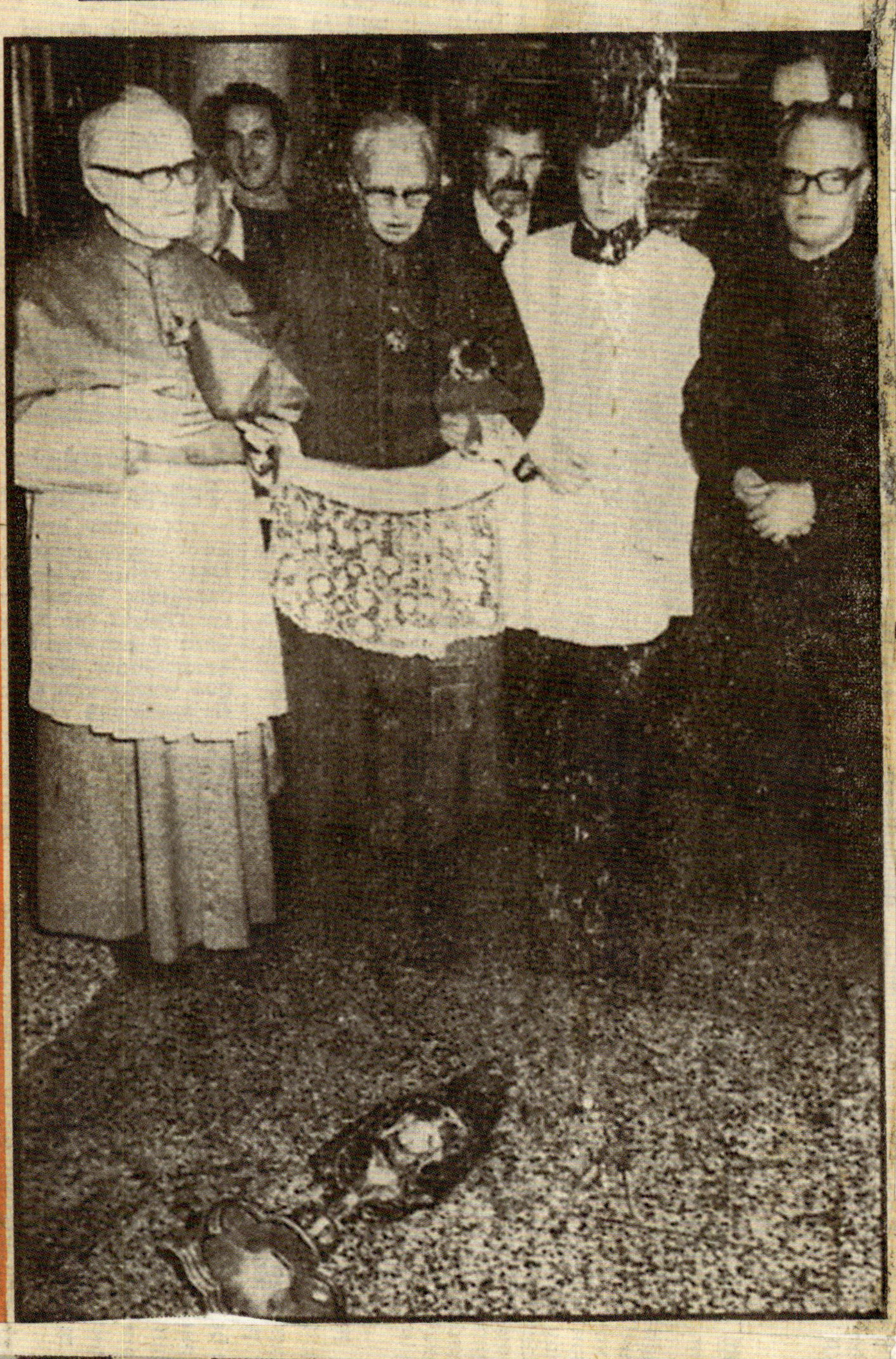

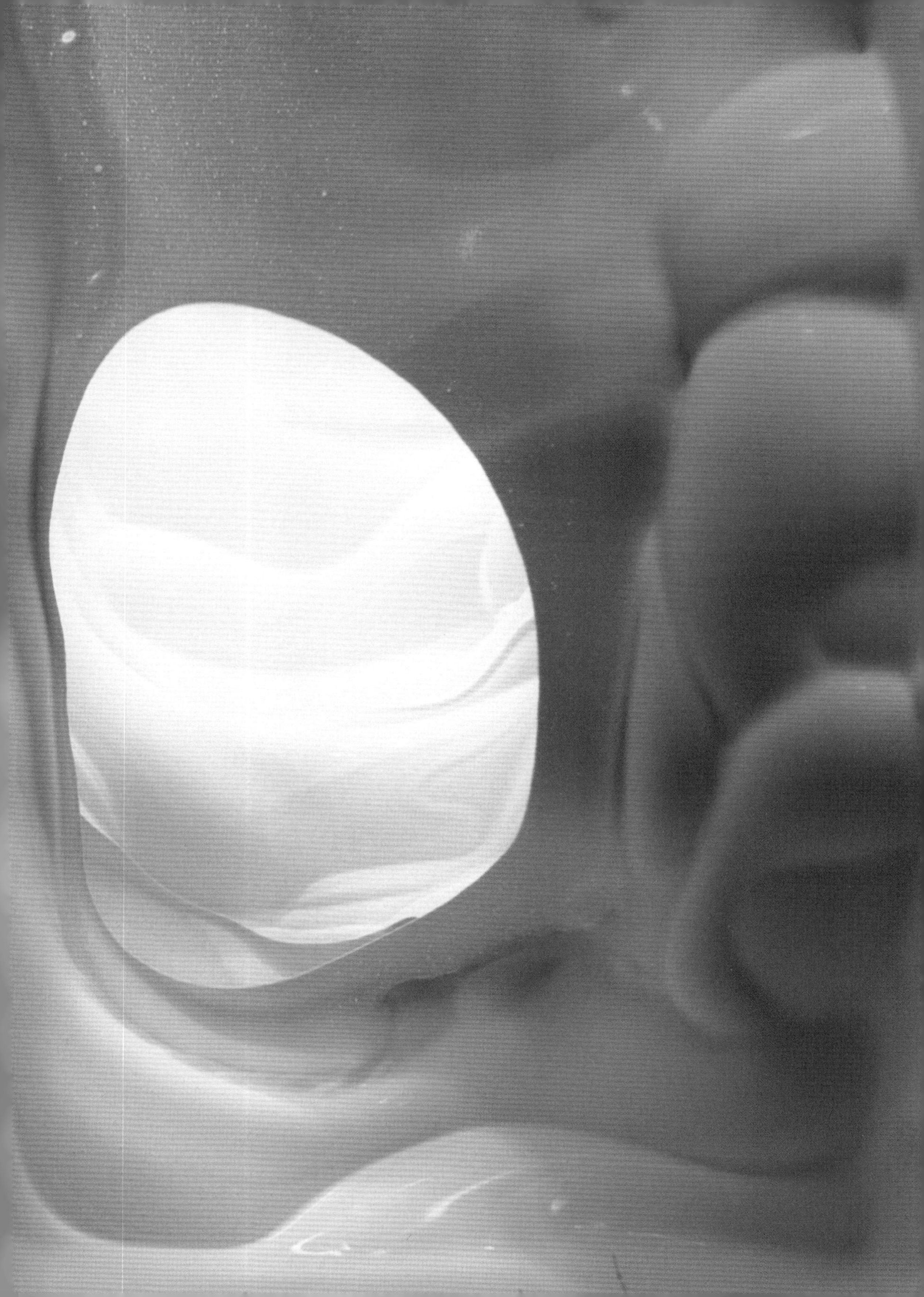

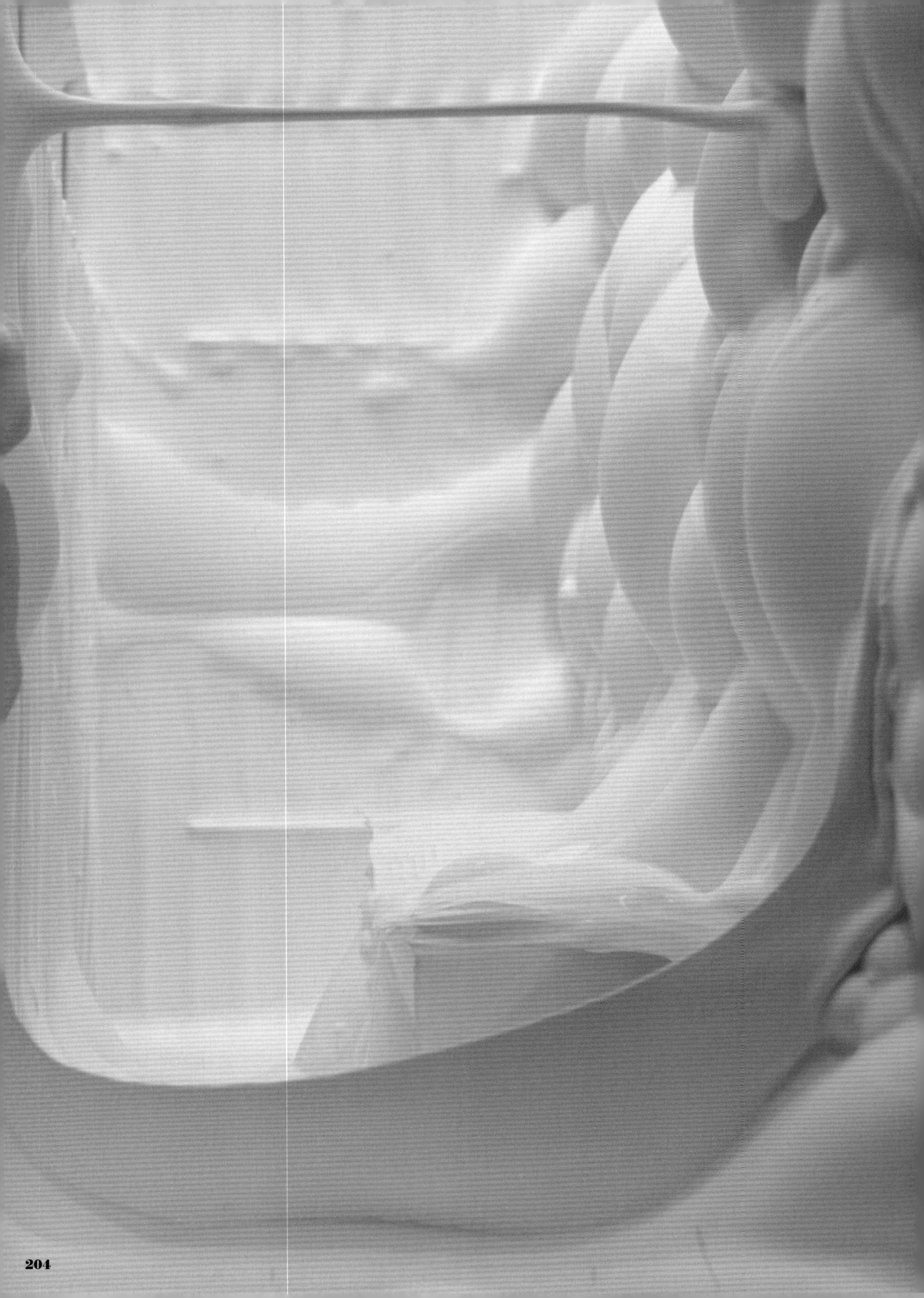

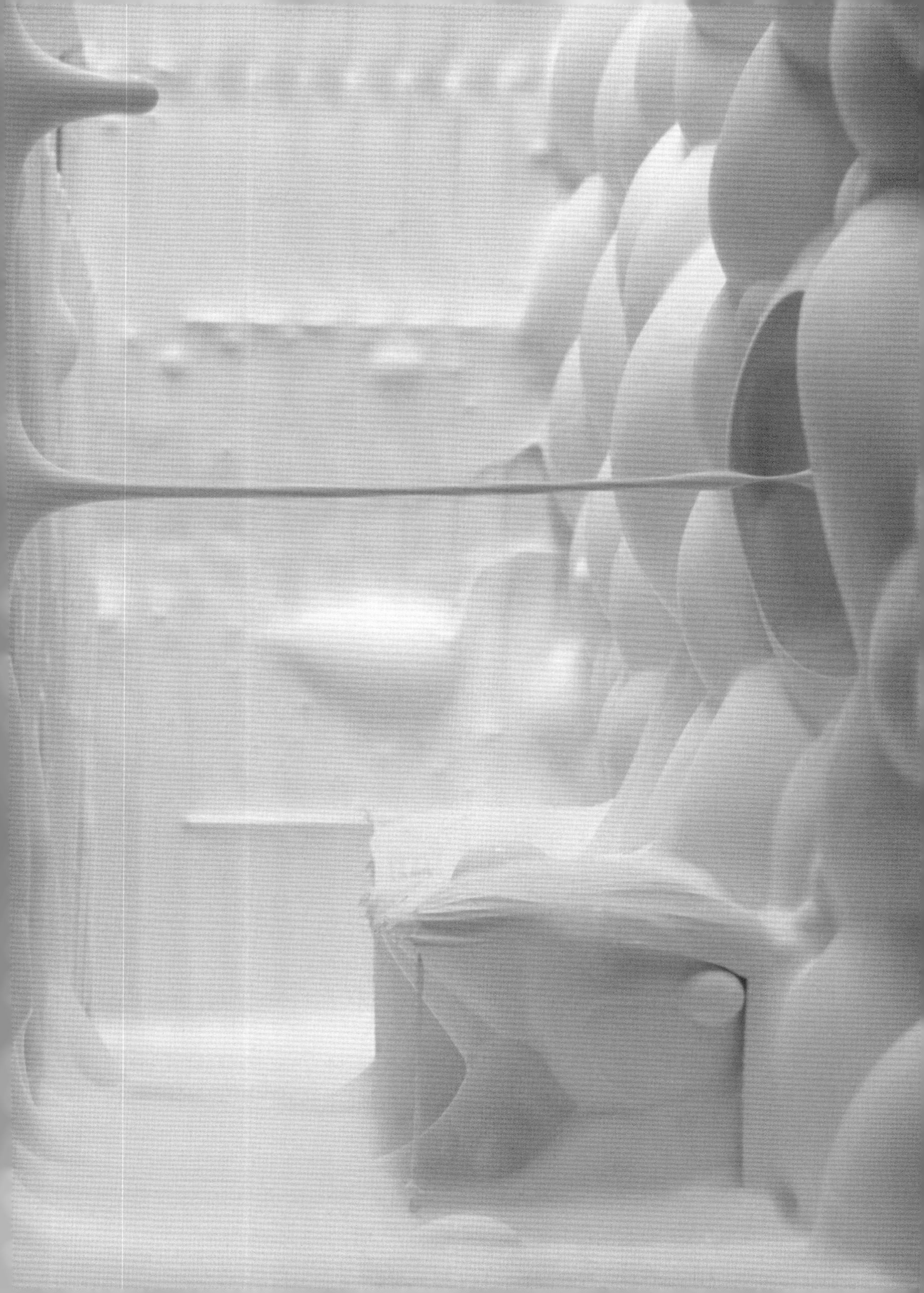

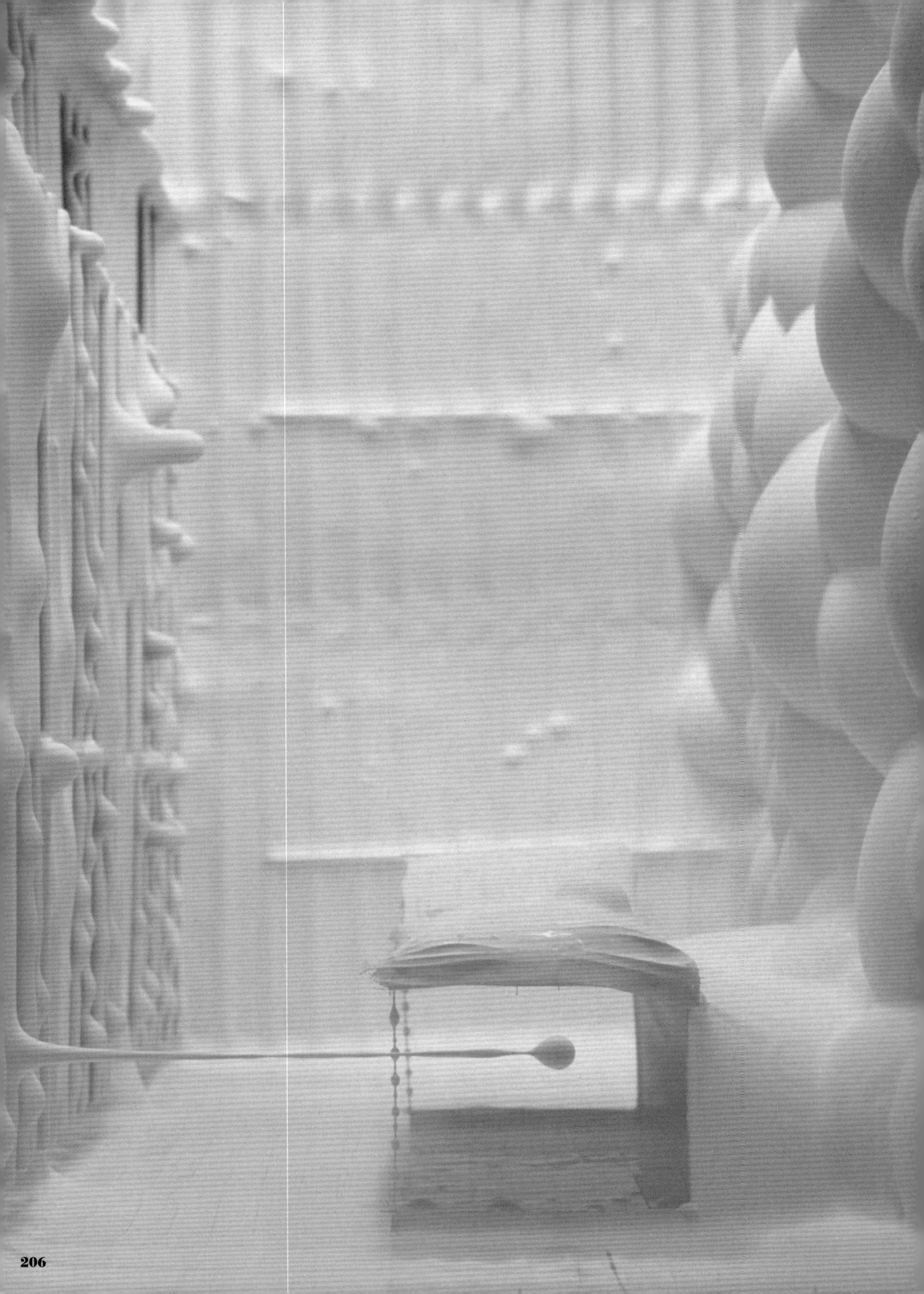

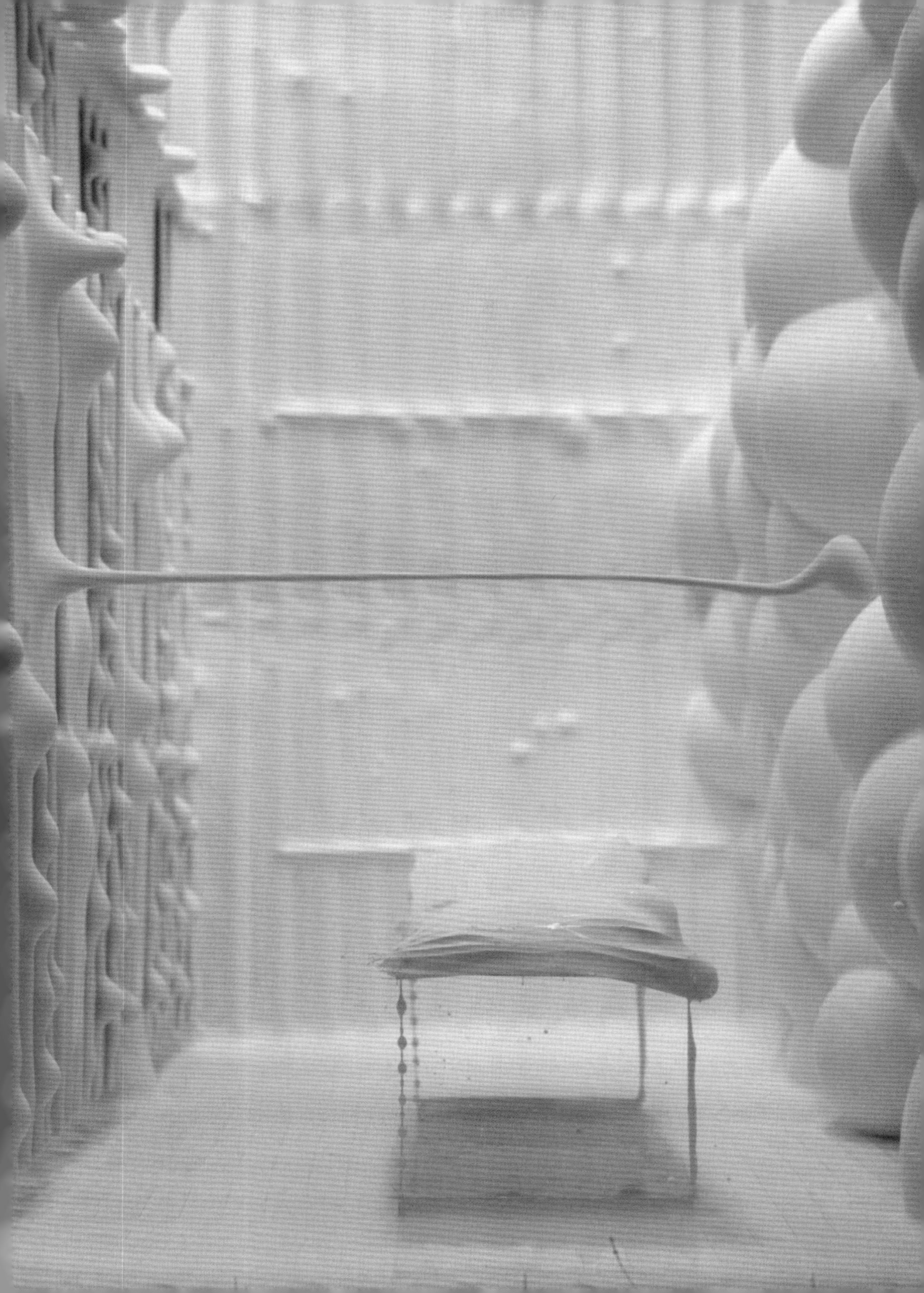

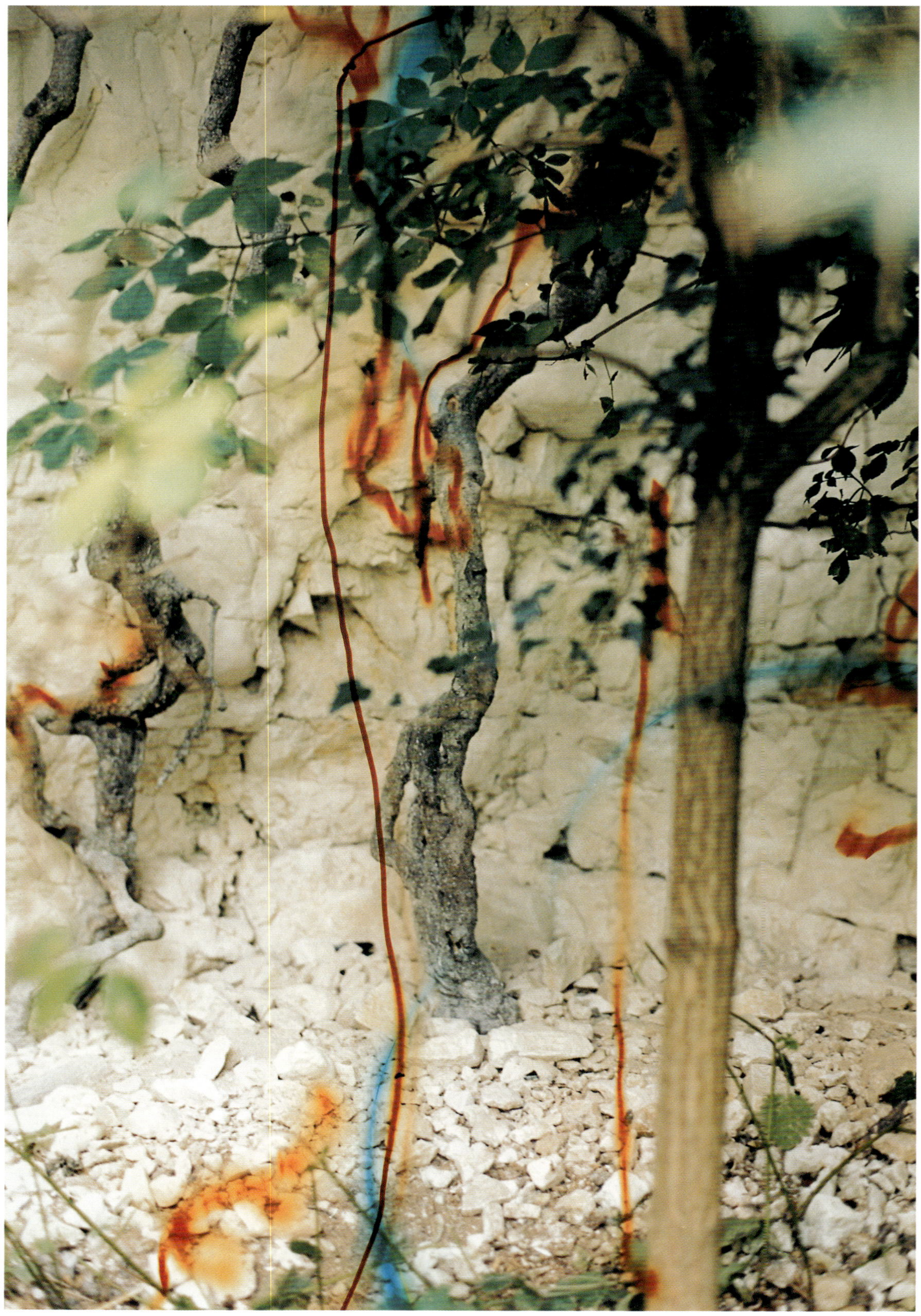

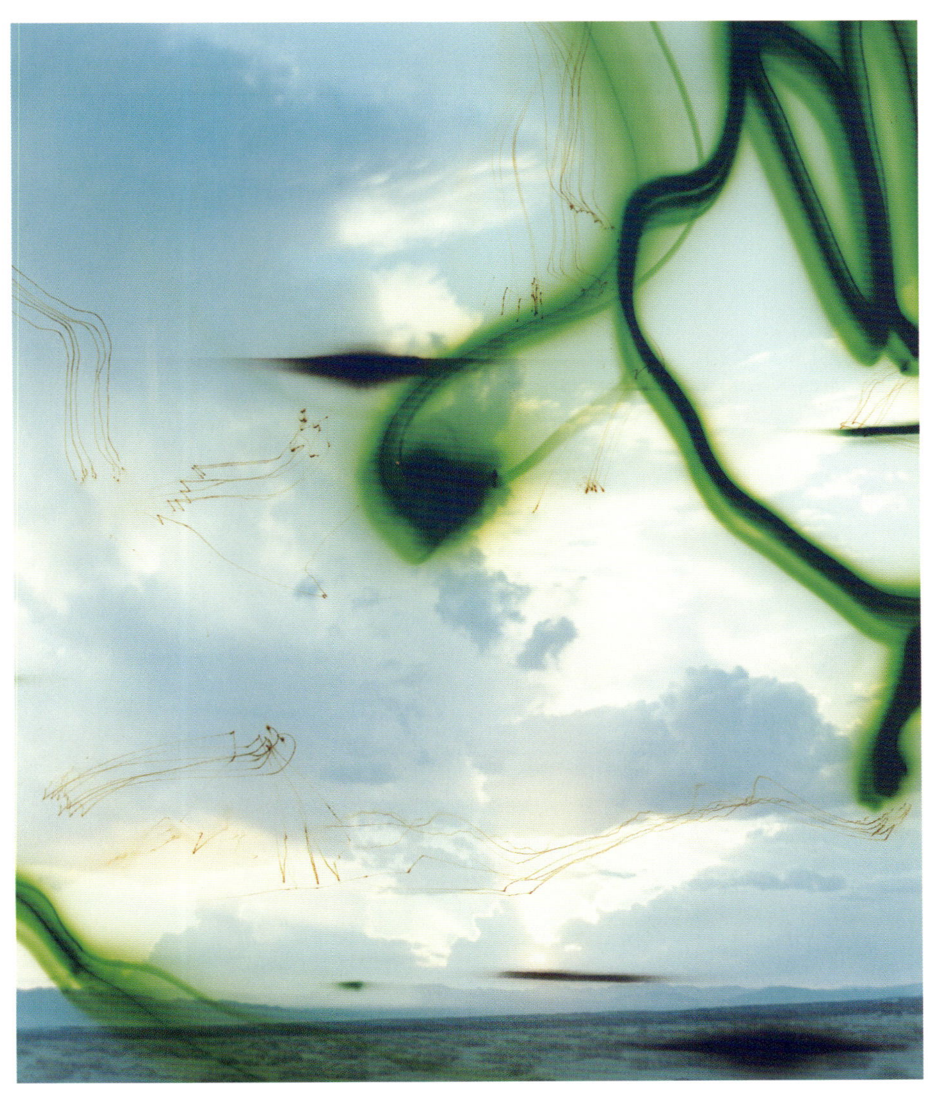

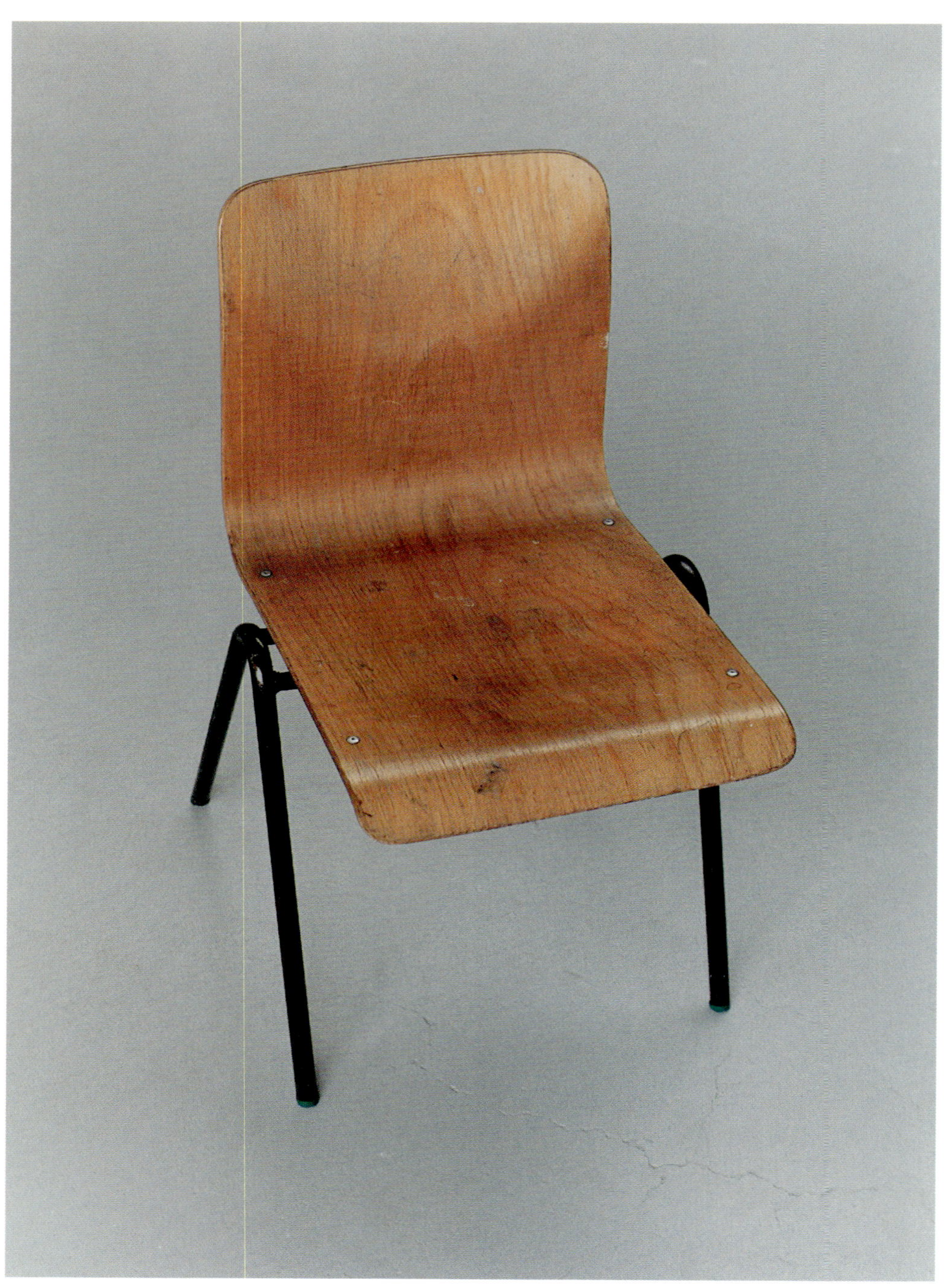

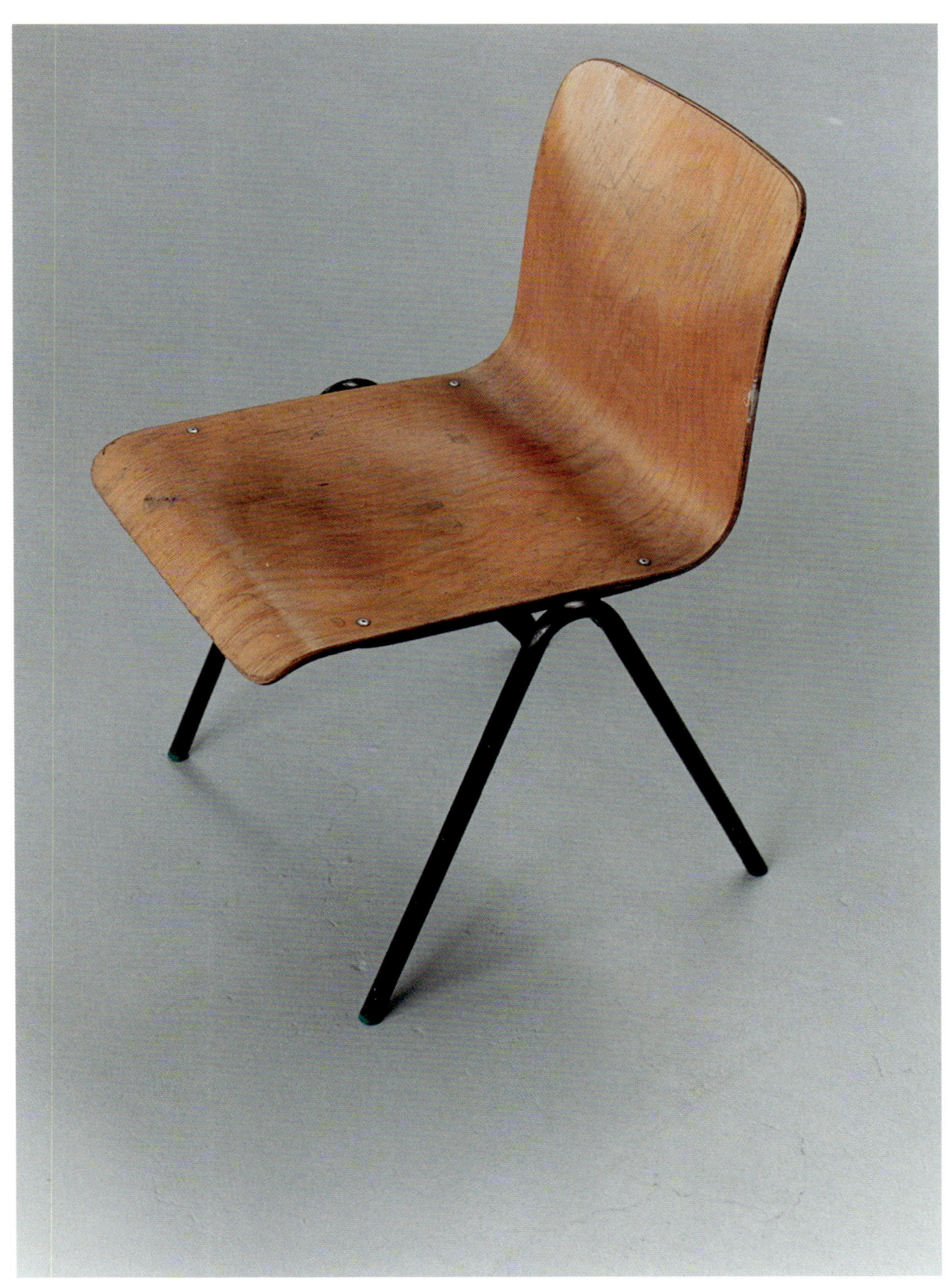

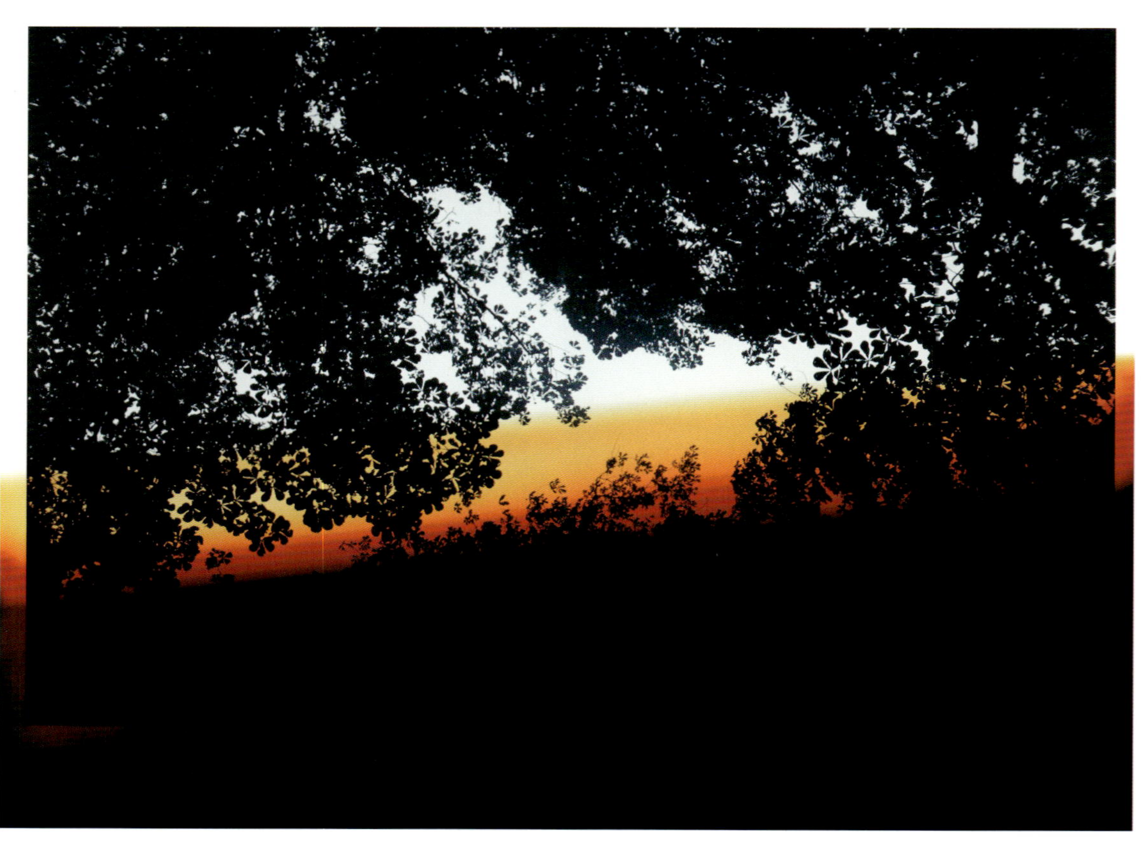

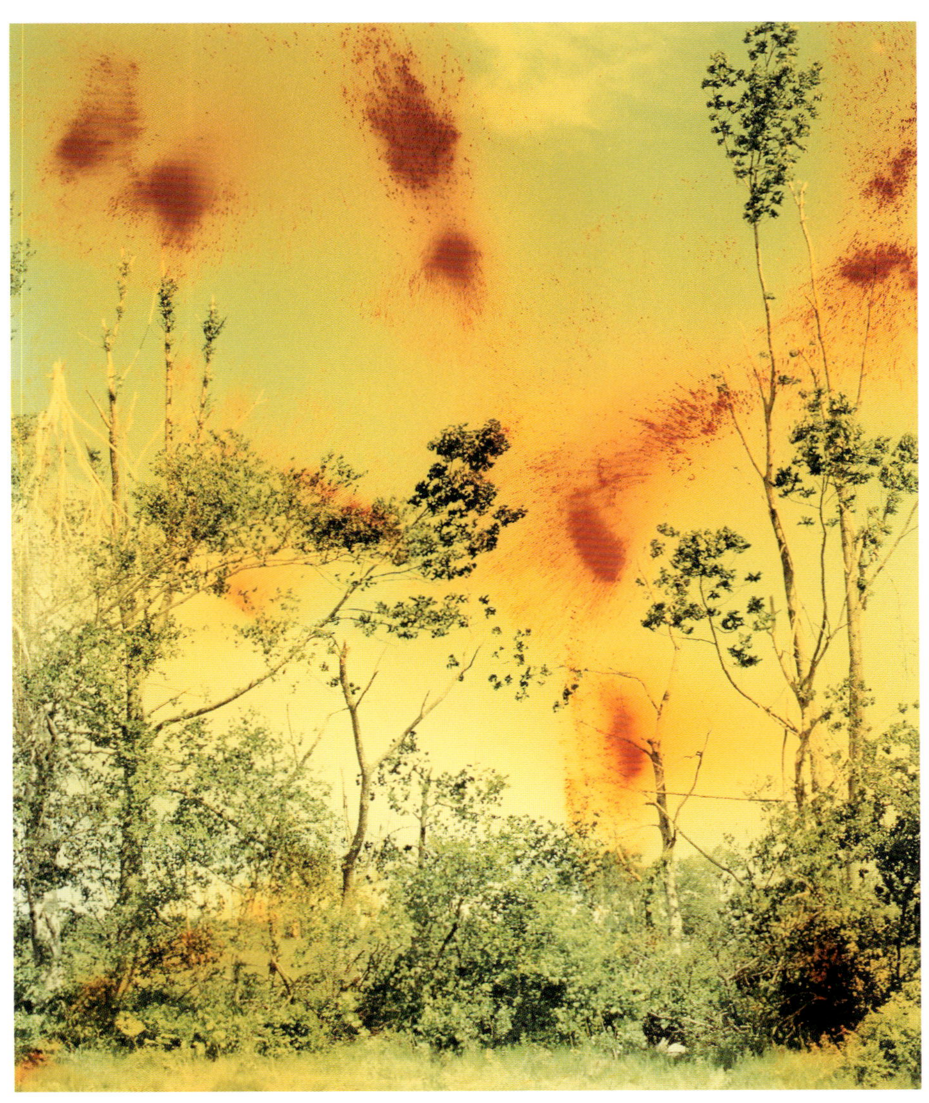

Most Needed

„Schönheit" ist ein prekärer Begriff des gegenwärtigen Kunstdiskurses. Nur selten taucht er in Texten und Vorträgen auf. Anstatt „ich finde das Kunstwerk schön" verwendet man andere, weniger subjektiv anmutende Redewendungen, wie „die Arbeit funktioniert" oder „ich schätze ihre/seine Position", um Zustimmung zu einem Kunstwerk auszudrücken. Diese Zurückhaltung trifft jedoch nicht nur auf den Begriff Schönheit zu. Überhaupt werden ästhetische Fragen in der Kunst wenig diskutiert und die zeitgenössische Kritik verfügt kaum über ein entsprechendes geeignetes Vokabular.
Sinnlichkeit, ästhetisches Vergnügen oder etwa das Potential der Kunst, die Betrachterinnen und Betrachter (auch) durch bildnerische Mittel zu berühren und neue Imaginationswelten zu erschließen, scheinen einer unmittelbaren Übertragung und Darstellung von Daten aus unserer sichtbaren Welt untergeordnet zu werden.

Dabei ist in den letzten Jahren das Interesse an ästhetischen Fragen, das sich unserer Begrifflichkeit so leicht entzieht, wieder gewachsen und eine Vielzahl von Künstlerinnen und Künstlern setzt sich verstärkt damit auseinander. Auch formale Aspekte spielen wieder eine größere Rolle. Ästhetischer Wert wird nicht mehr zwangsläufig als etwas betrachtet, das die Bedeutung einer künstlerischen Arbeit in Frage stellt oder gar mindert.

Sowohl historische, als auch aktuelle Entwicklungen haben ästhetische Fragen, und die Erscheinung des Schönen im besonderen, über lange Zeit in Misskredit geraten lassen. Vor allem aber hat die Auflösung einer normativen Ästhetik und das damit zusammenhängende Ende des autonomen Werkbegriffs dafür gesorgt, dass die ästhetische Erfahrung aus dem Blickfeld der Kunstkritik geraten ist und der Begriff „Schönheit" häufiger in Zusammenhang mit Sport, Massen- und Körperkultur als mit Kunst genannt wird. Bereits Immanuel Kant hatte in seiner *Kritik der Urteilskraft* (1790) das „Schöne" als eine dem „Erhabenen" untergeordnete Kategorie eingestuft. Während das Schöne „nur" attraktiv und unterhaltsam aber machtlos sei, könne das Erhabene eine emanzipatorische Wirkung ausüben. Mit der Avantgarde wurde – am radikalsten durch Marcel Duchamp – die klassische bürgerliche Ästhetik mit ihrer Neigung, die Kunst auf das Hervorbringen von Schönem zu reduzieren, durch eine Ästhetik des Negativen, des bewusst Nicht-Ästhetischen und Banalen abgelöst. Seitdem galt ästhetischer Genuss als konservativ und unvereinbar mit einer gesellschaftlich relevanten Kunst. Stattdessen stand die intellektuelle Ausrichtung der Kunst im Zentrum des Interesses.
Die vergangenen Jahrzehnte waren bestimmt von einem Dialog der Kunst mit der Alltags- und Massenkultur, vielfach darauf abzielend ein Teil derselben zu werden. Diese Auseinandersetzung war motiviert durch die Überzeugung, eine naturalistische Annäherung der Kunst an reale gesellschaftliche Prozesse könne die Gesellschaft am wirksamsten verändern und spiegelte sich auch im Verlassen des „White Cube" und der Hinwendung zu nicht-musealen Räumen wider.

Mit dieser Fokussierung beschränkte die Kunst sich jedoch zunehmend selbst und ein wichtiges Potential wurde in den Hintergrund gedrängt: die Fähigkeit, Vorstellungskraft, Un- und Unterbewusstes sowie Gefühle als Bestandteile der Reflexion und des Verstehens einzubeziehen.
Es scheint derzeit wichtig, dass Kunst wieder Freiräume schafft, sich abgrenzt und Zonen entstehen, die Platz lassen für Alternativen und Experimente, für Phantasie und Imagination und ein anderes Denken und Handeln. Dem kommt auch ein wiederaufgelebtes Interesse an Utopien entgegen, das Künstlerinnen und Künstler erneut das Potential der Kunst erkunden und mögliche Formen der Wirklichkeit entwerfen lässt. Statt – wie so häufig – unsere Alltagswahrnehmung zu bestätigen, könnte Kunst verstärkt ein Bereich für das Ungewöhnliche, Unerwartete sein und uns eine poetischere Sicht der Dinge ermöglichen.

Der *50. Jahresring* – das bedeutet, dass dieses Buch ein Jubiläumsband innerhalb einer Reihe mit einer langen Tradition ist. Ein Grund, sich nach vielen Bänden, die sich mit unterschiedlichen Aspekten der Kunstkritik befassten, der Kunst selbst zuzuwenden.
Wir haben für dieses besondere Buch 31 Künstlerinnen und Künstler verschiedener Generationen eingeladen. Ausgehend von Überlegungen zum Potential der Kunst und damit verbunden der aktuellen Bedeutung von Ästhetik haben wir sie gebeten, Beiträge für dieses Buch zu entwickeln. Dazu gehören auch die Fragen, unter welchen Bedingungen „Schönheit" heute erscheinen kann und ob Erfahrungen von Schönheit und Sinnlichkeit in diesem Kontext noch oder wieder relevant sind. Damit ist weder eine Rückkehr zu einer werkimmanenten Auffassung von Schönheit, noch die Wiederbelebung einer normativen Ästhetik gemeint. Im Gegenteil, die Künstlerbeiträge dieses Buches zeigen das Unbestimmte und wenig Kalkulierbare der Schönheit als einer Vorstellung, die ihre Veränderlichkeit schon in sich trägt.

Wir danken den Künstlerinnen und Künstlern, die dieses Buch möglich gemacht haben.

Marjorie Jongbloed, Brigitte Oetker, Christiane Schneider

Most Needed

"Beauty" is a precarious term in contemporary art discourse. It rarely occurs in lectures and essays. Instead of "in my view this work of art is beautiful" other, less subjective formulations – such as "the work functions well" or "I hold his/her position in high regard" – are used to express a positive opinion of a work of art. However, this restraint is not confined to the notion of Beauty. Aesthetic issues of any sort are scarcely addressed in contemporary art and, as a rule, critics today do not have a suitable range of vocabulary at their command. Sensuality, aesthetic pleasure and the potential of art to move the viewer by its visual impact and to open up new realms of imagination seem to have been ousted by unmediated exposition and presentation of data from our visible world.

Despite this, in recent years interest in aesthetic questions which so effectively elude our powers of expression has grown, and many artists are now grappling with these issues. By the same token, formal artistic considerations are also coming to the fore again. Aesthetic value is no longer necessarily viewed as something which jeopardises or diminishes the significance of a work of art.

Developments past and present, along with the phenomenon of Beauty itself, have over the years discredited aesthetic issues. But above all it has been the dissolution of a normative aesthetic and the concomitant demise of the notion of the autonomous work that account for the disappearance of "aesthetic experience" from art criticism and the fact that "beauty" is more often associated with sports, popular culture and body image than with art. As early as 1790, in his *Critique of Reason*, Immanuel Kant was already defining Beauty as a sub-category of the Sublime. While Beauty was "merely" appealing and entertaining – but intrinsically powerless – the Sublime held out the promise of emancipation. It was the 20th century avant-garde – with Marcel Duchamp as its most radical exponent – which established an aesthetic of negativity, promoting the non-aesthetic and the banal that displaced the prevailing classical aesthetic with its tendency to reduce art to the pursuit of Beauty. Following that, aesthetic pleasure was dismissed as conservative and incompatible with socially relevant art. As a result, the intellectual intentions of art took centre stage.
Recent decades have seen art entering into a dialogue with popular and mass culture, frequently in the hope of becoming part of the latter. This involvement was motivated by the conviction that art which most naturalistically replicated real social process could most effectively change society, and soon led to art's departure from the White Cube and the preference for non-museal spaces.

However, with this shift, art increasingly restricted its own potential and one important component was forced into the background, namely its capacity to integrate our powers of imagination, feelings, unconscious and subconscious, into our reflection and understanding.

It seems that the time has come for art to re-establish its room for manoeuvre, its domain and to create zones that can accommodate alternatives and experiments, fantasy and imagination, different ways of thinking and doing. In fact we can already see a revived interest in utopias, with artists exploring anew the full potential of art and proposing possible forms of reality. Instead of merely confirming our everyday perception of the world – as is so often the case – art could surely be an arena for the unusual and the unexpected and open up a more poetic view of things.

As the *fiftieth Jahresring* this is a special anniversary volume in a series with a long tradition and, after the many volumes dealing with various aspects of art criticism, now art itself should take the lime-light.
For this special edition, contributions were invited from thirty-one artists of different generations. In particular, they were asked to respond to the current interest in the potential of art and the ensuing importance of aesthetics, which in turn raises issues such as the conditions needed for Beauty today and whether the presence of Beauty and Sensuality are still (or once again) relevant in this context. This neither implies a return to the assumed immanence of Beauty in the work of art nor the resuscitation of a normative aesthetic. On the contrary, the artists' contributions in this volume demonstrate the indeterminate and largely incalculable nature of Beauty as a concept which is by definition intrinsically mercurial.

We would like to thank the artists who have made this book possible.

Marjorie Jongbloed, Brigitte Oetker, Christiane Schneider

Beiträge · Works

Curtis Anderson
***1956 USA, lebt und arbeitet in Köln · lives and works in Cologne**
Die Farbe des Wassers · The Colour of Water, 2003.

Richard Artschwager
***1923 Washington, lebt und arbeitet · lives and works in Hudson**
Paralleles Universum I (so etwa) und Paralleles Universum 2 · Parallel Universe I (well, approximately) and Parallel Universe II,
2003.

Olafur Eliasson
***1967 Kopenhagen, lebt und arbeitet · lives and works in Berlin**
Museums Are Radical, erste Veröffentlichung · first published in „Olafur Eliasson: The Weather Project", Tate Publishing, London 2003.

Luciano Fabro
***1936 Turin, lebt und arbeitet in Mailand · lives and works in Milan**
Aus: *Das Gewebe unter der Kruste,* Verlag Gachnang + Springer, Bern und · and Berlin, 1990, 146–149 /
Piedi senili, 2001 / *La lune s'allume sur l'onde qui ronde à bas jour,* 2002.

Hans-Peter Feldmann
***1941, lebt und arbeitet · lives and works in Düsseldorf**
Hans-Peter Feldmann zeigt ein paar Seiten, die aus einigen Dutzend auf einem Trödelmarkt gefundenen Kladden stammen, die von
jemand randvoll mit Zeitungsausschnitten beklebt wurden. · Hans-Peter Feldmann shows a couple of pages, which stem from some
copy books found at a fleamarket that somebody filled brim-full with newspaper clippings.

Peter Fischli / David Weiss
***1952 / *1946 Zürich, leben und arbeiten · live and work in Zürich**
Fotos aus dem Fundus · Photos from *Eine unerledigte Arbeit,* 2001–2003.

Ellen Gallagher
***1965 Providence, Rhode Island, lebt und arbeitet · lives and works in New York**
Aus: *Double Natural,* 2002, Plastilin, Kunstharz, Tusche und Papier auf Leinwand · Plasticine, resin, ink and paper on canvas.

Isa Genzken
***1948 Bad Oldesloe, lebt und arbeitet · lives and works in Berlin**
Schaufenster, 2003, 8 Collagen, 29,7 x 21 cm.

Tue Greenfort
***1973 Holbäk, lebt und arbeitet · lives and works in Frankfurt a. M. und · and Berlin**
Stufe · Step, 2002, Konstruktion für möglichen Übergang im Dionysoshof (Kölner Domplatte). Die Stufe wurde spontan von
Fußgängern genutzt und war im Laufe des Tages verschwunden. · Construction for possible passageway near the Cathedral of Cologne.
The step was used spontanously by pedestrians and disappeared during the day. Courtesy: Johann König, Berlin.

Charline von Heyl
***1960 Mainz, lebt und arbeitet · lives and works in New York**
Ohne Titel · Untitled, 2003, Tuschezeichnung und Collage · Ink drawing and collage.

On Kawara
Die letzten 6 Bilder aus · Latest Six Paintings out of *Today's Series*, 1966–,
Acryl auf Leinwand · Liquitex on canvas, 20,5 cm x 26,7 cm und · and 25,5 cm x 34,3 cm, Fotos · Photos: Hiro Ihara.

Job Koelewijn
***1962 Spakenburg, lebt und arbeitet · lives and works in Amsterdam**
Ohne Titel · Untitled, 2003, Installation in Neukirchen, Stiftung Kunstverein Springhornhof. Courtesy: Fons Welters, Amsterdam.

Isa Melsheimer
***1968 Neuss, lebt und arbeitet · lives and works in Berlin**
186: *Ohne Titel · Untitled*, 2002, Stoffe, Stickgarn, Perlen, Nähseide, Dachlatten, Kaninchendraht, Pappmaché · fabric, yarn, beads,
sewing thread, rabbit wire, paper-mâché, ca. 280 x 180 cm (Stoff · Fabric), ca. 65 x 25 x 70 cm (Objekt · Object) / 187: *Nr. f*, 2003,
Gouache und Tusche auf Papier · Gouache and ink on paper, 17 x 24 cm / 188: *Nr. e*, 2003, Gouache und Tusche auf Papier · Gouache
and ink on paper, 17 x 24 cm / 189: Detail aus · from *Ohne Titel · Untitled*, 2002. Courtesy: Galerie Barbara Wien, Berlin.

Jean-Luc Mylayne
***1946 Amiens, lebt und arbeitet mit seiner Frau Mylayne Mylayne · lives and works with his wife**
Mylayne Mylayne in Riez
91: *No. B10 Novembre Decémbre 2000 – Janvier 2001*, 2001; 93: *No. C4 Juillet Août 1982*, 1982 /
94: *No. 126 Septembre Octobre 2000*, 2000 / 95: *No. B5 Novembre Decémbre 2000 – Janvier 2001*, 2001 / 96: *No. C1 Juin Juillet 1981*,
1981. Courtesy: Monika Sprüth Galerie, Köln · Cologne und · and Barbara Gladstone Gallery, New York.

Saskia Olde Wolbers
***1971 Breda, lebt und arbeitet · lives and works in London**
Stills aus dem · from the Video *Placebo*, 2001, C-type prints. Courtesy: Künstler und · Artist and Diana Stigter Gallery.

Hanno Otten
***1954 Köln, lebt und arbeitet · lives and works in London**
Ohne Titel · Untitled, 2003, 24 x 102 cm, Offsetdruck auf Papier · Offset print on paper.

Jorge Pardo
***1963 Havanna, lebt und arbeitet · lives and works in Los Angeles**
Ohne Titel · Untitled, 2003.

Gerhard Richter
***1932 Dresden, lebt und arbeitet in Köln · lives and works in Cologne**
Acht Grau, 2002 (878), 8 grau emaillierte Glasscheiben auf Stahlträgern · 8 grey-enameled glass panels on steel supports,
je · each 500 x 270 x 50 cm, Deutsche Guggenheim Berlin, 11. Oktober 2002 – 5. Januar 2003. Fotos · Photos: Mathias Schormann.

Jeroen de Rijke / Willem de Rooij
***1970 Brouwershaven / *1969 Beverwijk, leben und arbeiten · live and work in Amsterdam**
Crystals (cloride of cobalt). Diaserie, zusammengestellt für diese Publikation. Die Bilder sind als Referenz an den Film *Crystals*
(2003, 15 Min., 16 mm Farbe, ohne Ton) gemacht worden. · Series of slides, selected for this publication. The images were made in
reference to the film *Crystals* (2003, 15 min, 16 mm colour film, mute). Courtesy: Galerie Daniel Buchholz, Köln · Cologne.

Bojan Sarcevic
***1974 Belgrad, lebt und arbeitet · lives and works in Berlin**
Trompe l'oeil, 2003. Courtesy: BQ, Köln · Cologne.

Andreas Schulze
***1955 Hannover, lebt und arbeitet in Köln · lives and works in Cologne**
Ohne Titel · Untitled, 2003, Mischtechnik · mixed media.

Thomas Schütte
***1954 Oldenburg, lebt und arbeitet · lives and works in Düsseldorf**
Aus: *Quengelware*, 2002, 7 Kupferdrucke (Radierungen) · Copper plate prints (etching)

Tino Sehgal
come into my world

Lily van der Stokker
***1954 's Hertogenbosch, lebt und arbeitet · lives and works in Amsterdam und · and New York**

8: *Easy Fun 2 (sketch for wallpainting + couch)*, 2001–2003 / 10: *Nice and easy in pink (sketch for wallpainting + couch)*, 2002–2003 **/** 12: *Couch + Blue flap (sketch for wallpainting + couch)*, 2002–2003 / 14: *Girly (sketch for wallpainting + doors)*, 2003, Buntstift auf Papier · Colour pencil on paper. Courtesy: Klosterfelde Berlin.

Inga Svala Thorsdottir
***1966 Island, lebt und arbeitet · lives and works in Hamburg**

7887 Minuten Vollmondschein und 13 Minuten Finsternis in BORG 21°W & 64°N 2003 · 7887 minutes of full-moonlight and 13 minutes of darkness in BORG 21°W & 64°N, 2003, 6 von 12 Zeichnungen · 6 drawings of 12.

Diana Thater
***1962 San Francisco, lebt und arbeitet · lives and works in Los Angeles**

Models, inszeniert von · staged by Diana Thater, 2003,
77: *the nape of her neck (London)*, Alexis Marguerite Teplin, Öl auf Tube-Plakat · Oil on Tube poster, 2003, 97,8 x 148,6 cm /
78: *Layered*, Jeremy Gilbert-Rolfe, 1991, Öl auf Leinwand · Oil on linen, 48,3 x 48,3 x 6,4 cm / 79: Charles James Cocktail Kleid ·
Charles James' cocktail dress, späte 40er Jahre · late 40s / 80: *Lemon, Yellow, Red Tomato*, T. Kelly Mason, 2002, Farbfotografie
auf Sintra · Chromogenic print on Sintra, 44,5 x 50,8 / 82: Charles James Abendkleid · Charles James' evening gown, 1952 /
83: *Model*, Jeremy Gilbert-Rolfe, 1994, Öl auf Leinwand · Oil on linen, 96,5 x 97,5 x 3,8 / 84: *L'amour É Où?(Paris)*, Alexis Marguerite
Teplin, Öl auf Metro-Plakat · Oil on Metro poster, 2003, 118,7 x 171,5 cm.

Wolfgang Tillmans
***1968 Remscheid, lebt und arbeitet · lives and works in London**

208: *Quarry*, 2001 / 209: *I don't want to get over you*, 2000 / 210: *Chair (part 1)*, 2001 / 211: *Chair (part 2)*, 2001 /
212: *Park Work VII*, 2001 / 213: *Icestorm*, 2001.

Rosemarie Trockel
***1952 Schwerte, lebt und arbeitet in Köln · lives and works in Cologne**

Mischtechnik · mixed media, 2003.

Richard Wright
***1960 London, lebt und arbeitet · lives and works in Glasgow**

Courtesy: BQ, Köln · Cologne.

**Jahresring 50
herausgegeben im Auftrag des
Kulturkreises der deutschen Wirtschaft im BDI e.V.
von Brigitte Oetker**

Jahresring 50
Jahrbuch für moderne Kunst

Herausgeber · Editors:
Marjorie Jongbloed, Brigitte Oetker, Christiane Schneider
Übersetzung · Translation: Fiona Elliot
Gestaltung · Design: Yvonne Quirmbach, Köln · Cologne
Lithografie · Reproduction works: Farbanalyse, Köln · Cologne
Druck · Printer: Druckerei Fries, Köln · Cologne

©2003, Künstler · Artists, Herausgeber · Editors, Oktagon Verlag, Köln · Cologne

Dank · Thanks:
Ann Artschwager, Hiro Ihara, Silke Heneka, Max Hetzler und Samia Saouma,
Kasper König, Isabel Podeschwa, Joseph Sappler

Die Deutsche Bibliothek – CIP-Einheitsaufnahme
Ein Titelsatz für diese Publikation ist bei
Der Deutschen Bibliothek erhältlich.

Printed in Germany

Vertrieb außerhalb Europas · Distribution outside Europe
D.A.P./Distributed Art Publishers, Inc., New York
155 Sixth Avenue, New York, NY 10013
Tel 212-627-1999, Fax 212-627-9484

ISBN 3-89611-104-3

Inhalt · Contents